WARREN ELLIS
WRITER

DECLAN SHALVEY
ARTIST

JORDIE BELLAIRE
COLOR

FONOGRAFIKS
LETTERING & DESIGN

ELLE POWER & EOIN MARRON
PRODUCTION ASSISTANTS

INJECTION, VOLUME TWO. First printing. August, 2016.

Published by Image Comics, Inc. Office of publication: 2001 Center Street, Sixth Floor, Berkeley, CA 94704. Originally published in single magazine form as INJECTION #6–10, by Image Comics.

Printed in the USA. For information regarding the CPSIA on this printed material call: 203-595-3636 and provide reference # RICH–696510. For international rights, contact: foreignlicensing@imagecomics.com. ISBN 978-1-63215-720-1. Big Bang Comics/Forbidden Planet variant ISBN 978-1-63215-967-0.

INJECTION

VOLUME TWO

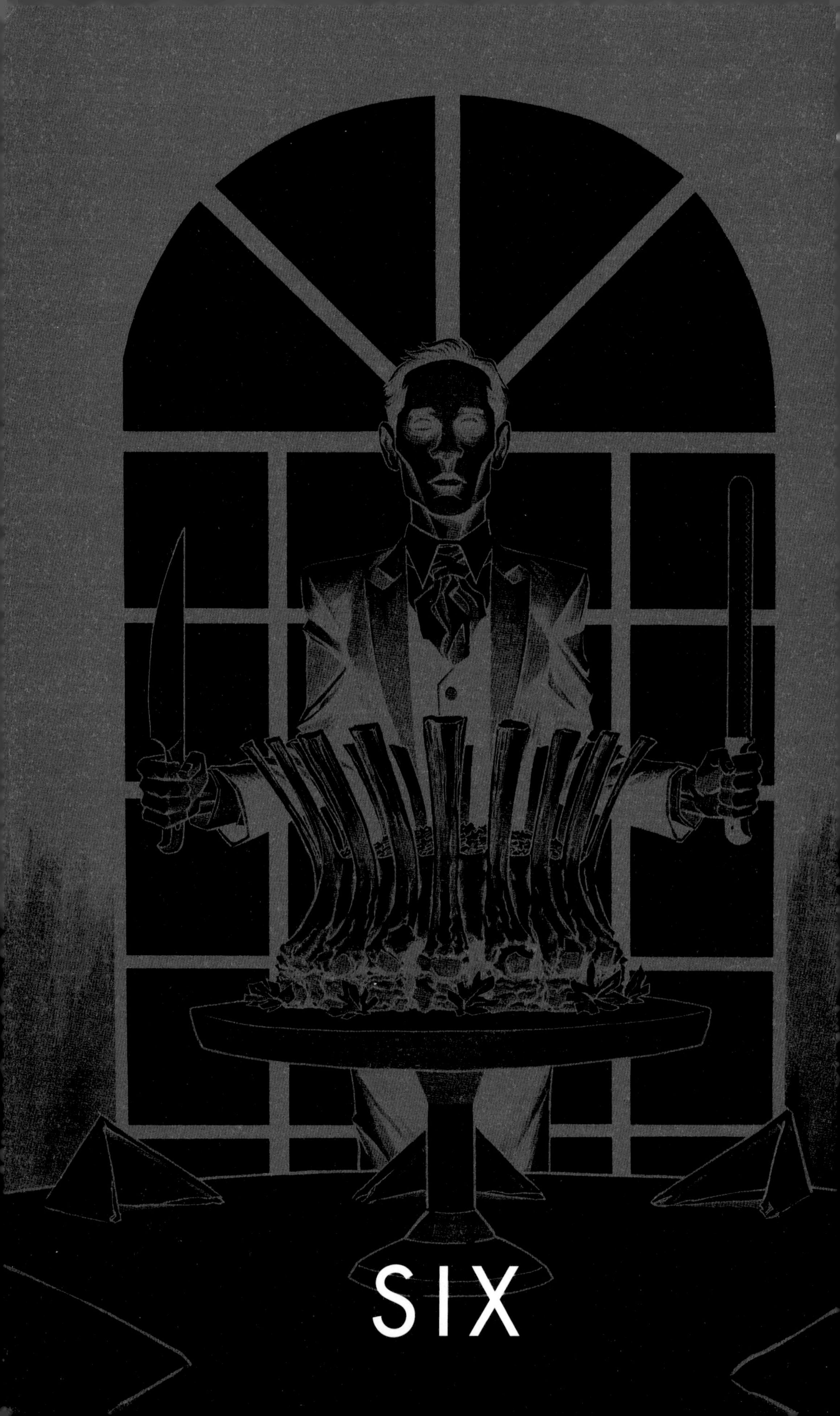

SIX

Here we go again.

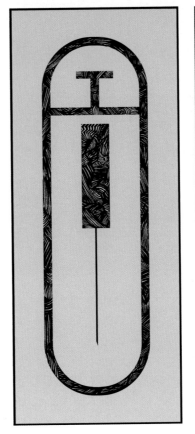

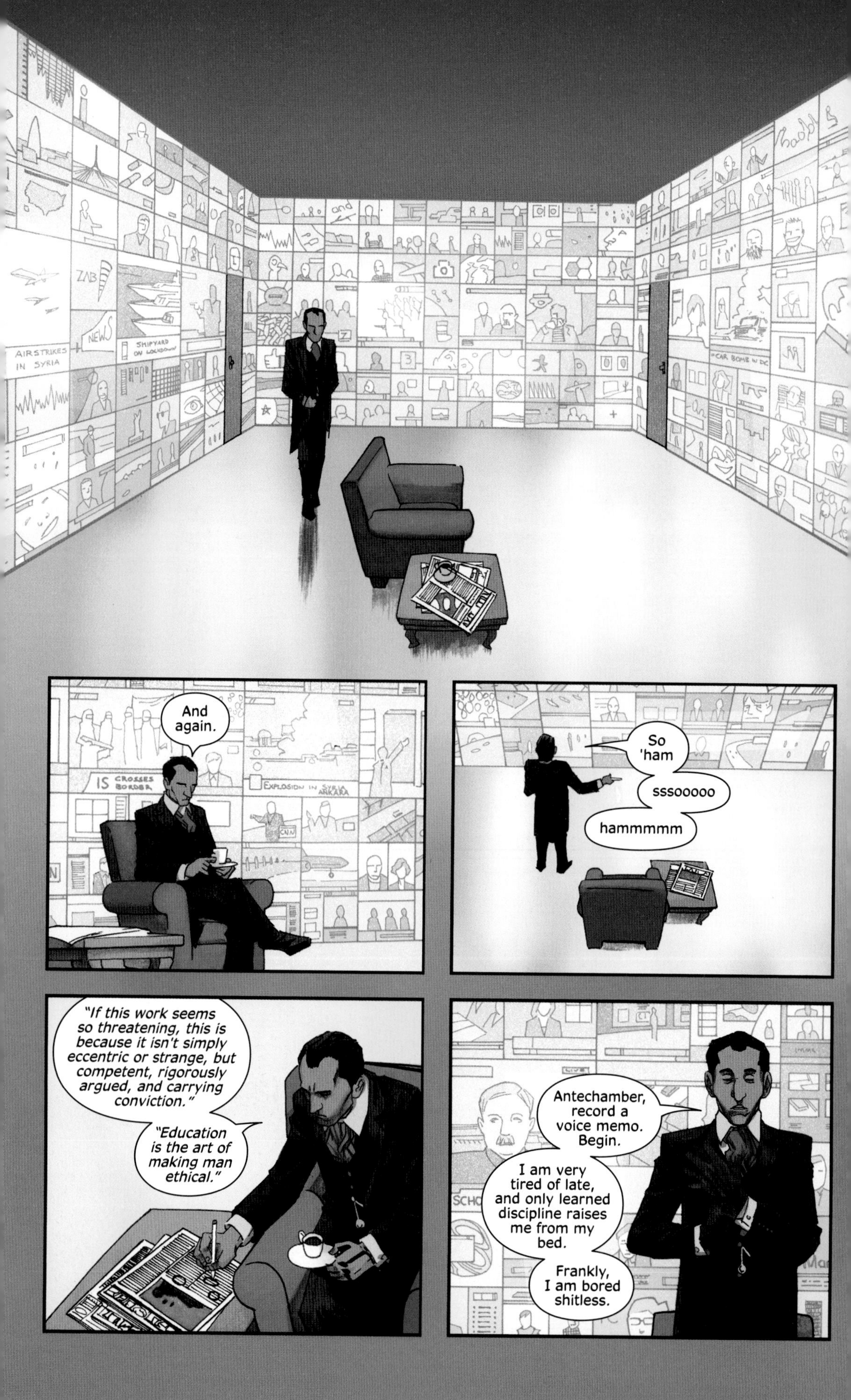
AIRSTRIKES IN SYRIA
SHIPYARD ON LOCKDOWN
NEWS
CAR BOMB IN DC
IS CROSSES BORDER
EXPLOSION IN SYRIA ANKARA
And again.
So 'ham
sssooooo
hammmmm
"If this work seems so threatening, this is because it isn't simply eccentric or strange, but competent, rigorously argued, and carrying conviction."
"Education is the art of making man ethical."
Antechamber, record a voice memo. Begin.
I am very tired of late, and only learned discipline raises me from my bed.
Frankly, I am bored shitless.

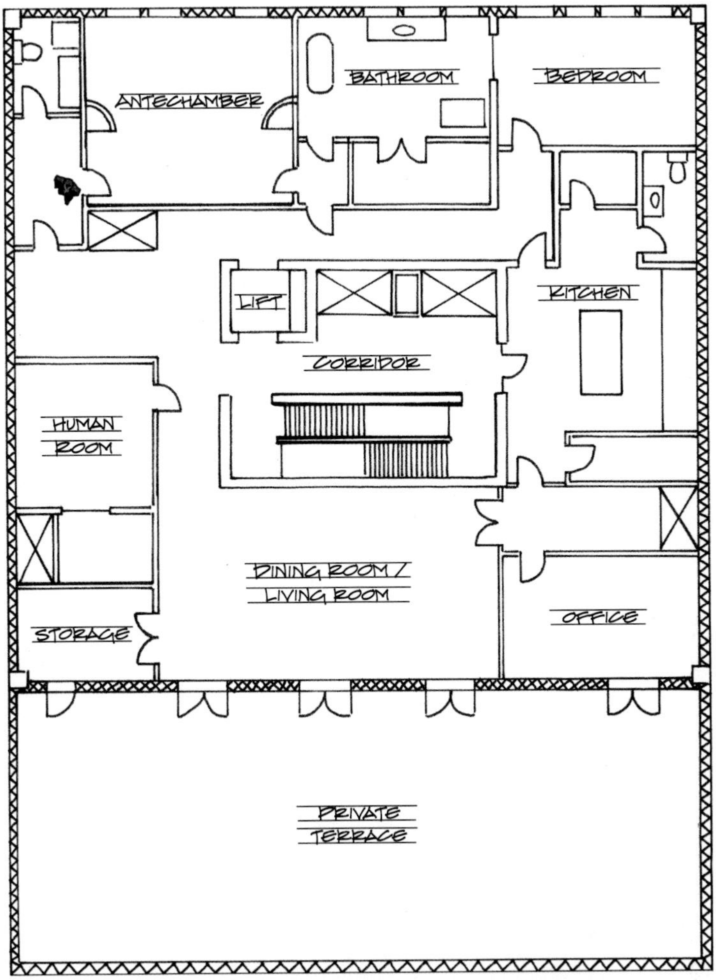
ANTECHAMBER
BATHROOM
BEDROOM
LIFT
KITCHEN
CORRIDOR
HUMAN ROOM
DINING ROOM / LIVING ROOM
OFFICE
STORAGE
PRIVATE TERRACE

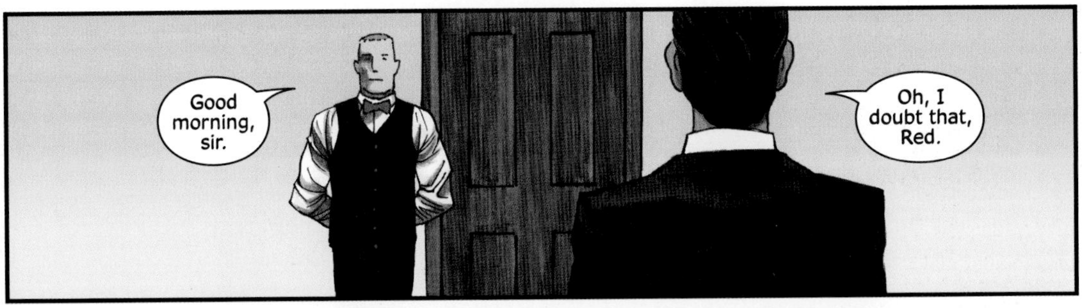
Good morning, sir.
Oh, I doubt that, Red.

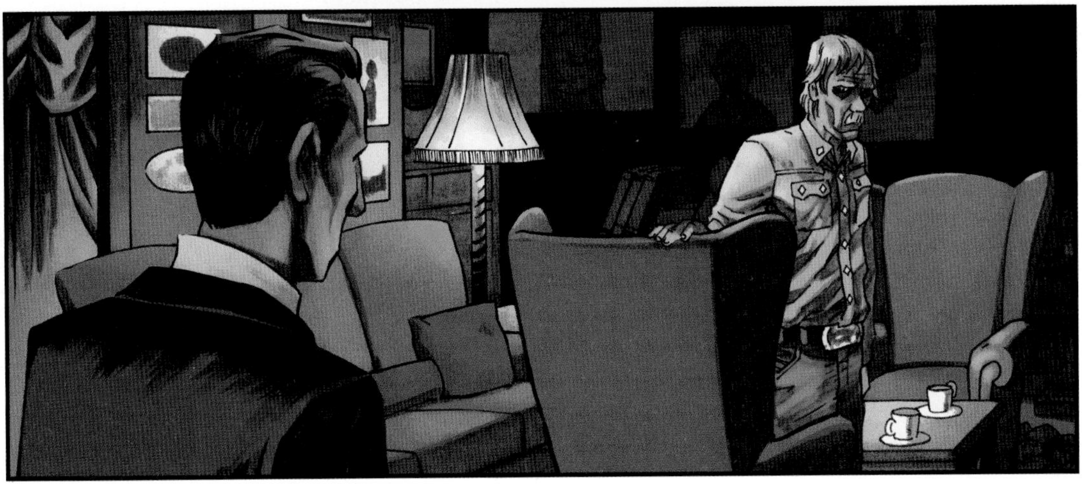

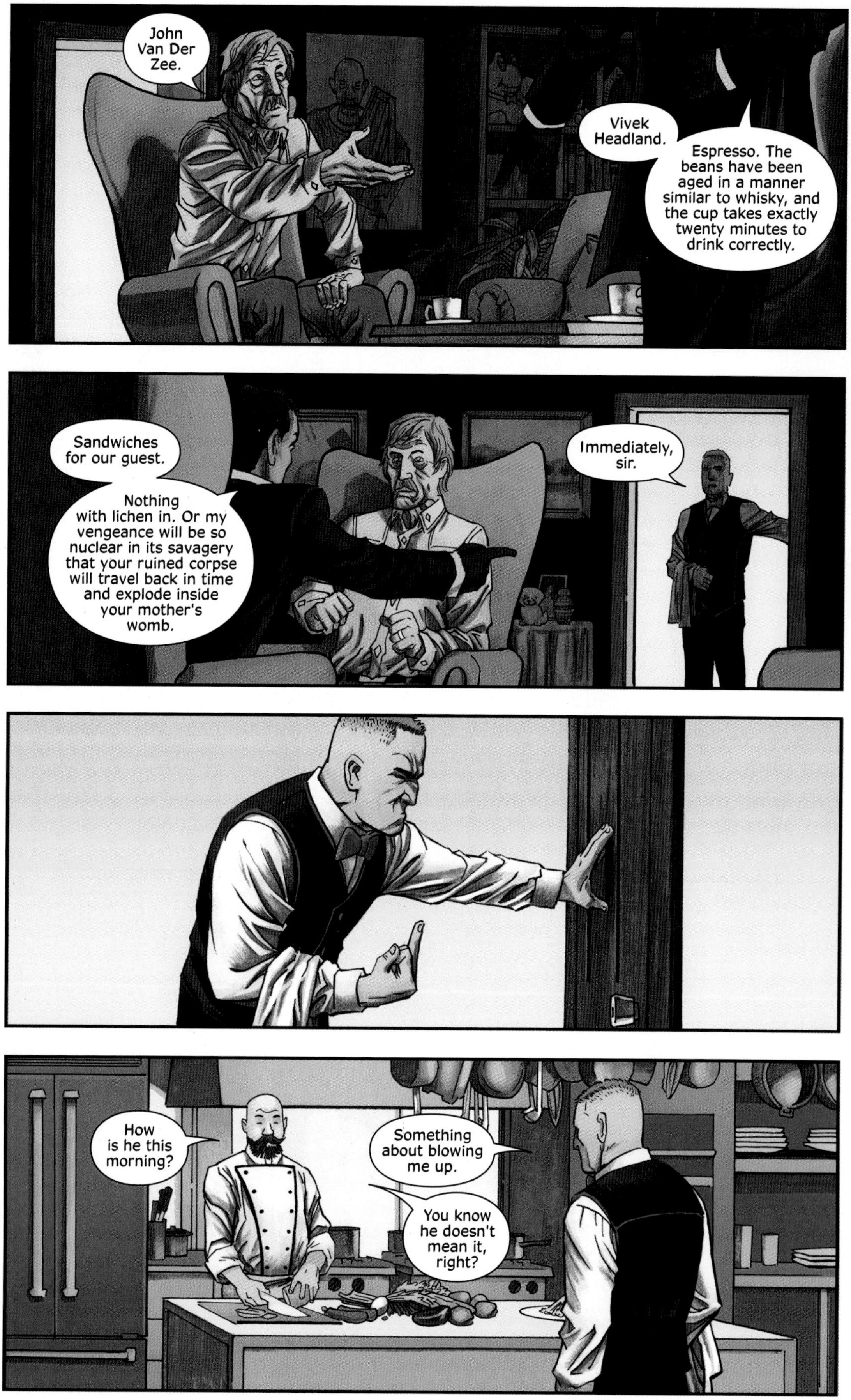
John Van Der Zee.
Vivek Headland.
Espresso. The beans have been aged in a manner similar to whisky, and the cup takes exactly twenty minutes to drink correctly.
Sandwiches for our guest.
Nothing with lichen in. Or my vengeance will be so nuclear in its savagery that your ruined corpse will travel back in time and explode inside your mother's womb.
Immediately, sir.
How is he this morning?
Something about blowing me up.
You know he doesn't mean it, right?

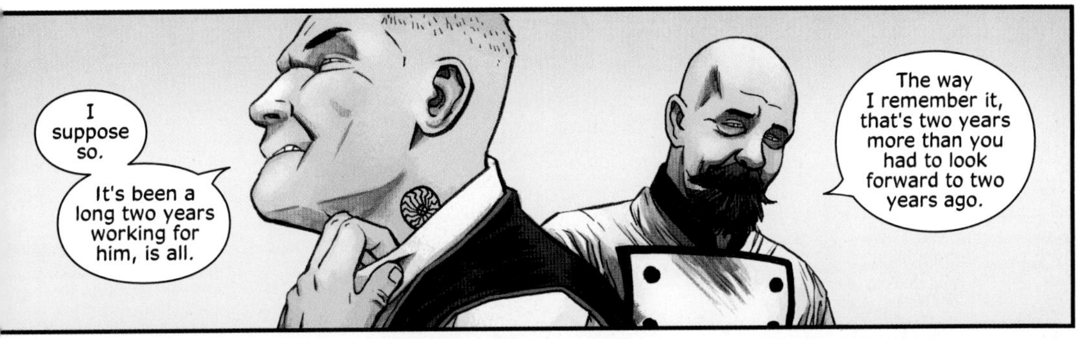
I suppose so.
It's been a long two years working for him, is all.
The way I remember it, that's two years more than you had to look forward to two years ago.

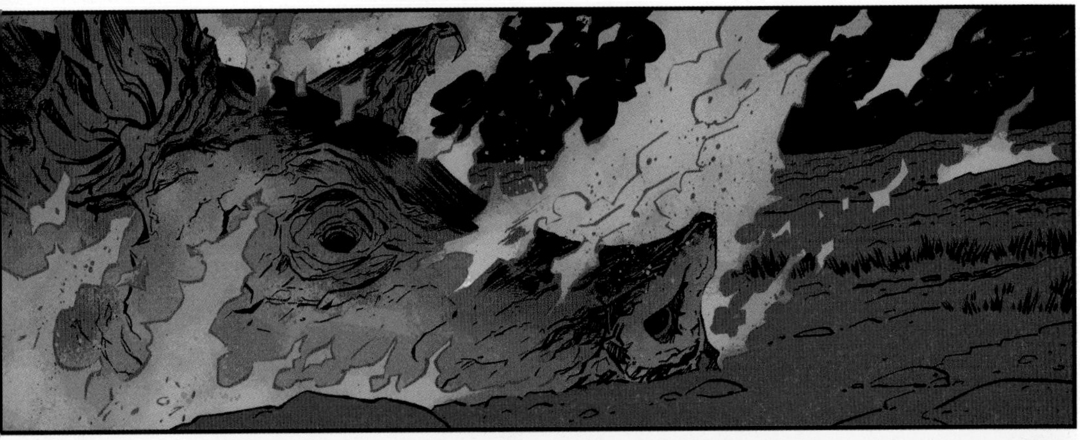

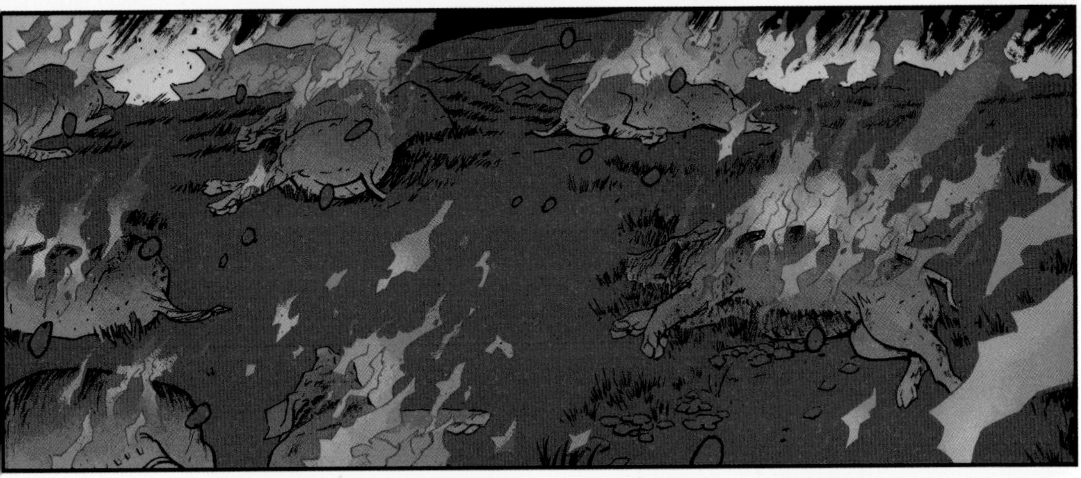

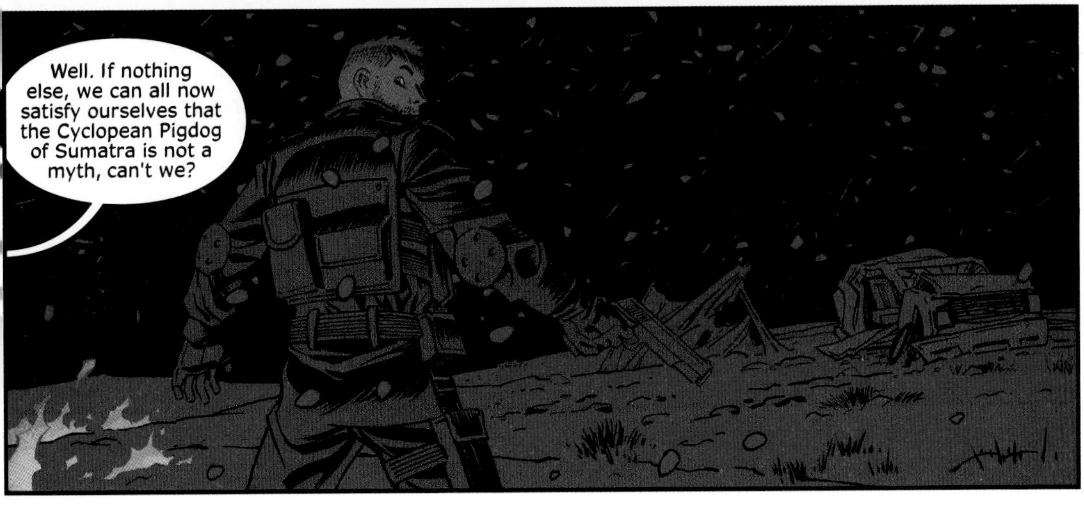
Well. If nothing else, we can all now satisfy ourselves that the Cyclopean Pigdog of Sumatra is not a myth, can't we?

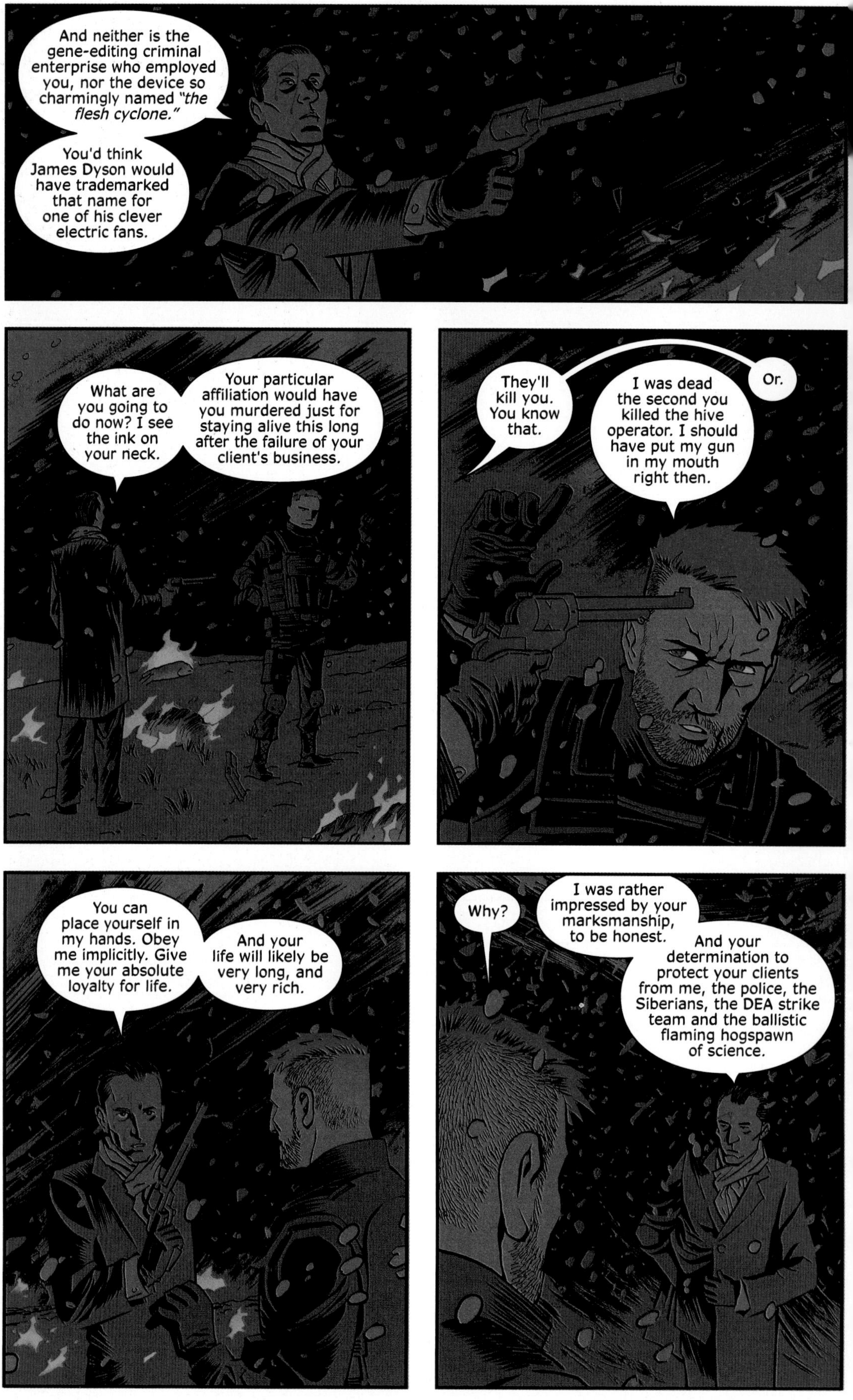

And neither is the gene-editing criminal enterprise who employed you, nor the device so charmingly named *"the flesh cyclone."*
You'd think James Dyson would have trademarked that name for one of his clever electric fans.
What are you going to do now? I see the ink on your neck.
Your particular affiliation would have you murdered just for staying alive this long after the failure of your client's business.
They'll kill you. You know that.
I was dead the second you killed the hive operator. I should have put my gun in my mouth right then.
Or.
You can place yourself in my hands. Obey me implicitly. Give me your absolute loyalty for life.
And your life will likely be very long, and very rich.
Why?
I was rather impressed by your marksmanship, to be honest.
And your determination to protect your clients from me, the police, the Siberians, the DEA strike team and the ballistic flaming hogspawn of science.

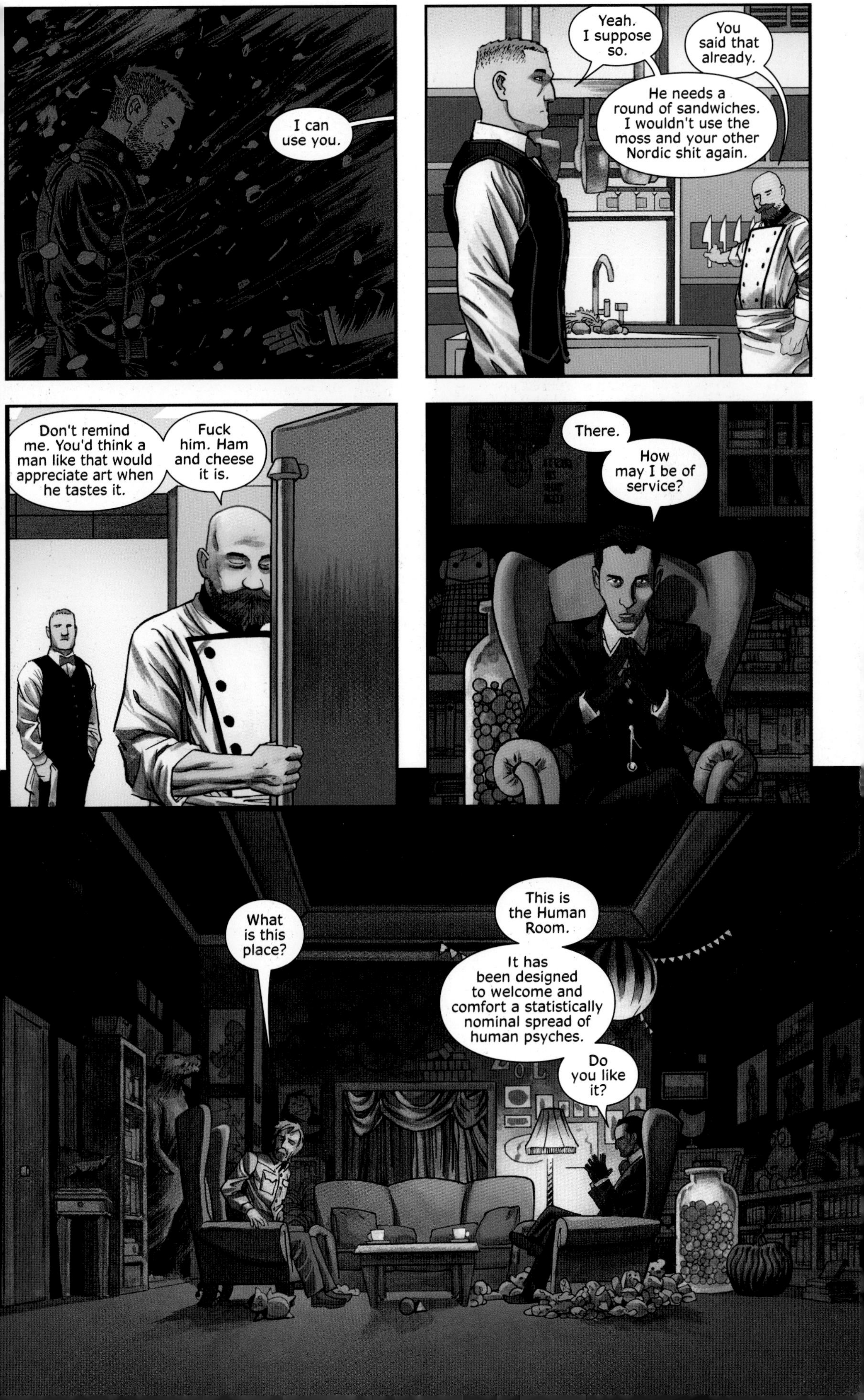
I can use you.
Yeah. I suppose so.
You said that already.
He needs a round of sandwiches. I wouldn't use the moss and your other Nordic shit again.
Don't remind me. You'd think a man like that would appreciate art when he tastes it.
Fuck him. Ham and cheese it is.
There.
How may I be of service?
What is this place?
This is the Human Room.
It has been designed to welcome and comfort a statistically nominal spread of human psyches.
Do you like it?

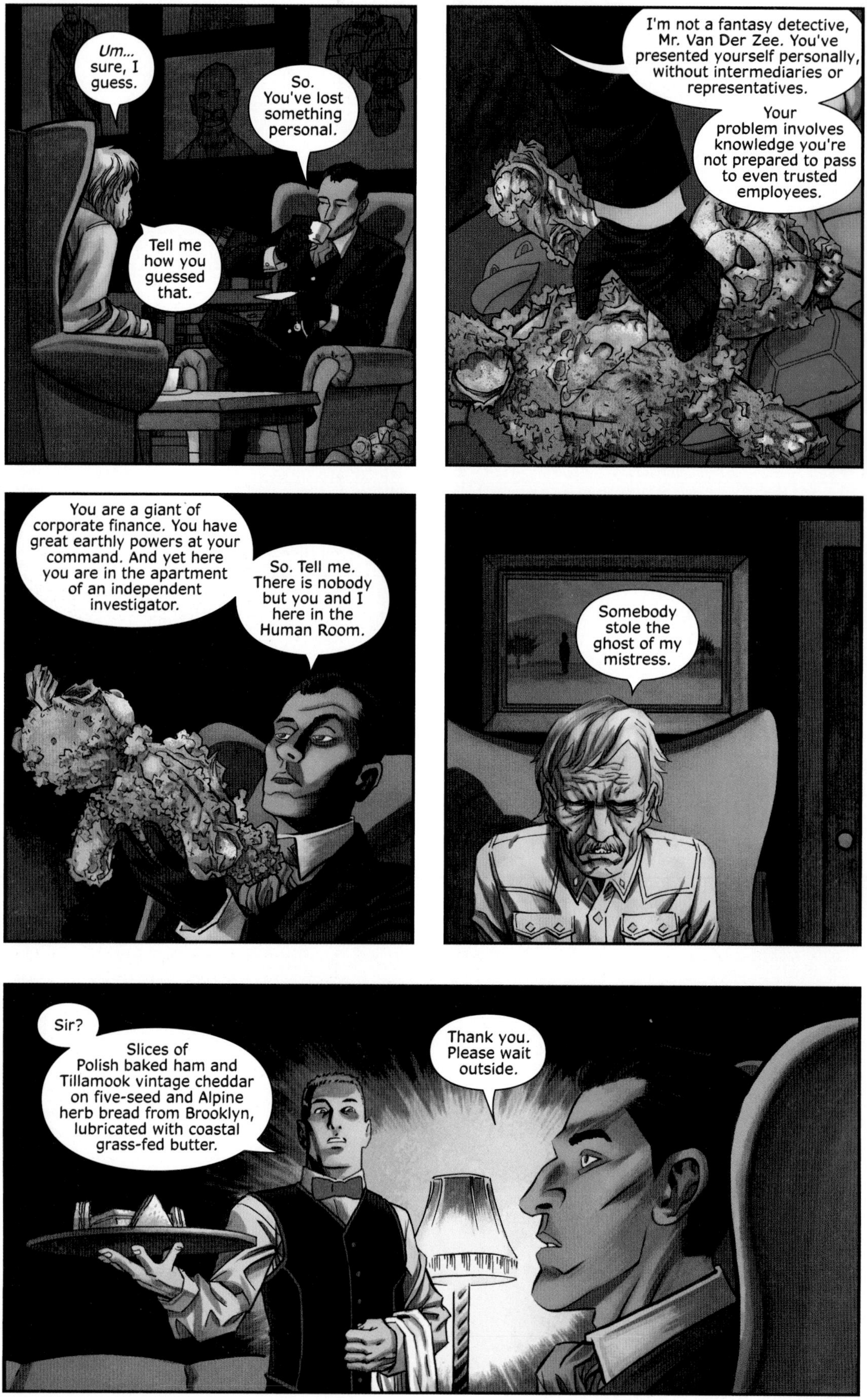

Um... sure, I guess.
So. You've lost something personal.
Tell me how you guessed that.
I'm not a fantasy detective, Mr. Van Der Zee. You've presented yourself personally, without intermediaries or representatives.
Your problem involves knowledge you're not prepared to pass to even trusted employees.
You are a giant of corporate finance. You have great earthly powers at your command. And yet here you are in the apartment of an independent investigator.
So. Tell me. There is nobody but you and I here in the Human Room.
Somebody stole the ghost of my mistress.
Sir?
Slices of Polish baked ham and Tillamook vintage cheddar on five-seed and Alpine herb bread from Brooklyn, lubricated with coastal grass-fed butter.
Thank you. Please wait outside.

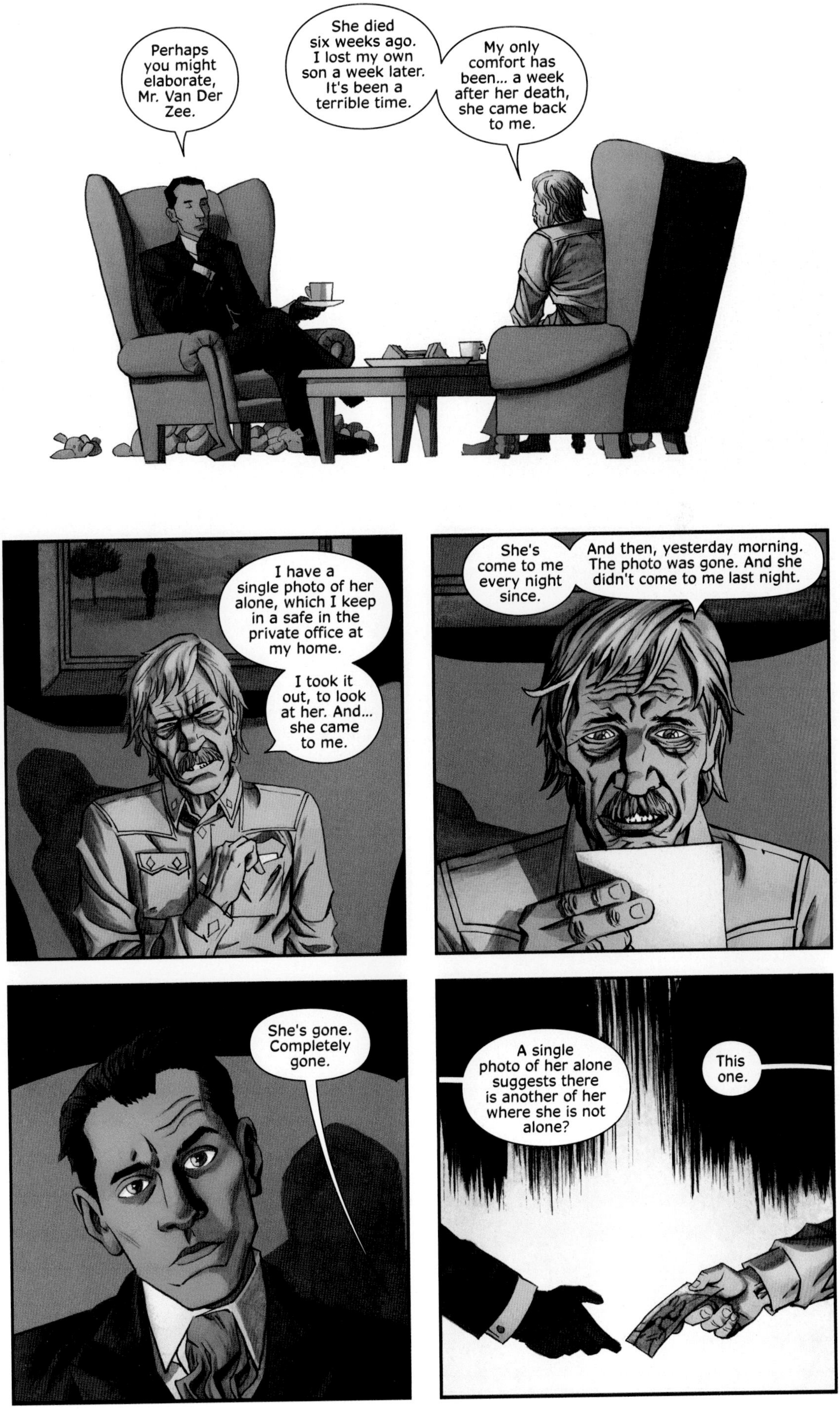
Perhaps you might elaborate, Mr. Van Der Zee.
She died six weeks ago. I lost my own son a week later. It's been a terrible time.
My only comfort has been... a week after her death, she came back to me.
I have a single photo of her alone, which I keep in a safe in the private office at my home.
I took it out, to look at her. And... she came to me.
She's come to me every night since.
And then, yesterday morning. The photo was gone. And she didn't come to me last night.
She's gone. Completely gone.
A single photo of her alone suggests there is another of her where she is not alone?
This one.

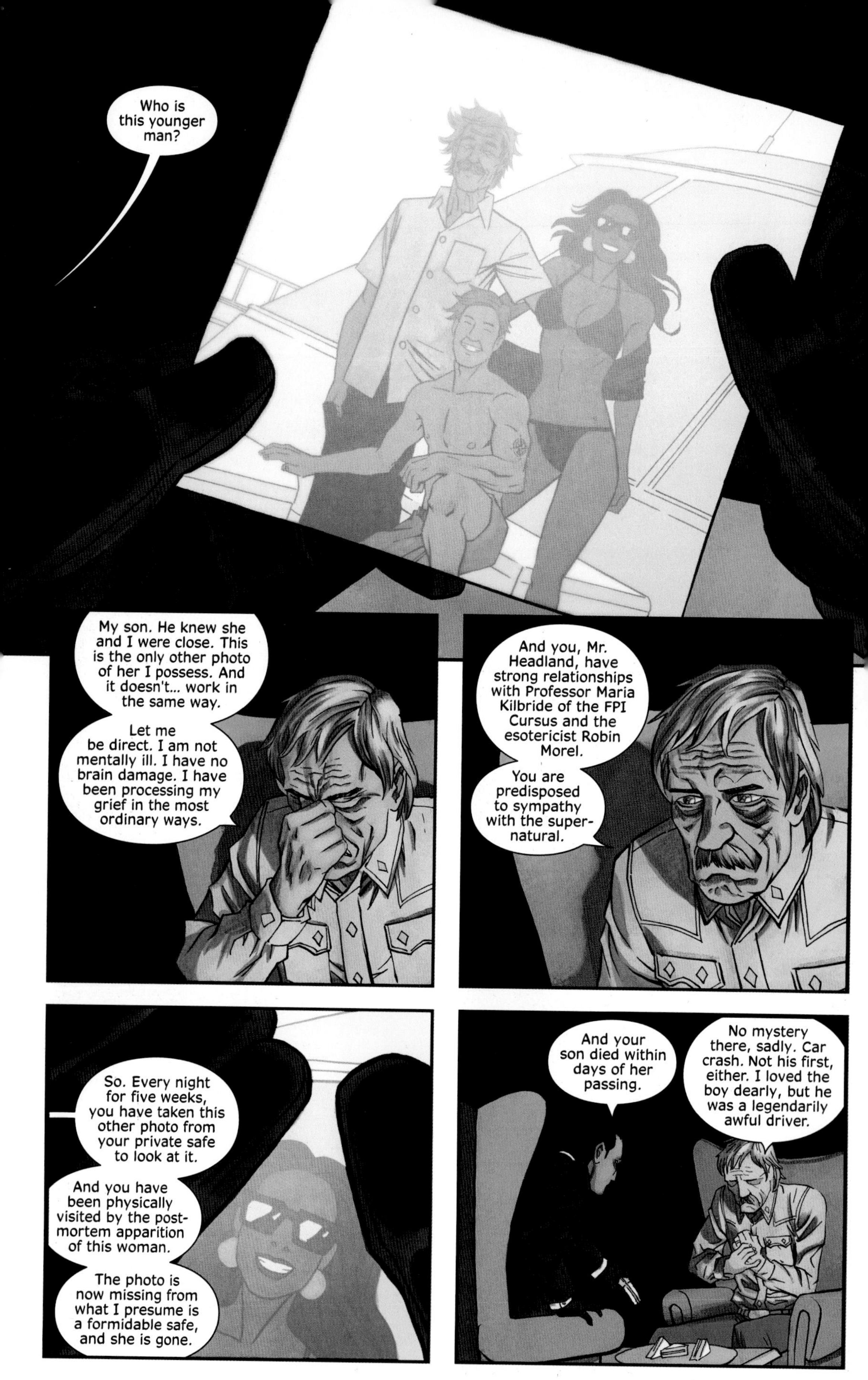
Who is this younger man?
My son. He knew she and I were close. This is the only other photo of her I possess. And it doesn't... work in the same way.
Let me be direct. I am not mentally ill. I have no brain damage. I have been processing my grief in the most ordinary ways.
And you, Mr. Headland, have strong relationships with Professor Maria Kilbride of the FPI Cursus and the esotericist Robin Morel.
You are predisposed to sympathy with the super-natural.
So. Every night for five weeks, you have taken this other photo from your private safe to look at it.
And you have been physically visited by the post-mortem apparition of this woman.
The photo is now missing from what I presume is a formidable safe, and she is gone.
And your son died within days of her passing.
No mystery there, sadly. Car crash. Not his first, either. I loved the boy dearly, but he was a legendarily awful driver.

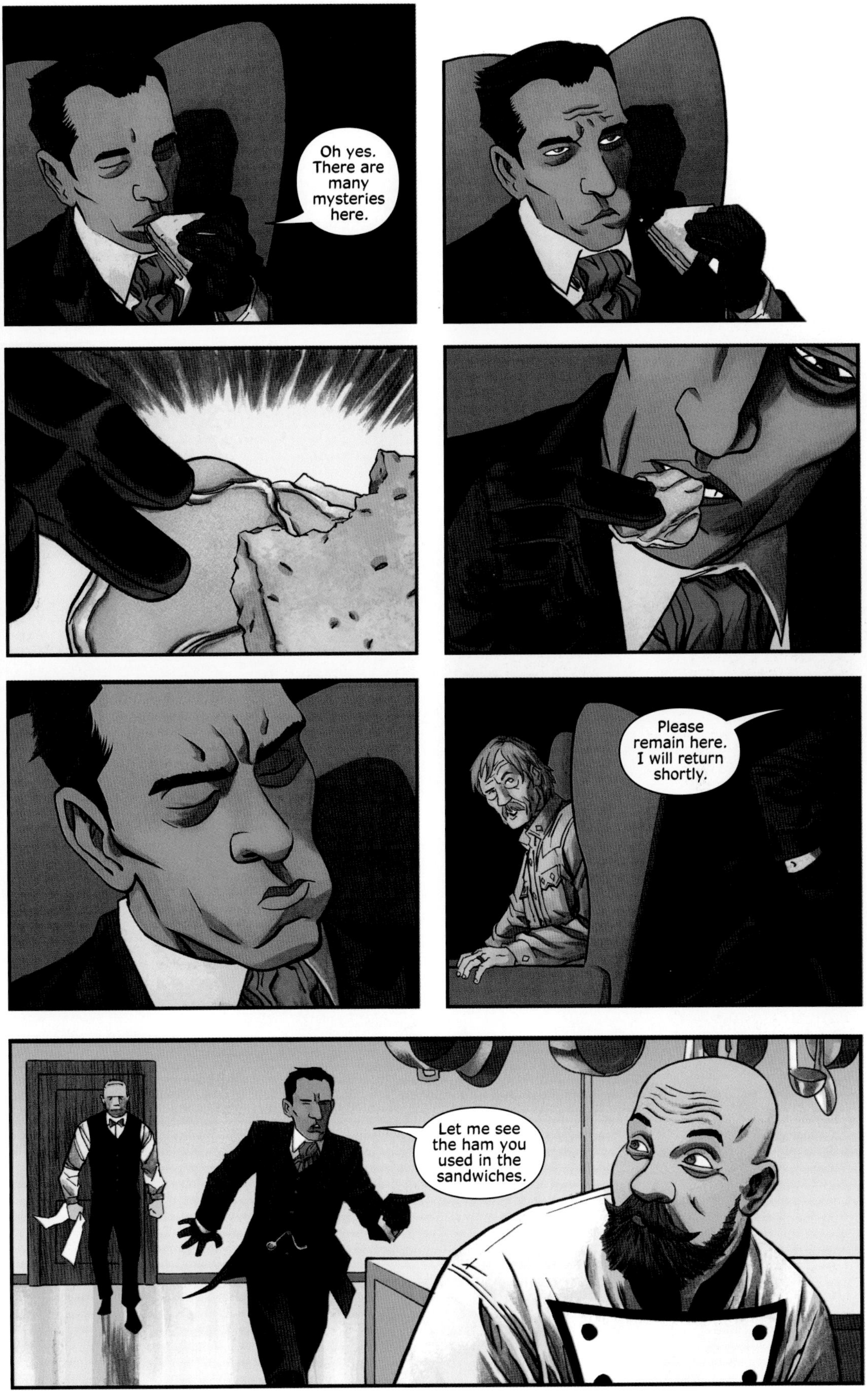
Oh yes. There are many mysteries here.
Please remain here. I will return shortly.
Let me see the ham you used in the sandwiches.

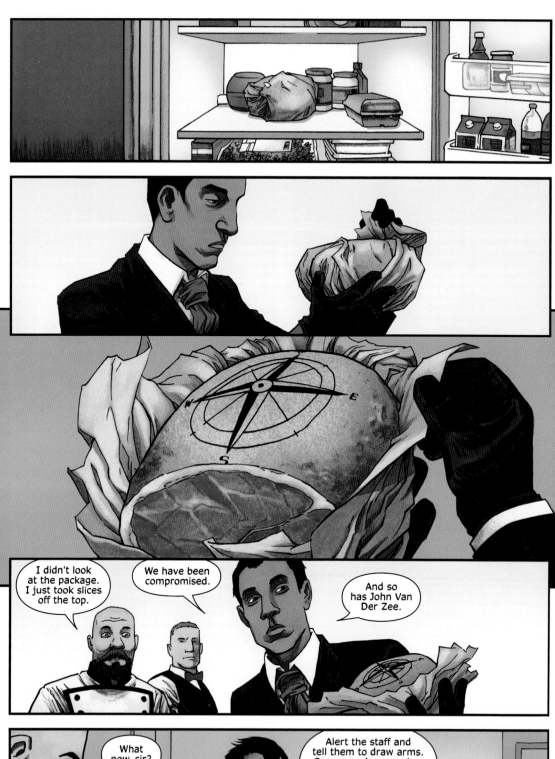

I didn't look at the package. I just took slices off the top.

We have been compromised.

And so has John Van Der Zee.

What now, sir?

Alert the staff and tell them to draw arms. Our new adversary is a monster. Nobody should adulterate a sandwich with human ham.

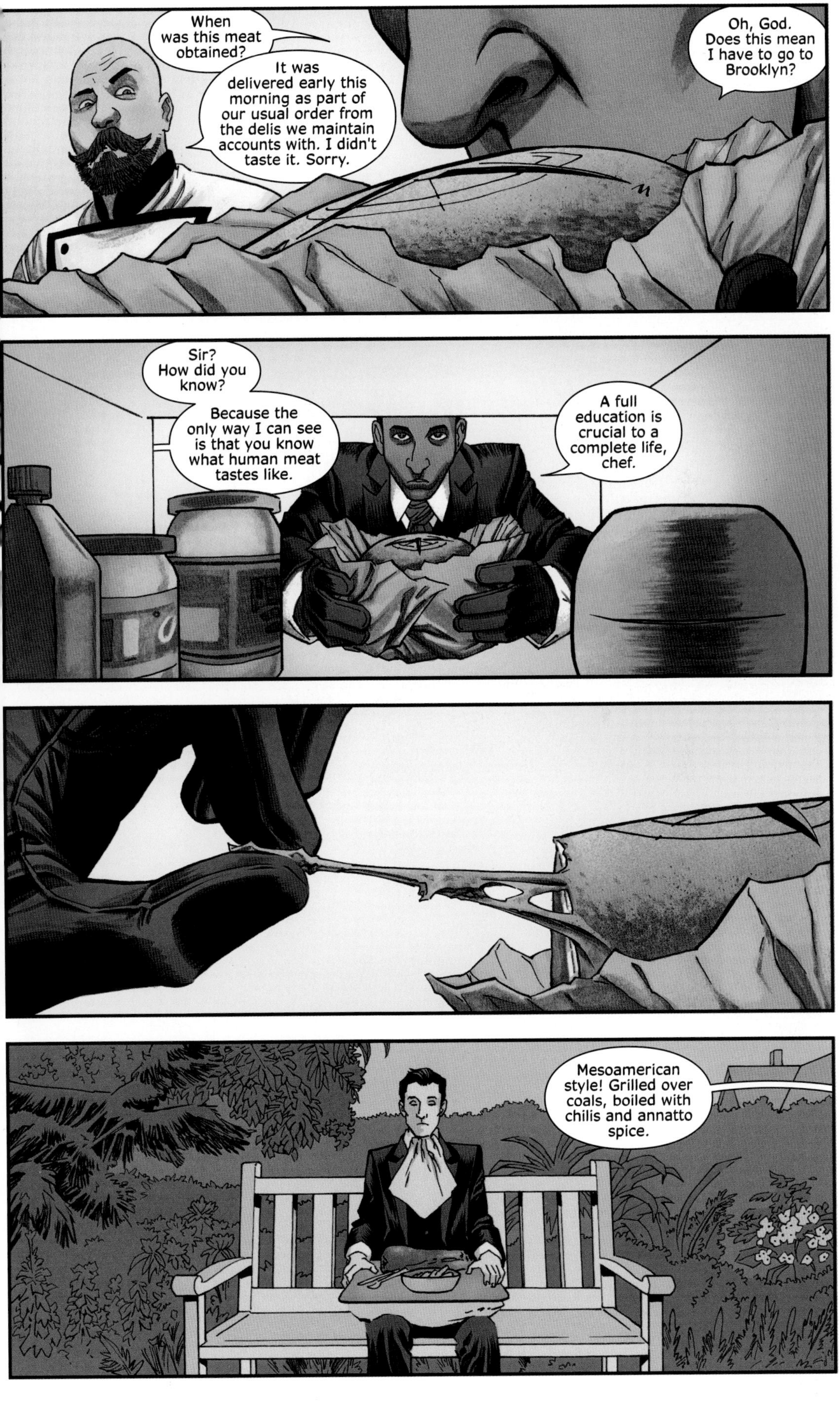
When was this meat obtained?
It was delivered early this morning as part of our usual order from the delis we maintain accounts with. I didn't taste it. Sorry.
Oh, God. Does this mean I have to go to Brooklyn?
Sir? How did you know?
Because the only way I can see is that you know what human meat tastes like.
A full education is crucial to a complete life, chef.
Mesoamerican style! Grilled over coals, boiled with chilis and annatto spice.

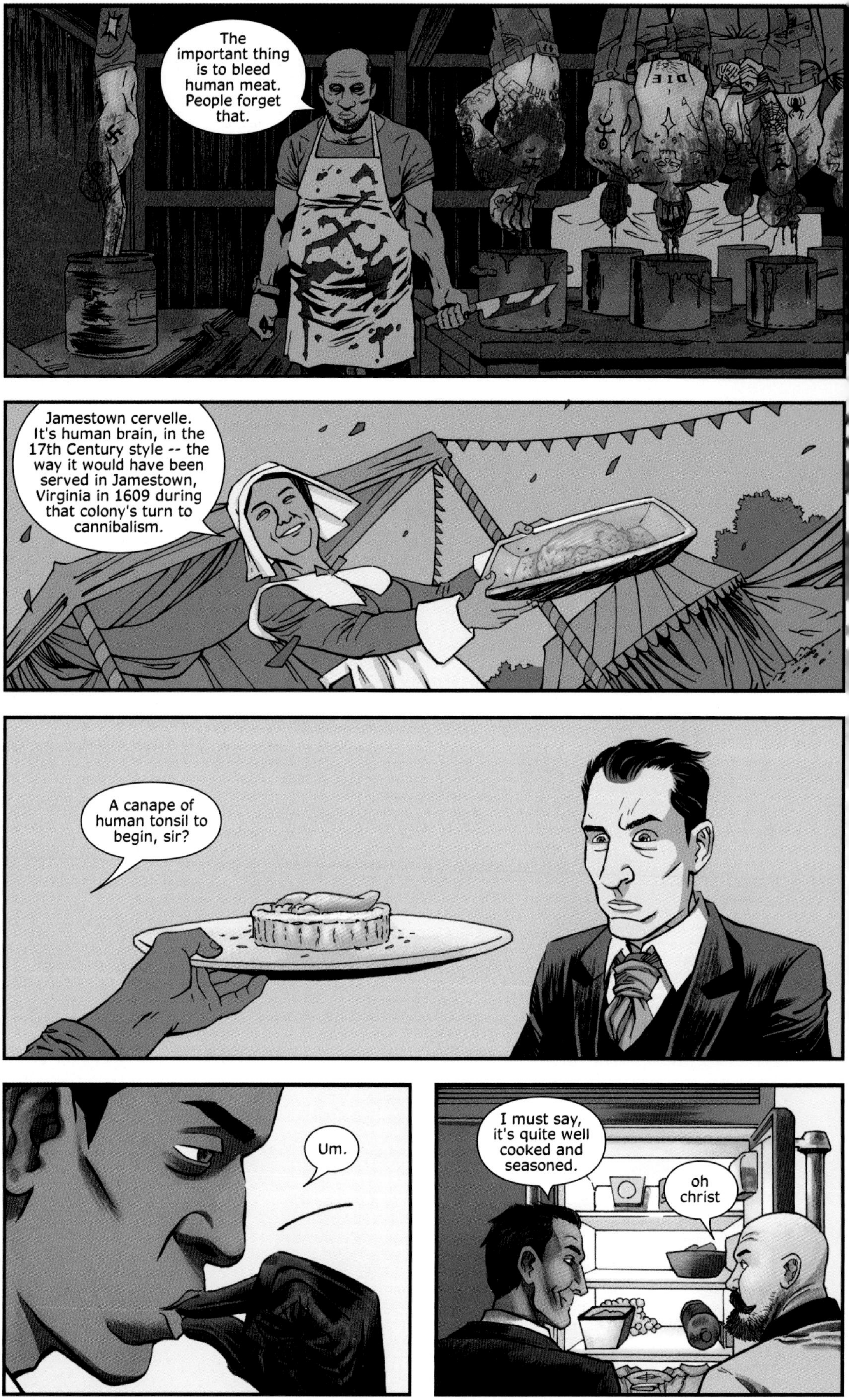
The important thing is to bleed human meat. People forget that.
Jamestown cervelle. It's human brain, in the 17th Century style -- the way it would have been served in Jamestown, Virginia in 1609 during that colony's turn to cannibalism.
A canape of human tonsil to begin, sir?
Um.
I must say, it's quite well cooked and seasoned.
oh christ

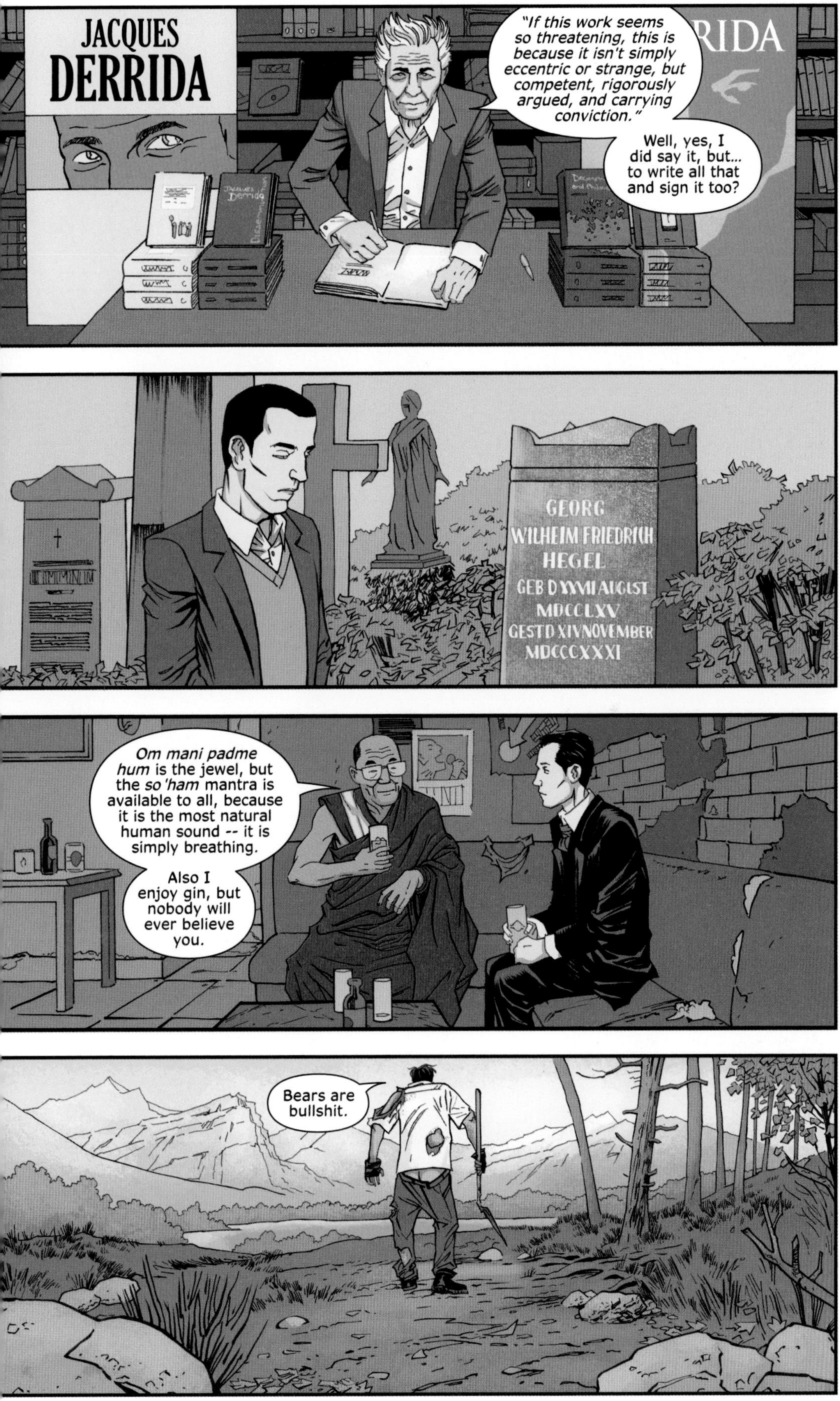
JACQUES
DERRIDA
RIDA
"If this work seems so threatening, this is because it isn't simply eccentric or strange, but competent, rigorously argued, and carrying conviction."
Well, yes, I did say it, but... to write all that and sign it too?
GEORG
WILHELM FRIEDRICH
HEGEL
GEB D XXVII AUGUST
MDCCLXX
GESTD XIV NOVEMBER
MDCCCXXXI
Om mani padme hum is the jewel, but the *so'ham* mantra is available to all, because it is the most natural human sound -- it is simply breathing.
Also I enjoy gin, but nobody will ever believe you.
Bears are bullshit.

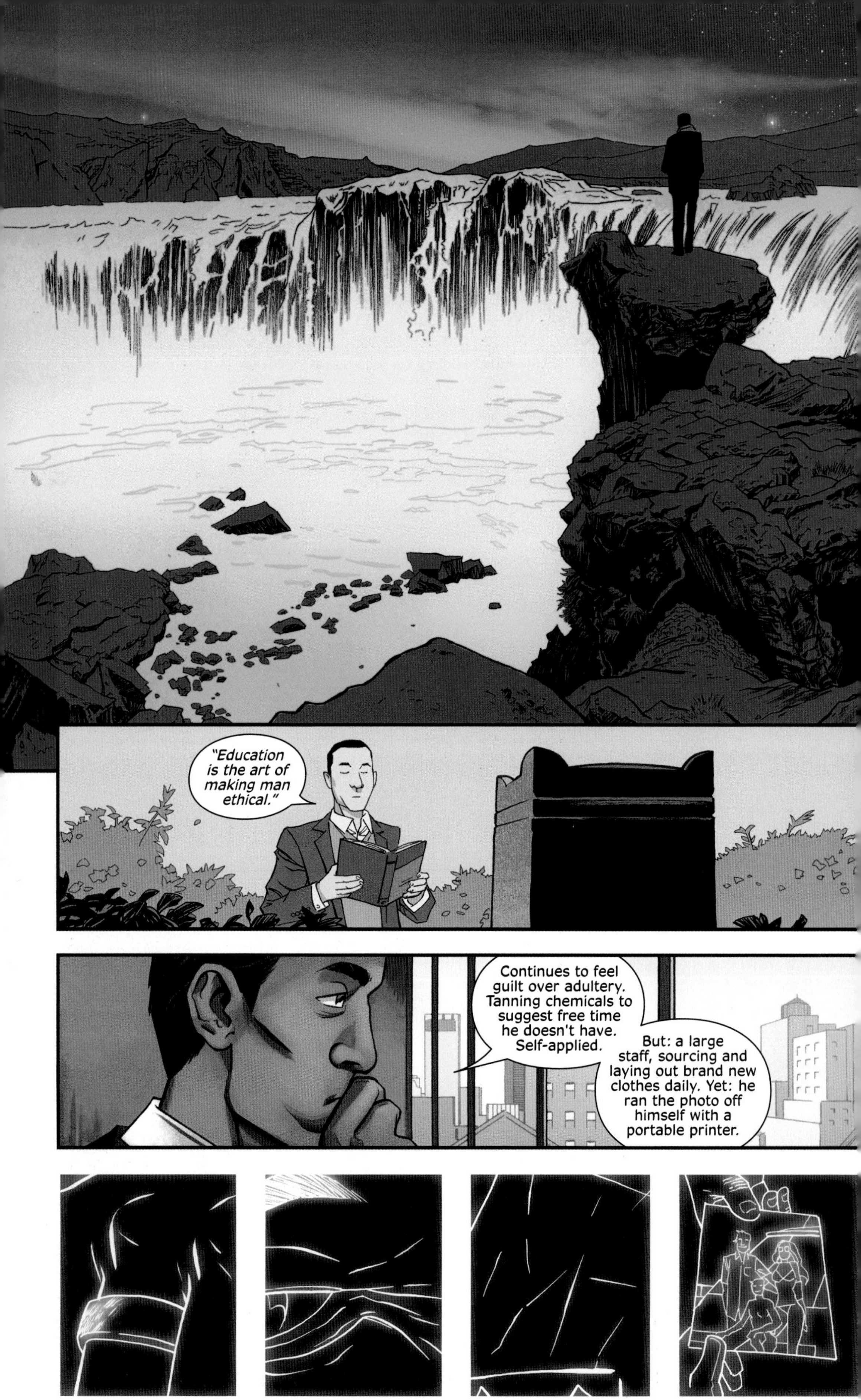
"Education is the art of making man ethical."
Continues to feel guilt over adultery. Tanning chemicals to suggest free time he doesn't have. Self-applied.
But: a large staff, sourcing and laying out brand new clothes daily. Yet: he ran the photo off himself with a portable printer.

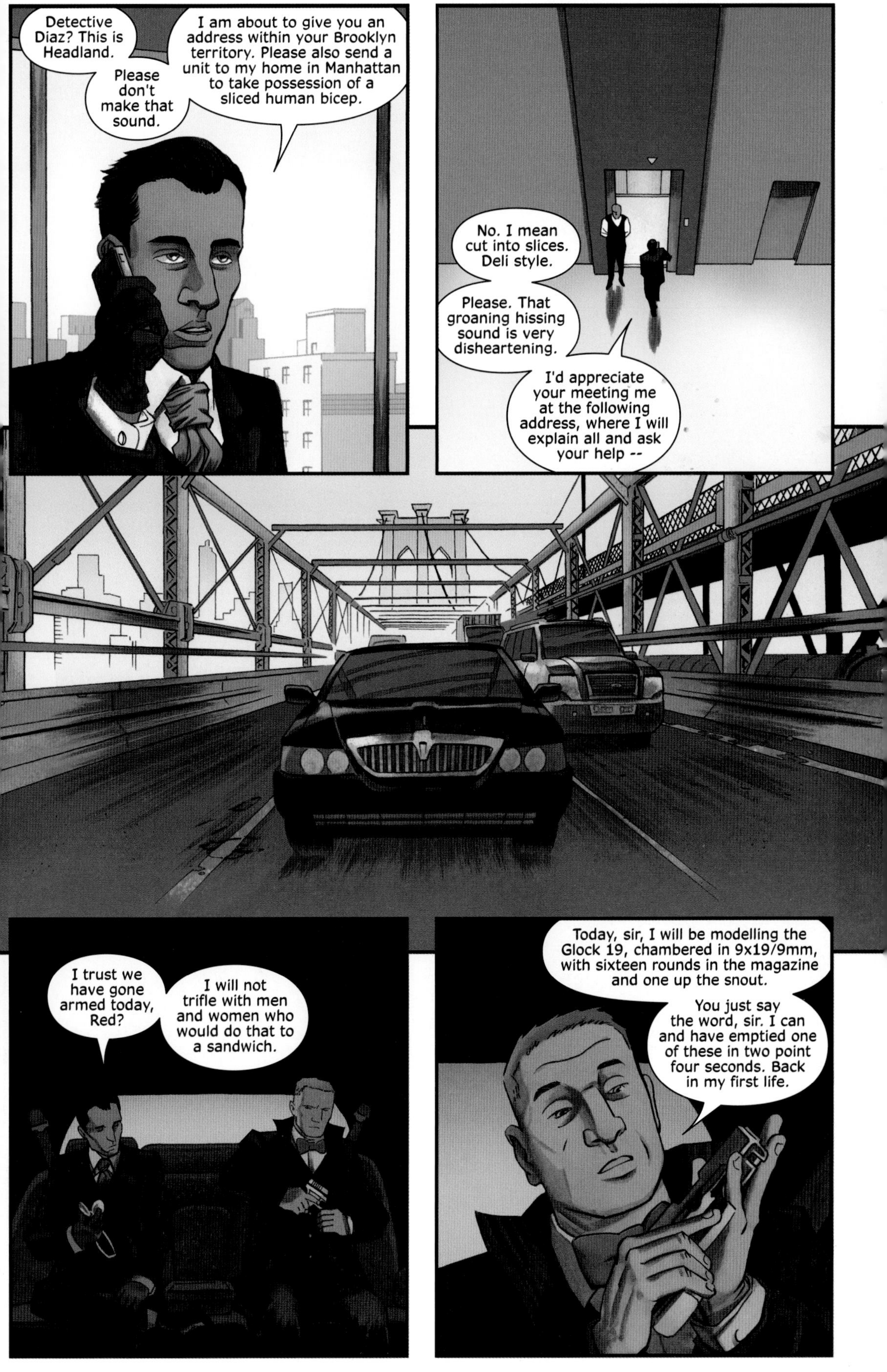
Detective Diaz? This is Headland.
Please don't make that sound.
I am about to give you an address within your Brooklyn territory. Please also send a unit to my home in Manhattan to take possession of a sliced human bicep.
No. I mean cut into slices. Deli style.
Please. That groaning hissing sound is very disheartening.
I'd appreciate your meeting me at the following address, where I will explain all and ask your help --
I trust we have gone armed today, Red?
I will not trifle with men and women who would do that to a sandwich.
Today, sir, I will be modelling the Glock 19, chambered in 9x19/9mm, with sixteen rounds in the magazine and one up the snout.
You just say the word, sir. I can and have emptied one of these in two point four seconds. Back in my first life.

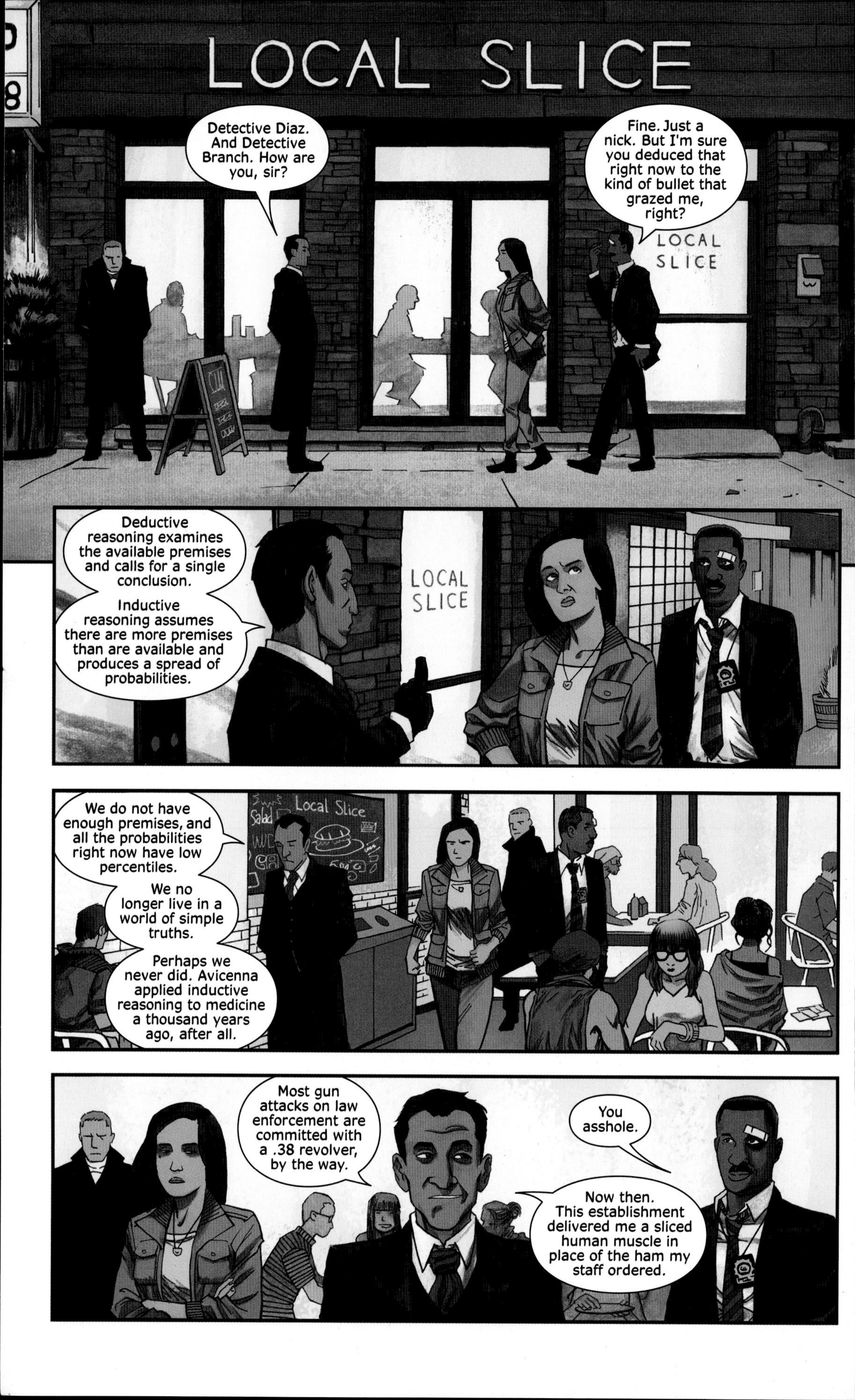
LOCAL SLICE
Detective Diaz. And Detective Branch. How are you, sir?
Fine. Just a nick. But I'm sure you deduced that right now to the kind of bullet that grazed me, right?
LOCAL SLICE
Deductive reasoning examines the available premises and calls for a single conclusion.
Inductive reasoning assumes there are more premises than are available and produces a spread of probabilities.
LOCAL SLICE
We do not have enough premises, and all the probabilities right now have low percentiles.
We no longer live in a world of simple truths.
Perhaps we never did. Avicenna applied inductive reasoning to medicine a thousand years ago, after all.
Local Slice
Most gun attacks on law enforcement are committed with a .38 revolver, by the way.
You asshole.
Now then. This establishment delivered me a sliced human muscle in place of the ham my staff ordered.

The muscle belonged to the son of a new client of mine. The son died some weeks ago. The client is unaware of the criminal food order.

And now? Over to you.

Thanks for that nice hot plate of shit for breakfast, Viv.

Police. I'm going to need to see the owner.

NO ENTRY

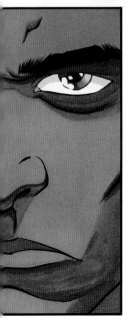

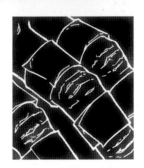

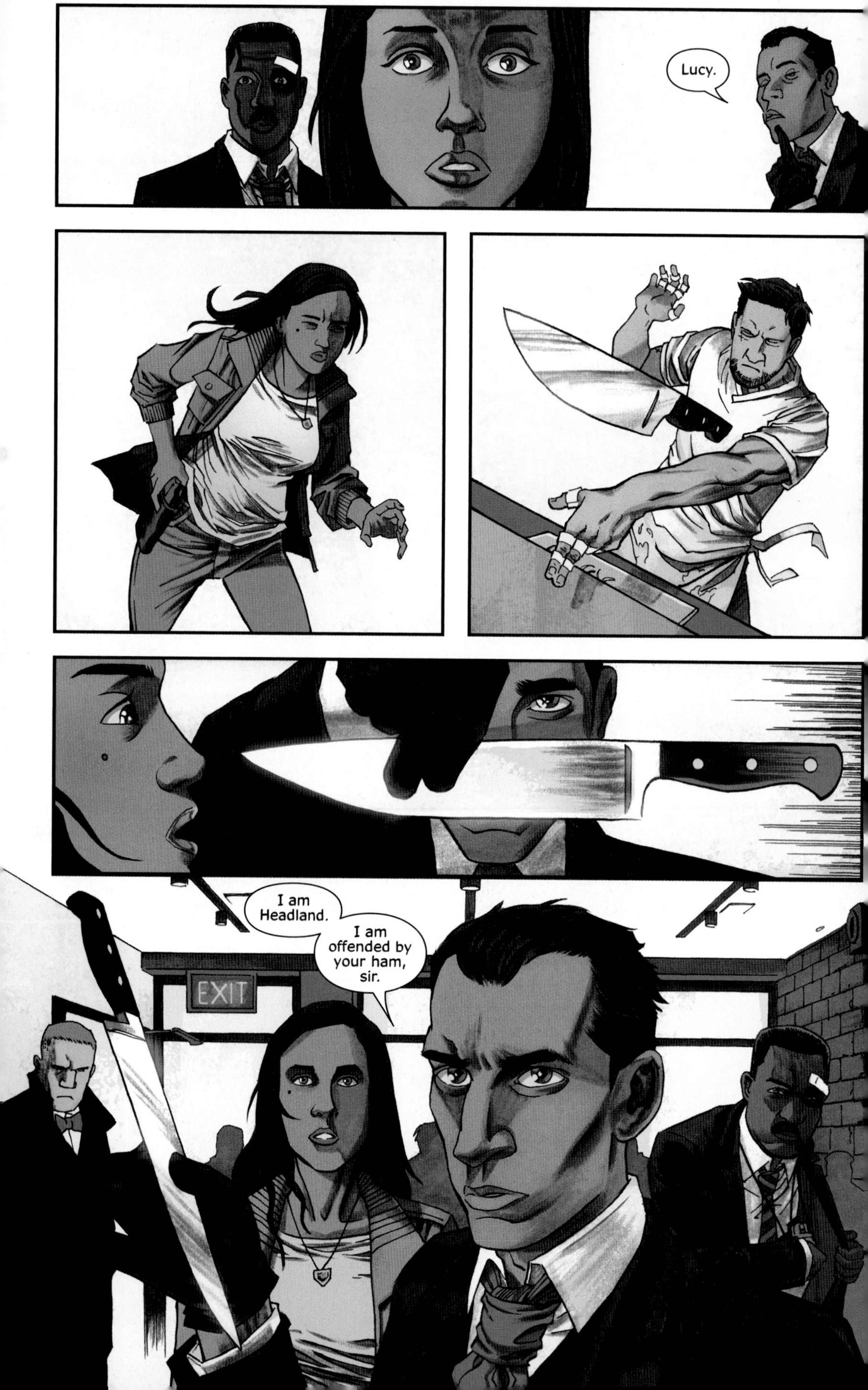
Lucy.
I am Headland.
I am offended by your ham, sir.
EXIT

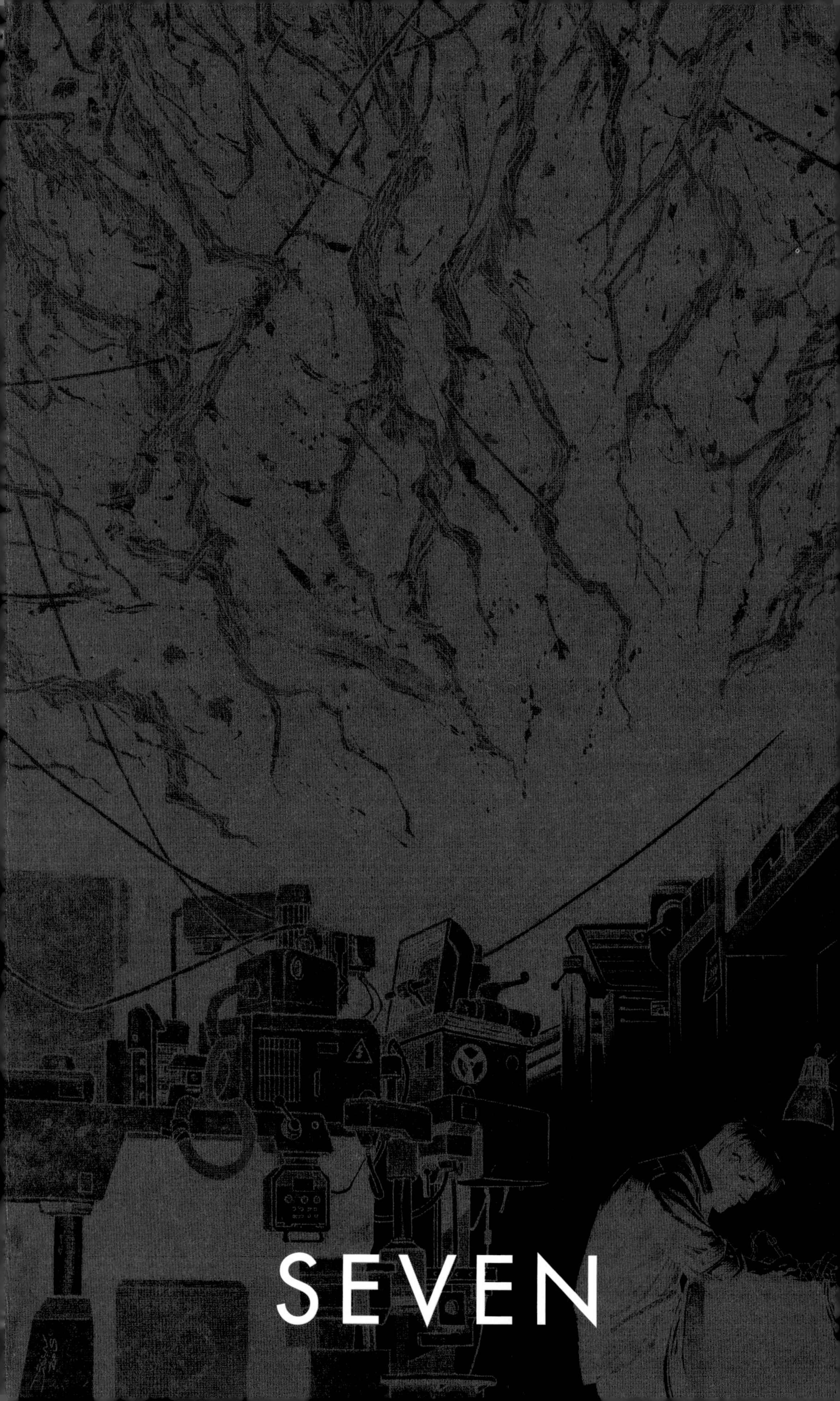

SEVEN

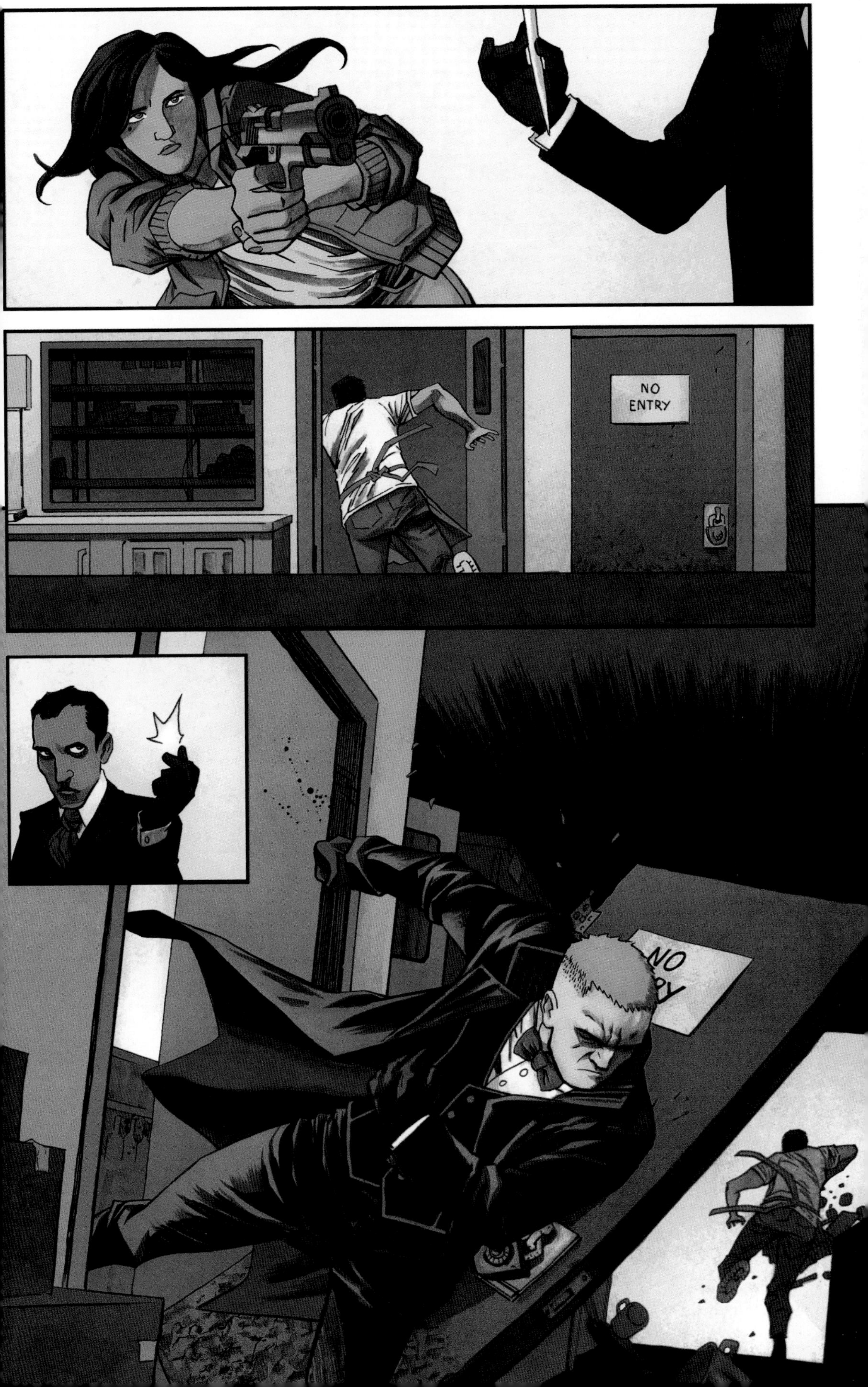

NO
ENTRY

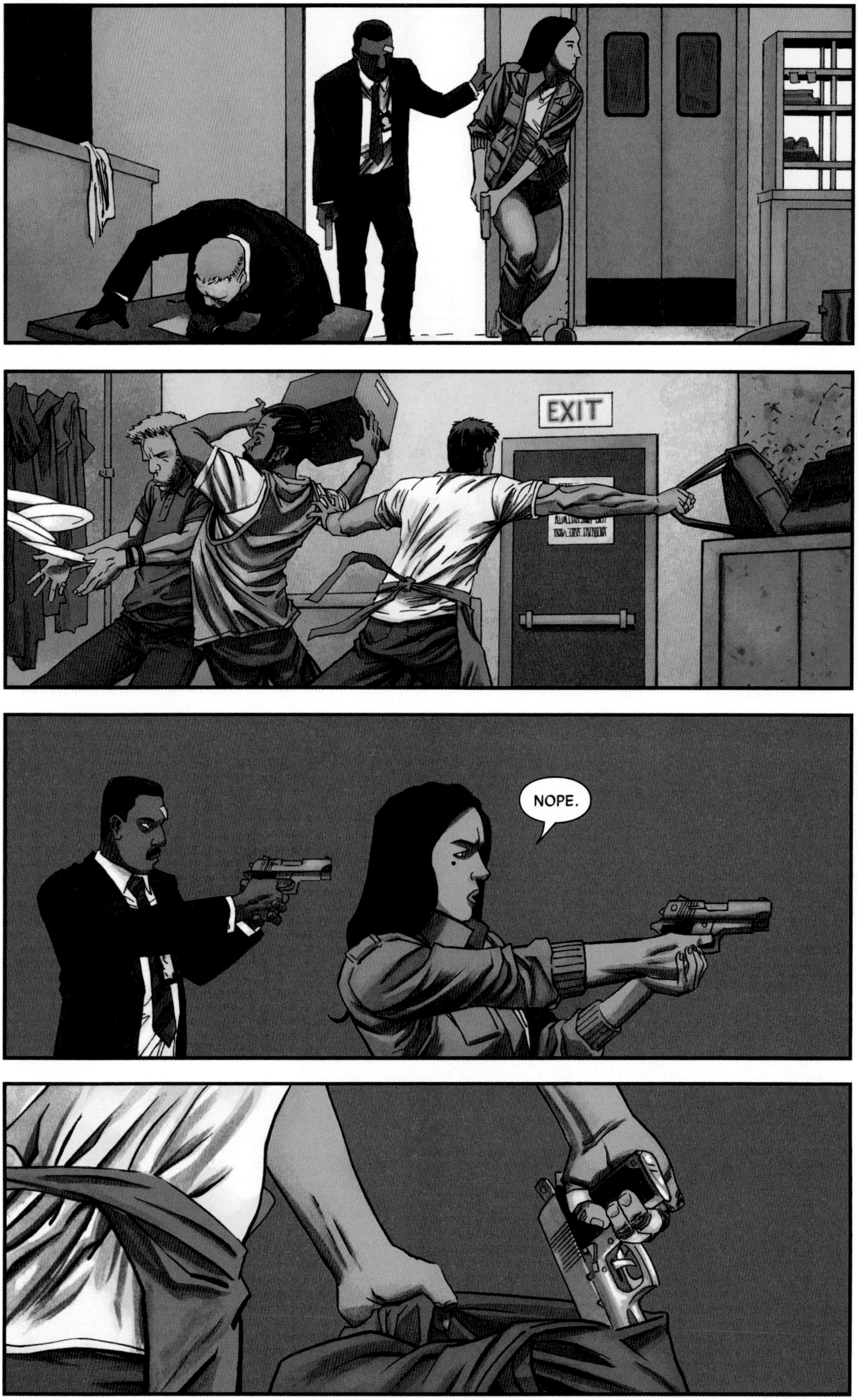

EXIT
NOPE.

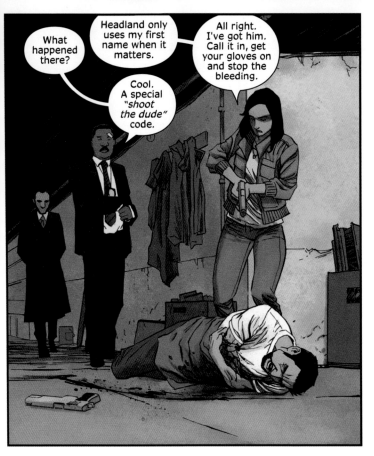

What happened there?

Headland only uses my first name when it matters.

All right. I've got him. Call it in, get your gloves on and stop the bleeding.

Cool. A special *shoot the dude"* code.

This is all going to take a little while now. We'll seal the kitchen. I'll call you when he's ready to be questioned?

I would ask that you allow this to be applied as per my Confidential Informant contract. Let me follow through with this.

Deal.

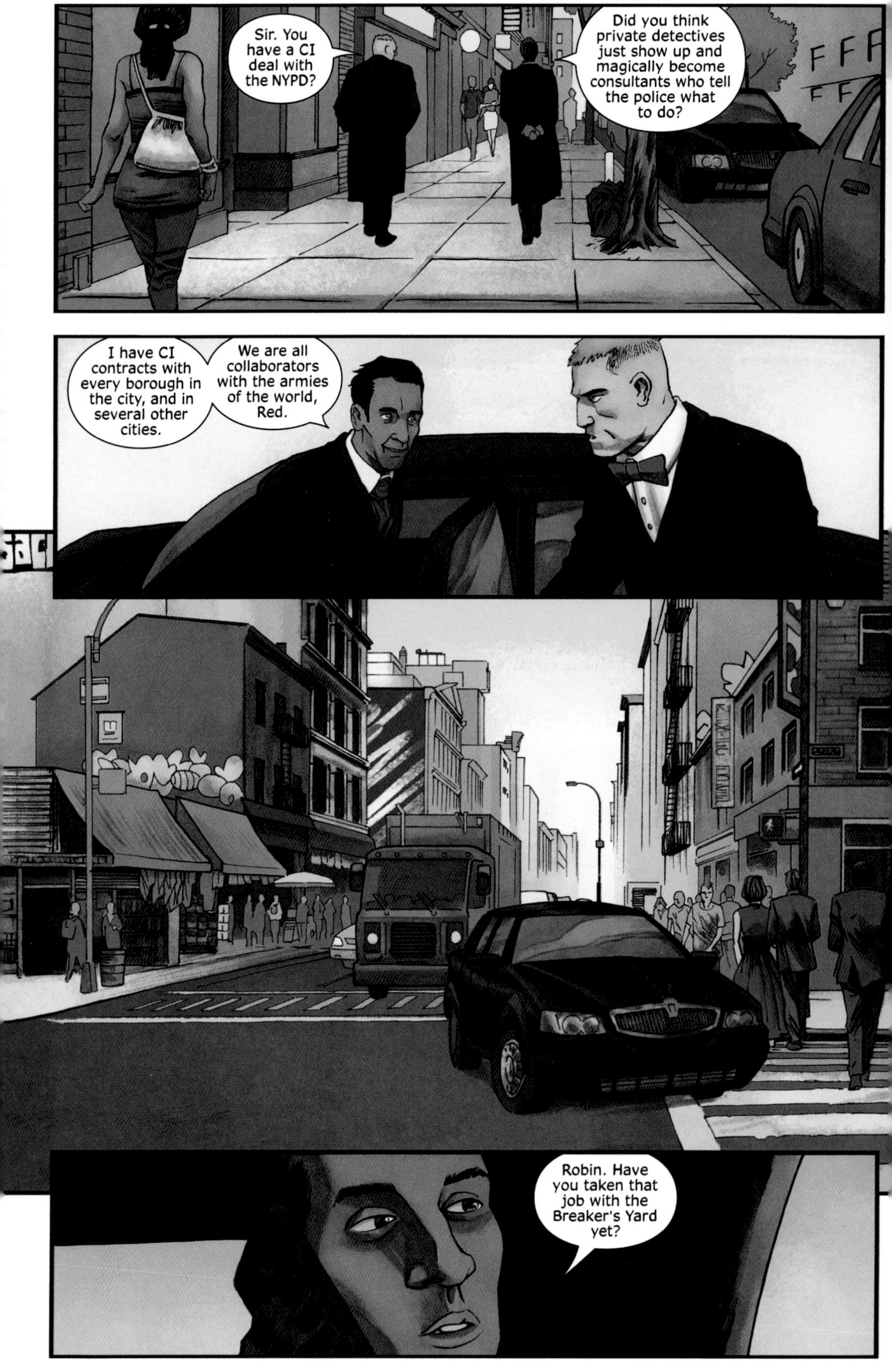
Sir. You have a CI deal with the NYPD?
Did you think private detectives just show up and magically become consultants who tell the police what to do?
I have CI contracts with every borough in the city, and in several other cities.
We are all collaborators with the armies of the world, Red.
Robin. Have you taken that job with the Breaker's Yard yet?

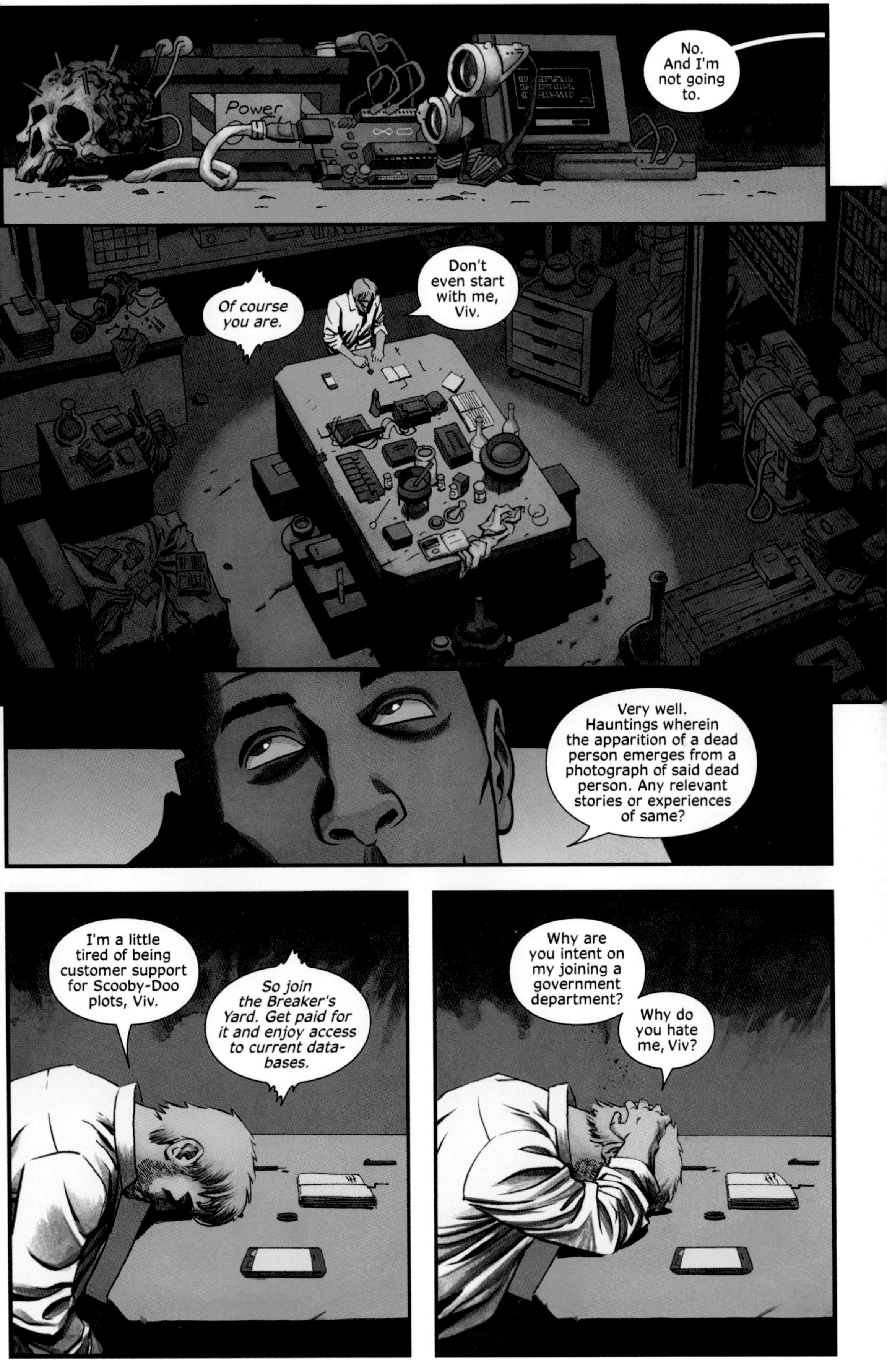

Power
No. And I'm not going to.
Of course you are.
Don't even start with me, Viv.
Very well. Hauntings wherein the apparition of a dead person emerges from a photograph of said dead person. Any relevant stories or experiences of same?
I'm a little tired of being customer support for Scooby-Doo plots, Viv.
So join the Breaker's Yard. Get paid for it and enjoy access to current data-bases.
Why are you intent on my joining a government department?
Why do you hate me, Viv?

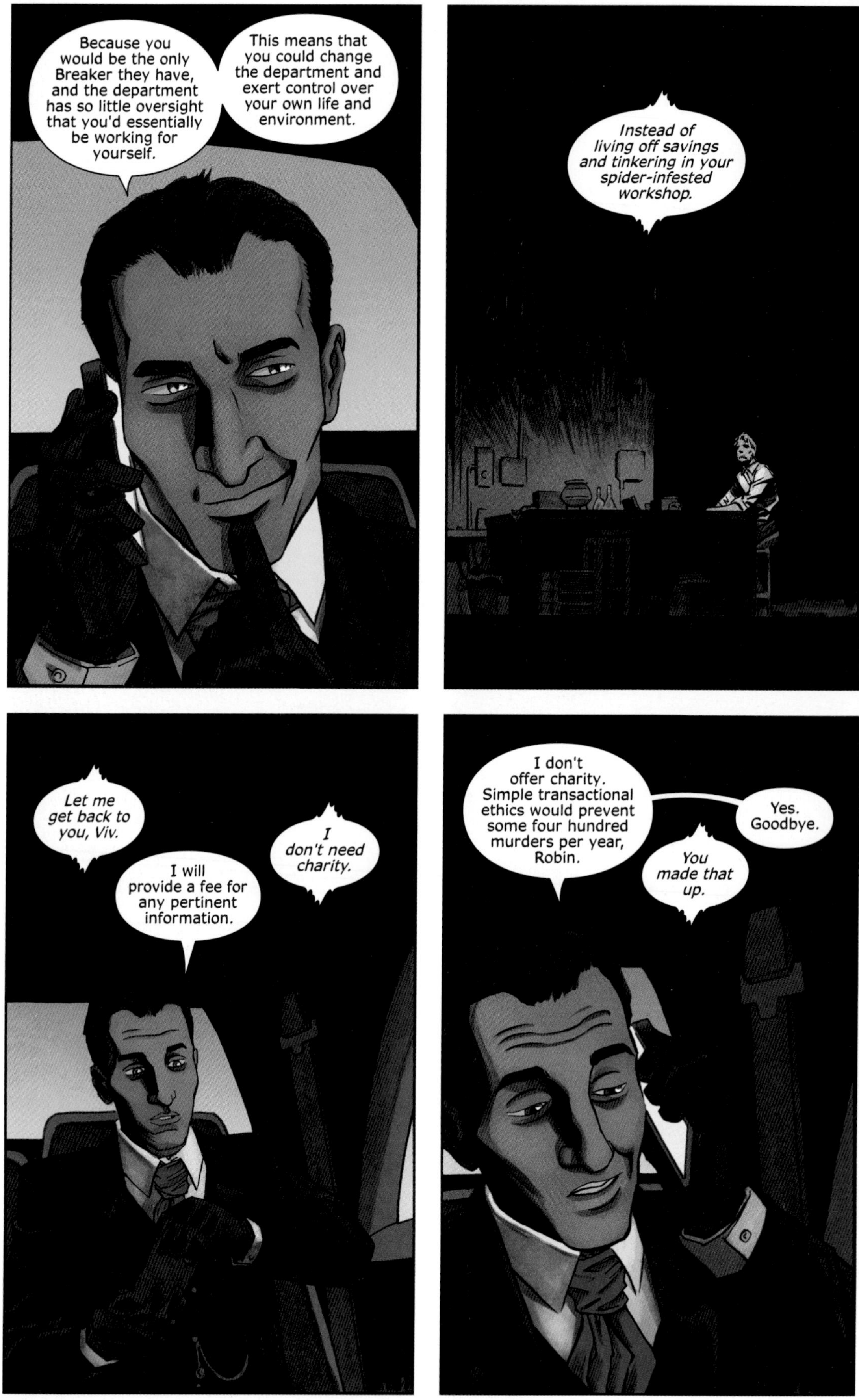
Because you would be the only Breaker they have, and the department has so little oversight that you'd essentially be working for yourself.
This means that you could change the department and exert control over your own life and environment.
Instead of living off savings and tinkering in your spider-infested workshop.
Let me get back to you, Viv.
I will provide a fee for any pertinent information.
I don't need charity.
I don't offer charity. Simple transactional ethics would prevent some four hundred murders per year, Robin.
You made that up.
Yes. Goodbye.

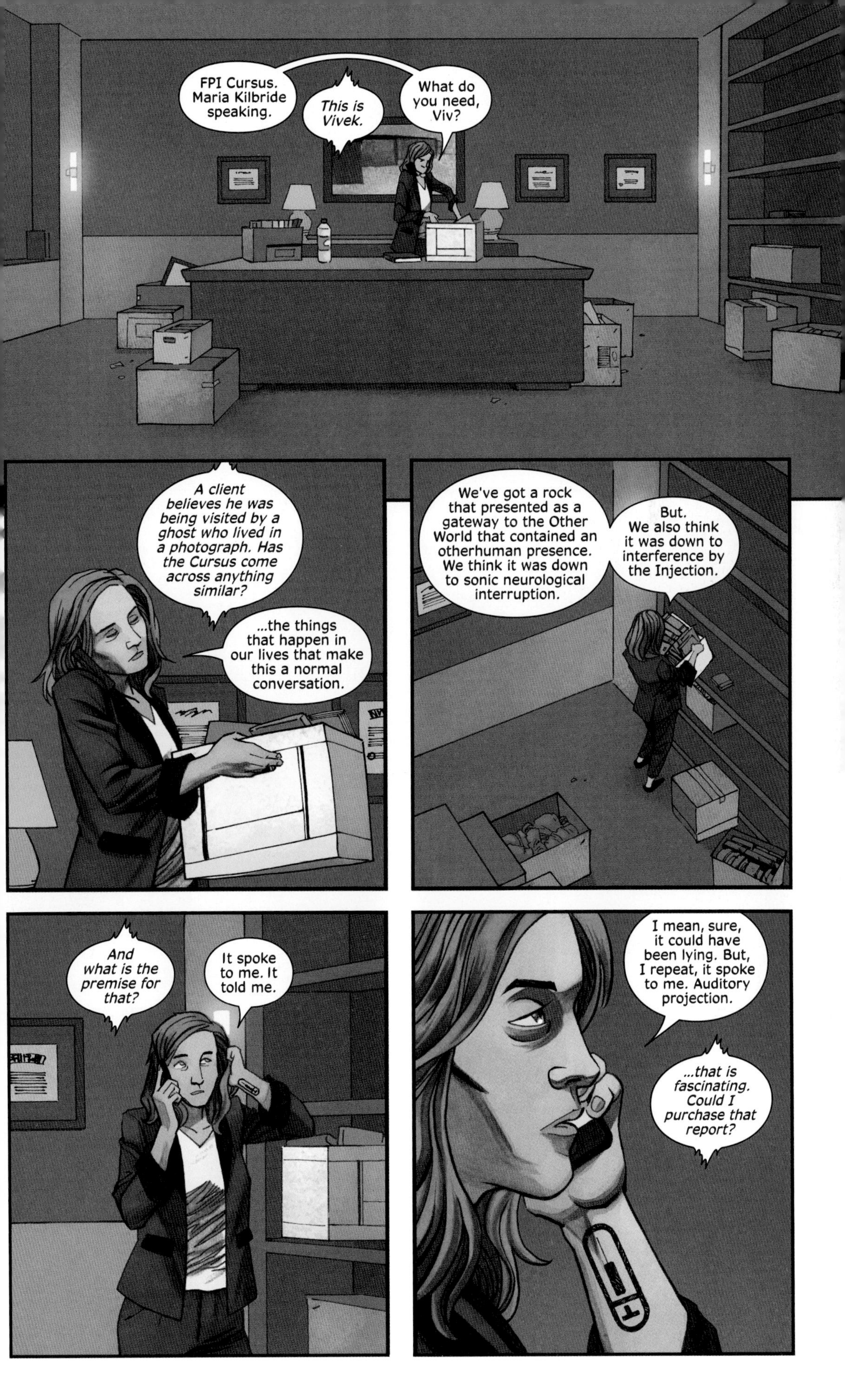

FPI Cursus. Maria Kilbride speaking.
This is Vivek.
What do you need, Viv?
A client believes he was being visited by a ghost who lived in a photograph. Has the Cursus come across anything similar?
...the things that happen in our lives that make this a normal conversation.
We've got a rock that presented as a gateway to the Other World that contained an otherhuman presence. We think it was down to sonic neurological interruption.
But. We also think it was down to interference by the Injection.
And what is the premise for that?
It spoke to me. It told me.
I mean, sure, it could have been lying. But, I repeat, it spoke to me. Auditory projection.
...that is fascinating. Could I purchase that report?

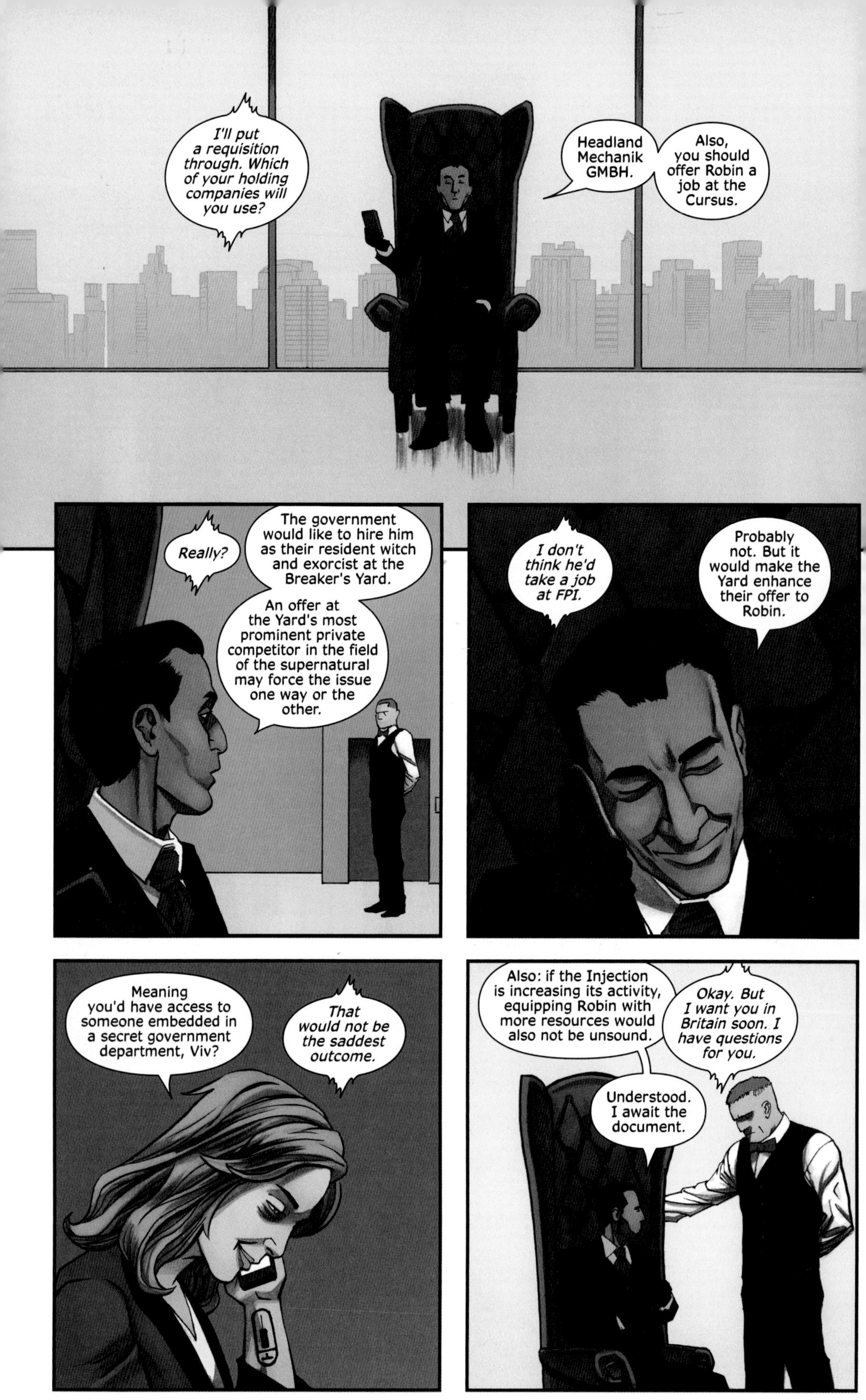

I'll put a requisition through. Which of your holding companies will you use?
Headland Mechanik GMBH.
Also, you should offer Robin a job at the Cursus.
Really?
The government would like to hire him as their resident witch and exorcist at the Breaker's Yard.
An offer at the Yard's most prominent private competitor in the field of the supernatural may force the issue one way or the other.
I don't think he'd take a job at FPI.
Probably not. But it would make the Yard enhance their offer to Robin.
Meaning you'd have access to someone embedded in a secret government department, Viv?
That would not be the saddest outcome.
Also: if the Injection is increasing its activity, equipping Robin with more resources would also not be unsound.
Okay. But I want you in Britain soon. I have questions for you.
Understood. I await the document.

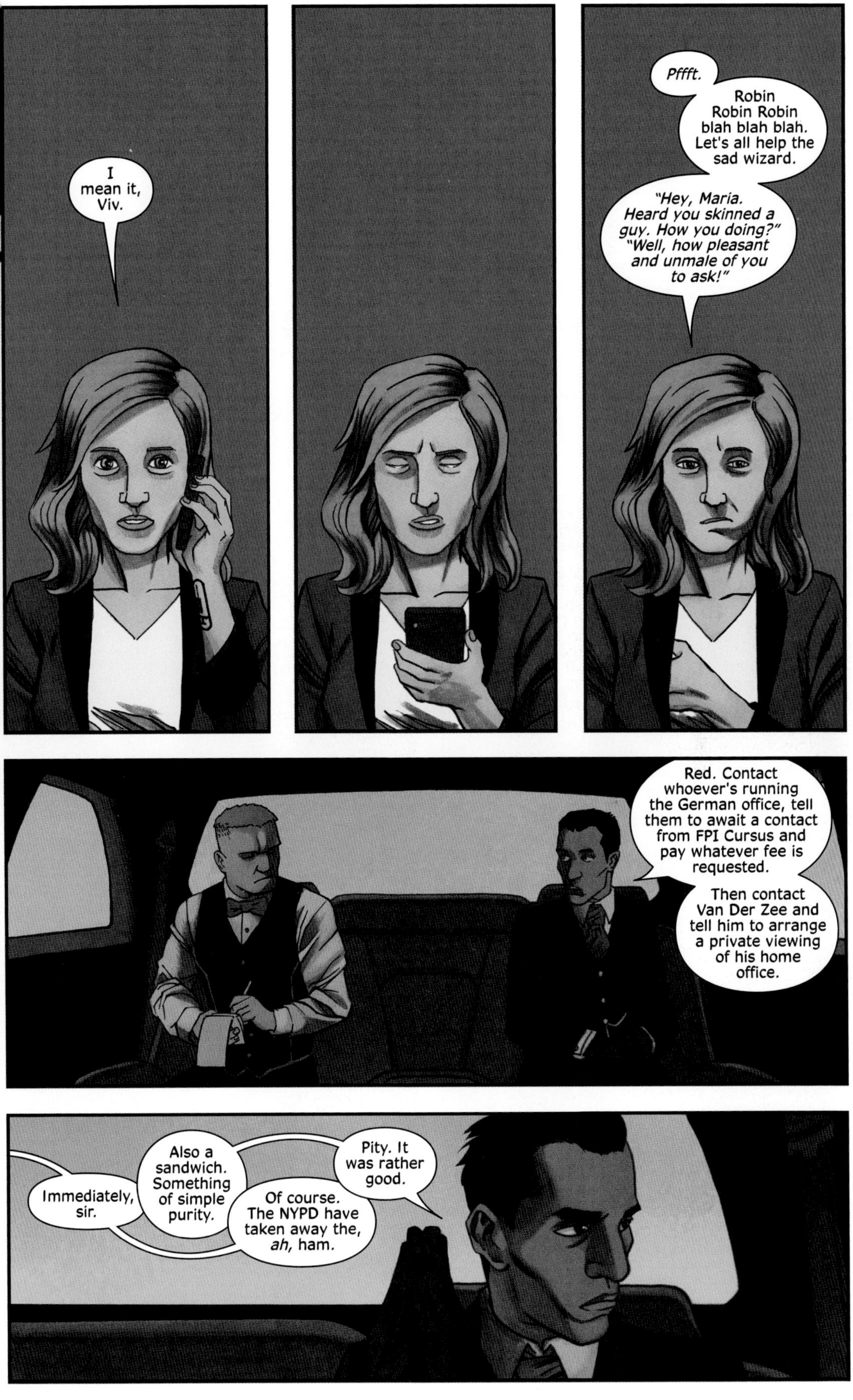
I mean it, Viv.
Pffft.
Robin Robin Robin blah blah blah. Let's all help the sad wizard.
"Hey, Maria. Heard you skinned a guy. How you doing?" "Well, how pleasant and unmale of you to ask!"
Red. Contact whoever's running the German office, tell them to await a contact from FPI Cursus and pay whatever fee is requested.
Then contact Van Der Zee and tell him to arrange a private viewing of his home office.
Immediately, sir.
Also a sandwich. Something of simple purity.
Of course. The NYPD have taken away the, *ah,* ham.
Pity. It was rather good.

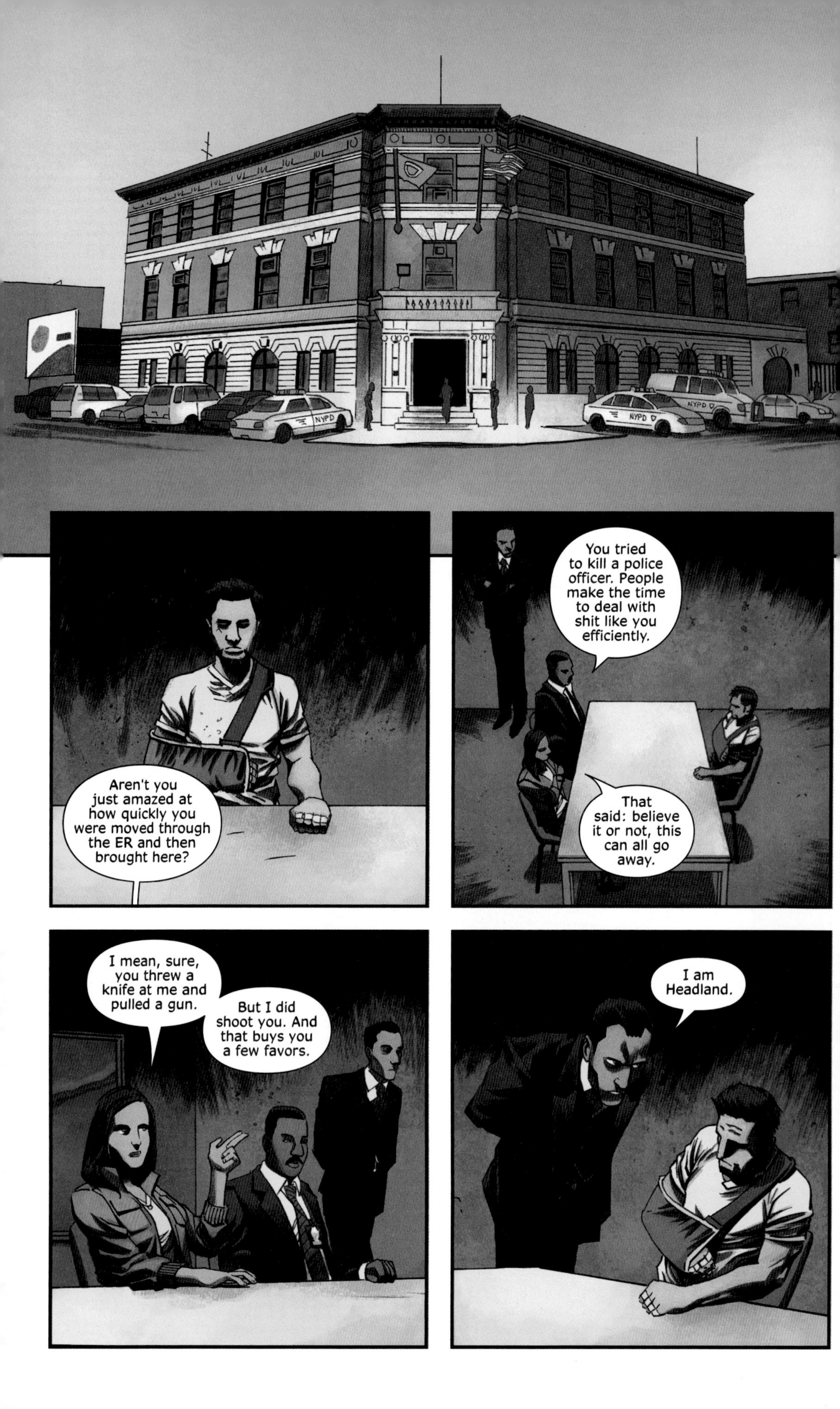
Aren't you just amazed at how quickly you were moved through the ER and then brought here?
You tried to kill a police officer. People make the time to deal with shit like you efficiently.
That said: believe it or not, this can all go away.
I mean, sure, you threw a knife at me and pulled a gun.
But I did shoot you. And that buys you a few favors.
I am Headland.
NYPD
NYPD
NYPD

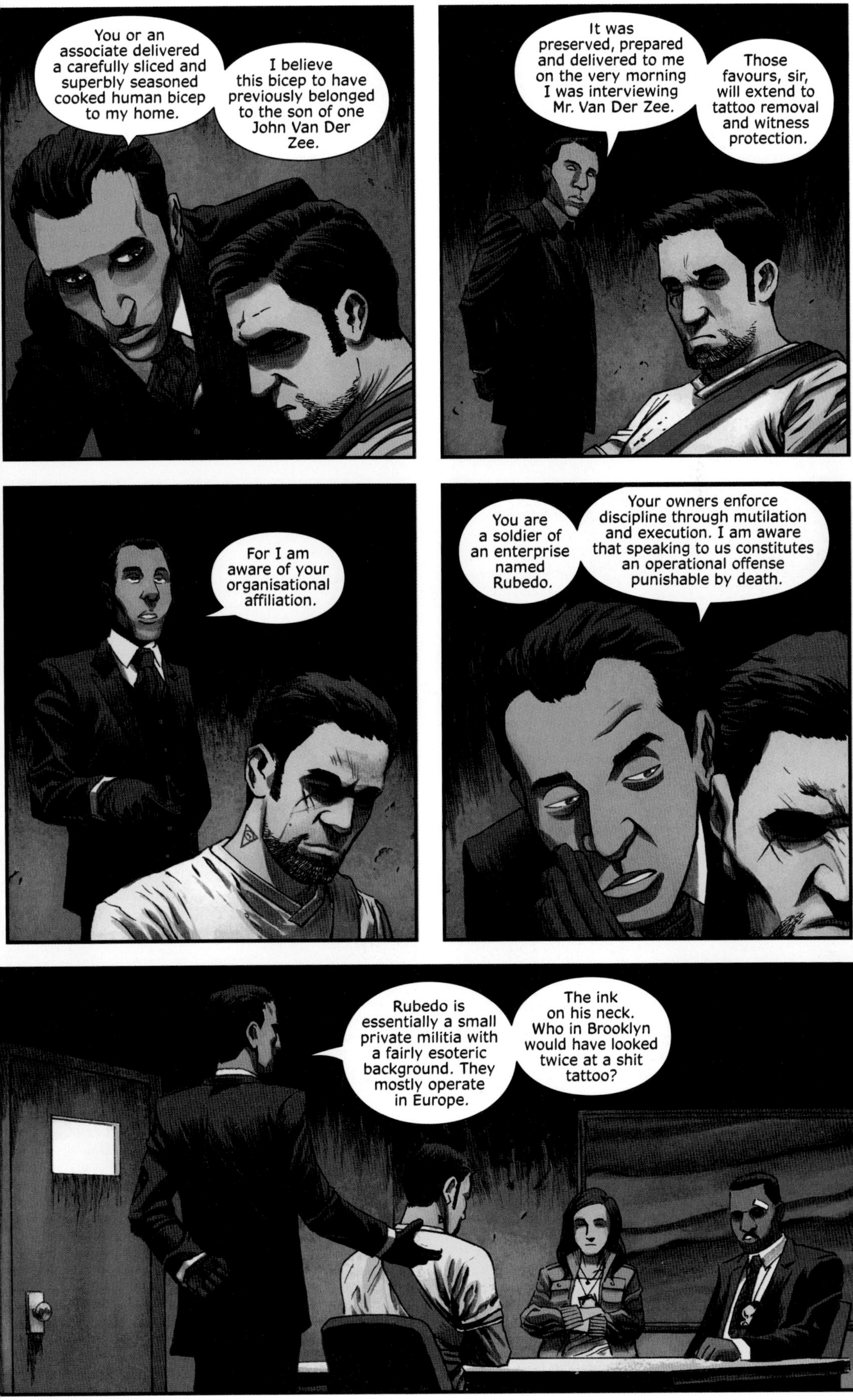

You or an associate delivered a carefully sliced and superbly seasoned cooked human bicep to my home.
I believe this bicep to have previously belonged to the son of one John Van Der Zee.
It was preserved, prepared and delivered to me on the very morning I was interviewing Mr. Van Der Zee.
Those favours, sir, will extend to tattoo removal and witness protection.
For I am aware of your organisational affiliation.
You are a soldier of an enterprise named Rubedo.
Your owners enforce discipline through mutilation and execution. I am aware that speaking to us constitutes an operational offense punishable by death.
Rubedo is essentially a small private militia with a fairly esoteric background. They mostly operate in Europe.
The ink on his neck. Who in Brooklyn would have looked twice at a shit tattoo?

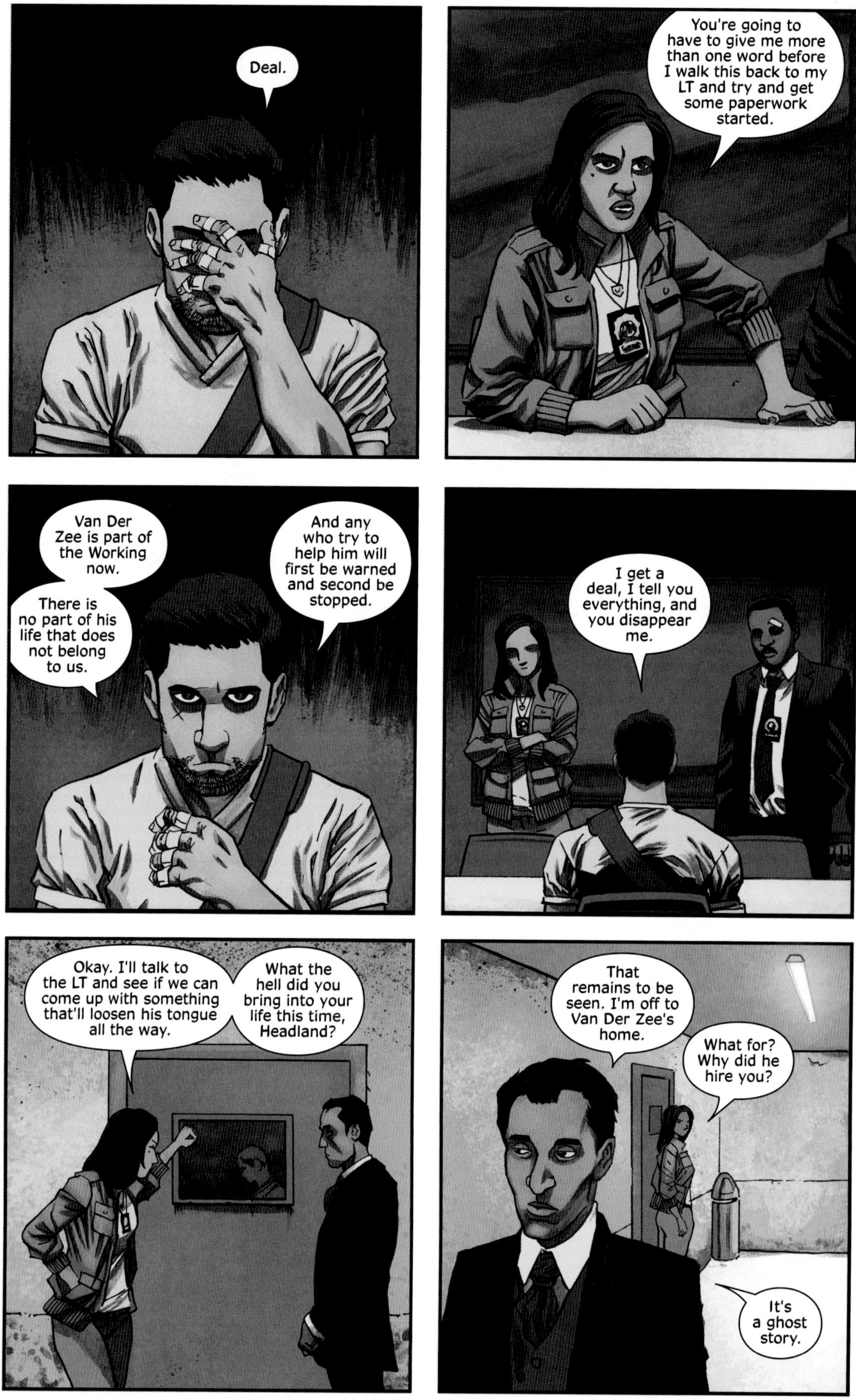
Deal.
You're going to have to give me more than one word before I walk this back to my LT and try and get some paperwork started.
Van Der Zee is part of the Working now.
There is no part of his life that does not belong to us.
And any who try to help him will first be warned and second be stopped.
I get a deal, I tell you everything, and you disappear me.
Okay. I'll talk to the LT and see if we can come up with something that'll loosen his tongue all the way.
What the hell did you bring into your life this time, Headland?
That remains to be seen. I'm off to Van Der Zee's home.
What for? Why did he hire you?
It's a ghost story.

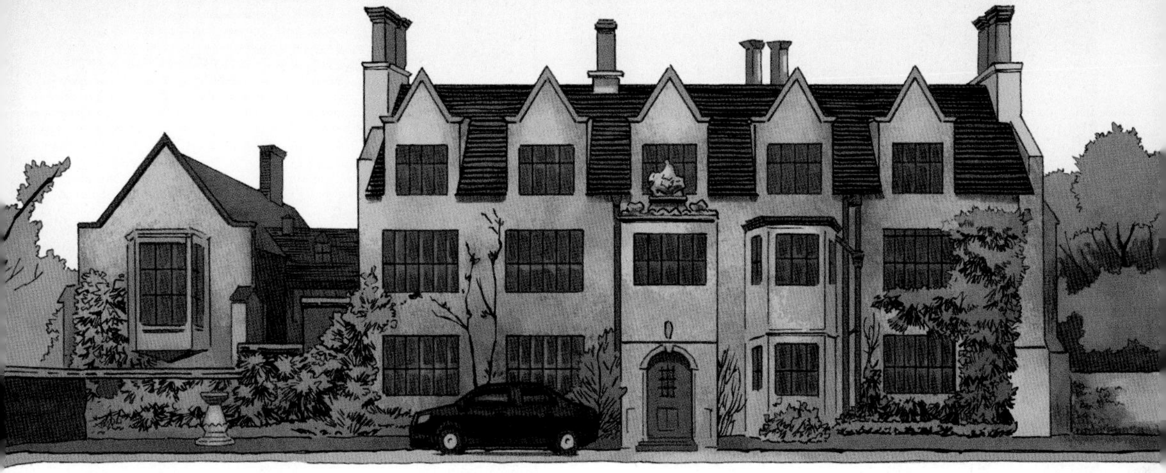

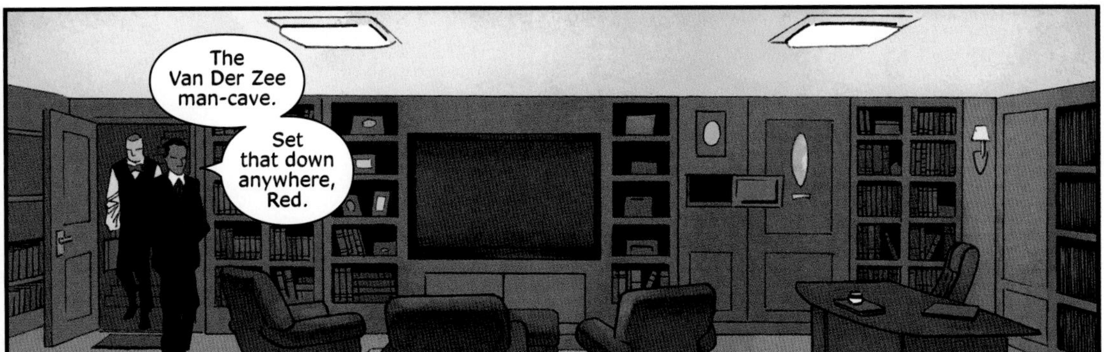

The Van Der Zee man-cave.
Set that down anywhere, Red.

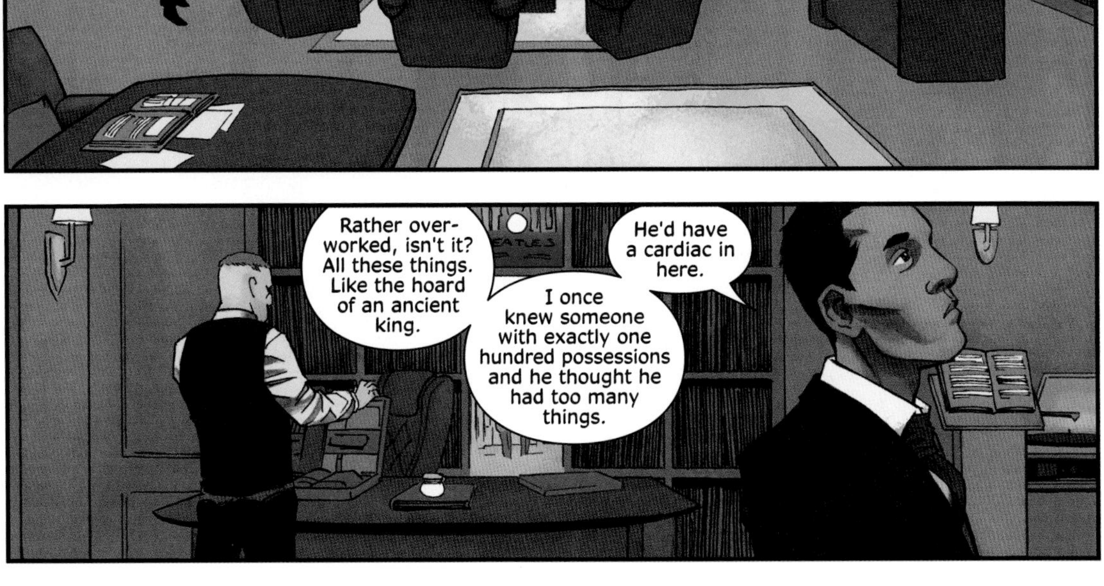

Rather over-worked, isn't it? All these things. Like the hoard of an ancient king.
He'd have a cardiac in here.
I once knew someone with exactly one hundred possessions and he thought he had too many things.

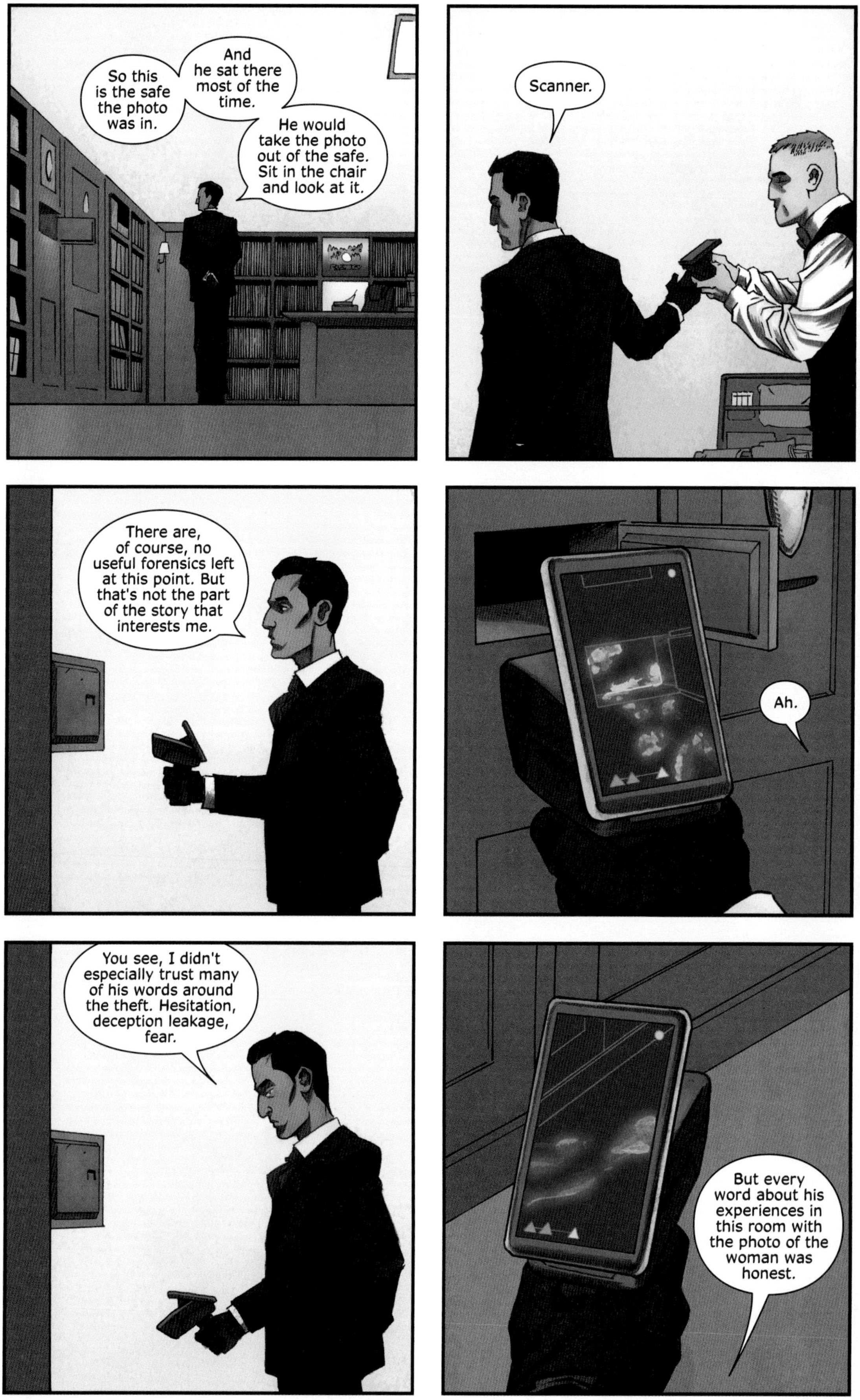
So this is the safe the photo was in.
And he sat there most of the time.
He would take the photo out of the safe. Sit in the chair and look at it.
Scanner.
There are, of course, no useful forensics left at this point. But that's not the part of the story that interests me.
Ah.
You see, I didn't especially trust many of his words around the theft. Hesitation, deception leakage, fear.
But every word about his experiences in this room with the photo of the woman was honest.

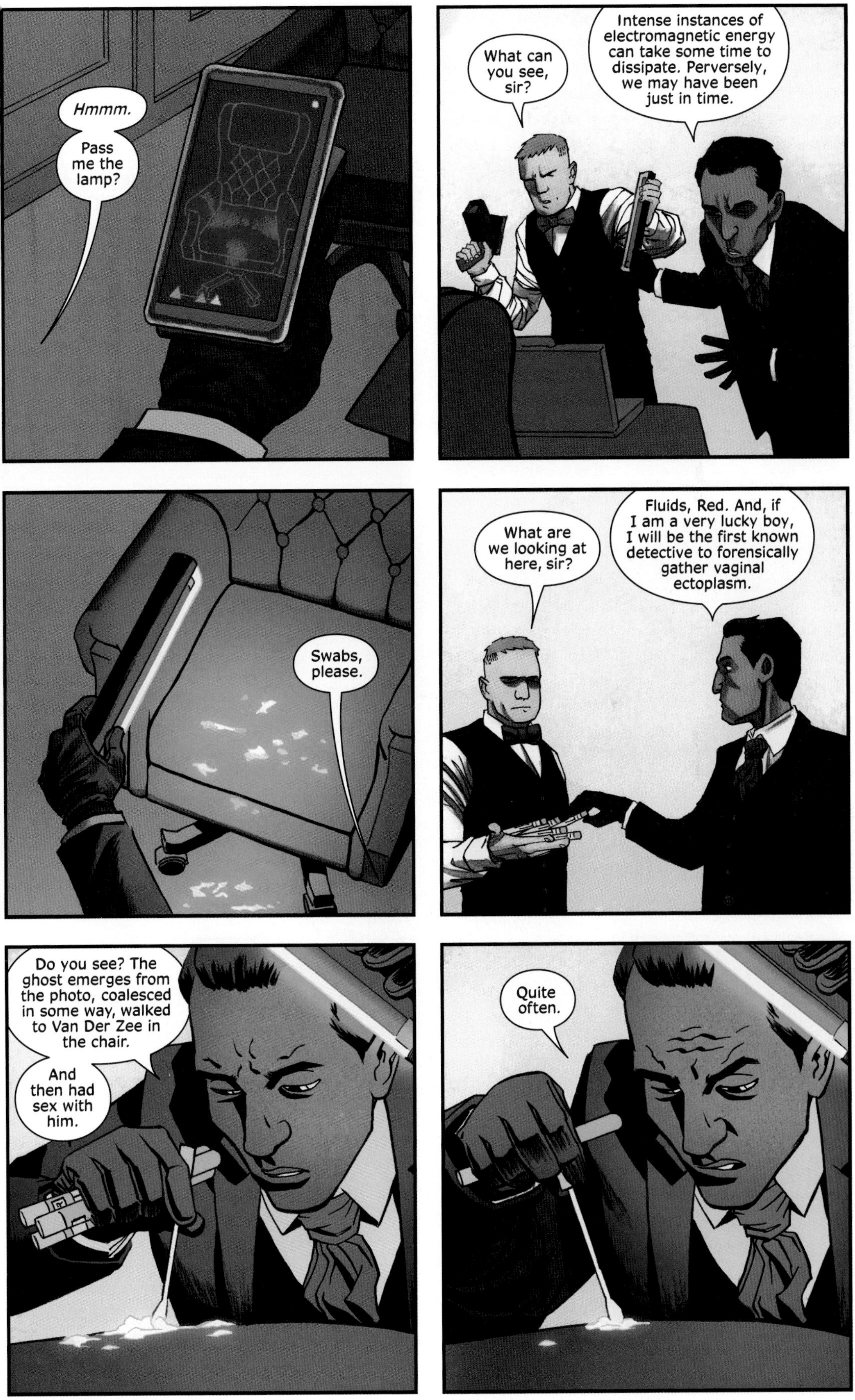

Hmmm.
Pass me the lamp?
What can you see, sir?
Intense instances of electromagnetic energy can take some time to dissipate. Perversely, we may have been just in time.
Swabs, please.
What are we looking at here, sir?
Fluids, Red. And, if I am a very lucky boy, I will be the first known detective to forensically gather vaginal ectoplasm.
Do you see? The ghost emerges from the photo, coalesced in some way, walked to Van Der Zee in the chair.
And then had sex with him.
Quite often.

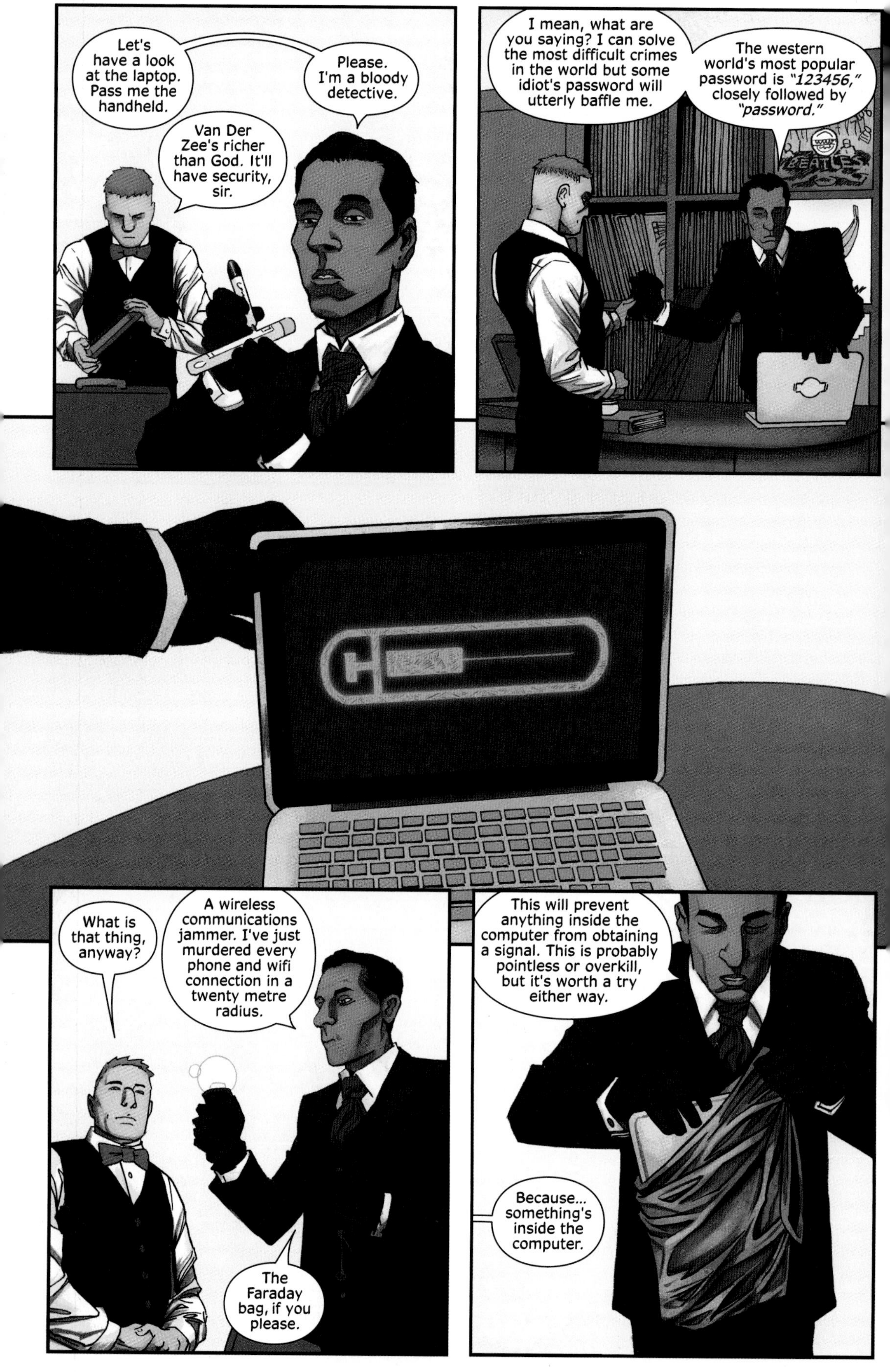
Let's have a look at the laptop. Pass me the handheld.
Please. I'm a bloody detective.
Van Der Zee's richer than God. It'll have security, sir.
I mean, what are you saying? I can solve the most difficult crimes in the world but some idiot's password will utterly baffle me.
The western world's most popular password is *"123456,"* closely followed by *"password."*
BEATLES
What is that thing, anyway?
A wireless communications jammer. I've just murdered every phone and wifi connection in a twenty metre radius.
The Faraday bag, if you please.
This will prevent anything inside the computer from obtaining a signal. This is probably pointless or overkill, but it's worth a try either way.
Because... something's inside the computer.

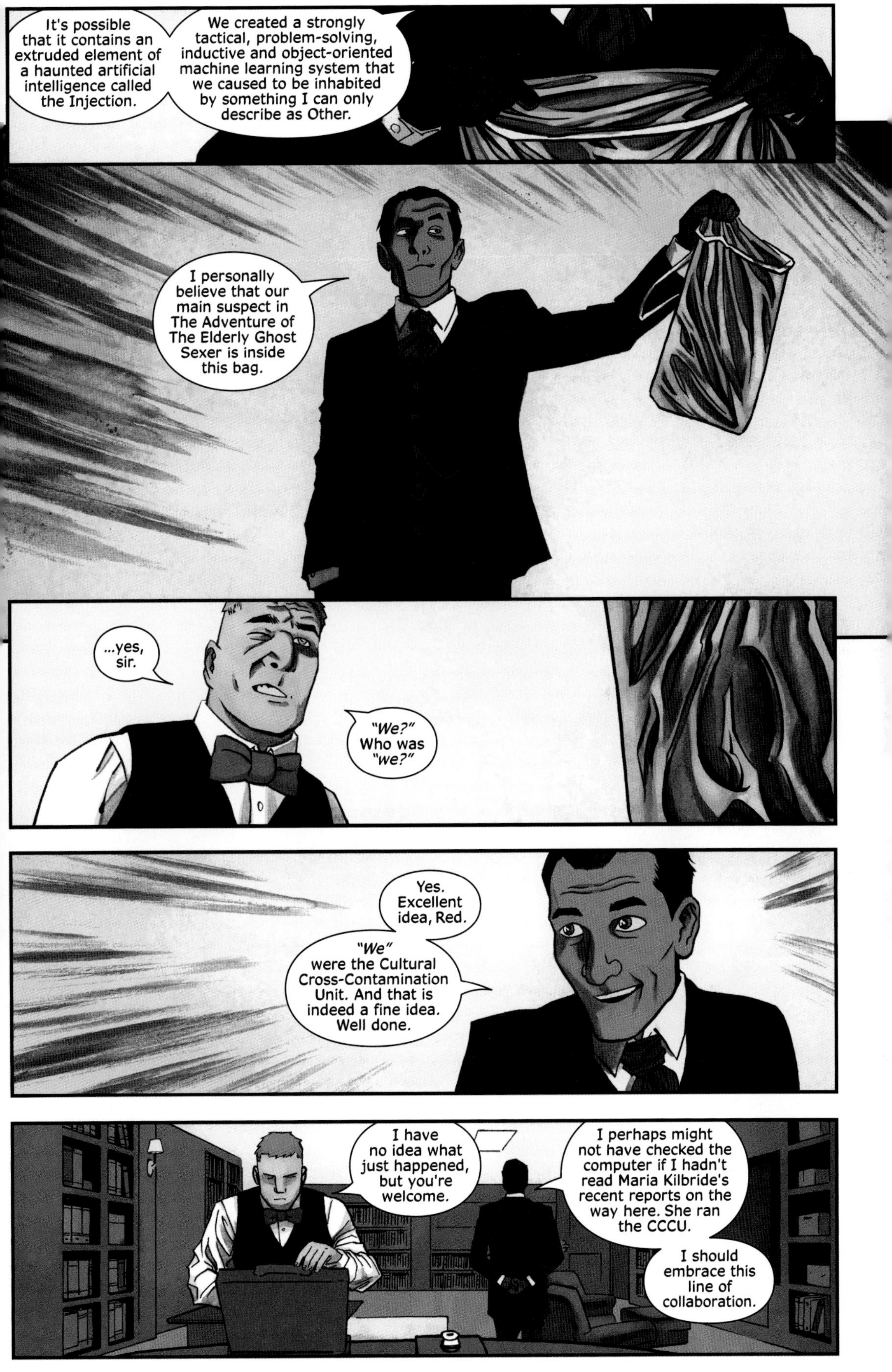
It's possible that it contains an extruded element of a haunted artificial intelligence called the Injection.
We created a strongly tactical, problem-solving, inductive and object-oriented machine learning system that we caused to be inhabited by something I can only describe as Other.
I personally believe that our main suspect in The Adventure of The Elderly Ghost Sexer is inside this bag.
...yes, sir.
"We?" Who was "we?"
Yes. Excellent idea, Red.
"We" were the Cultural Cross-Contamination Unit. And that is indeed a fine idea. Well done.
I have no idea what just happened, but you're welcome.
I perhaps might not have checked the computer if I hadn't read Maria Kilbride's recent reports on the way here. She ran the CCCU.
I should embrace this line of collaboration.

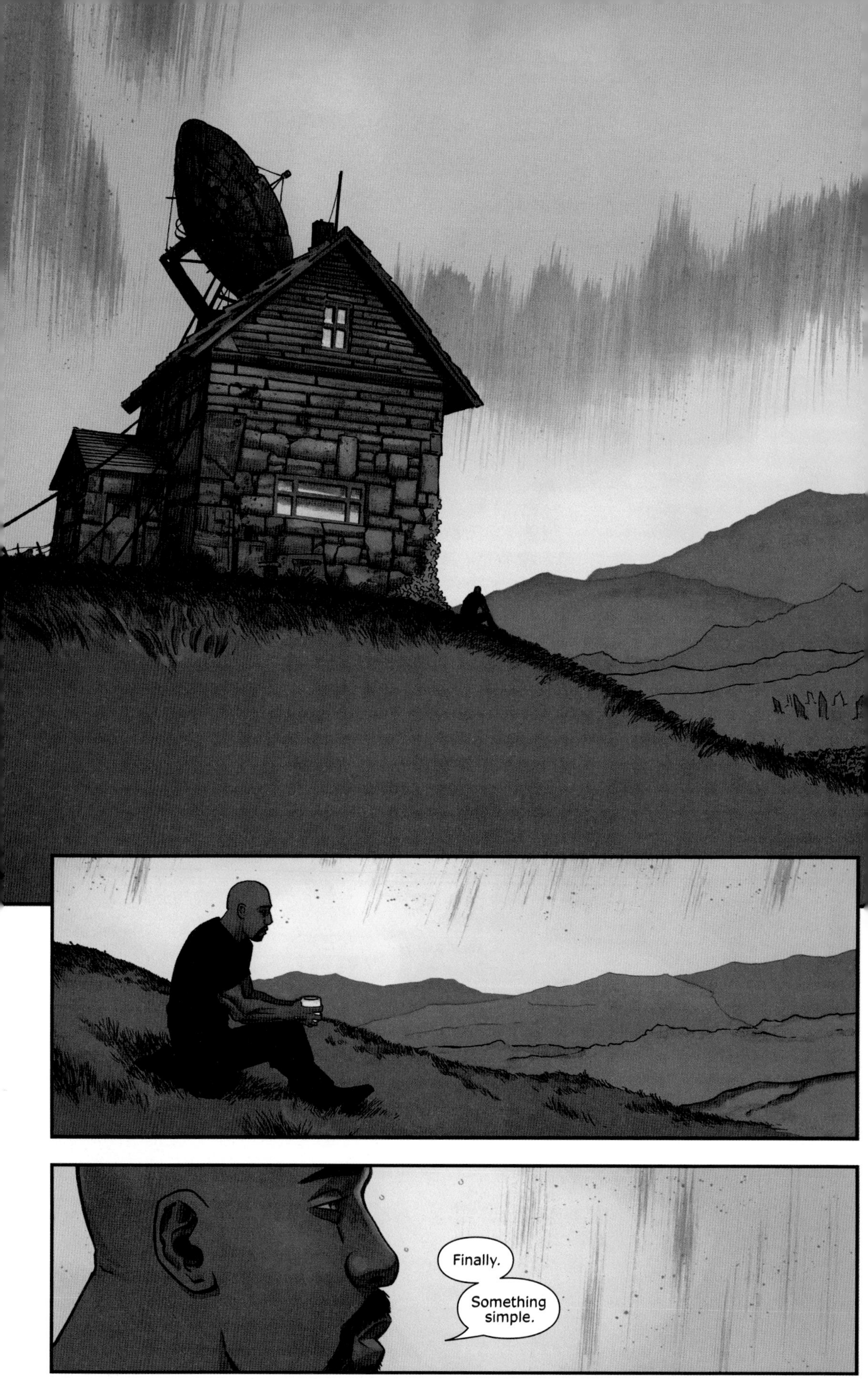
Finally.
Something simple.

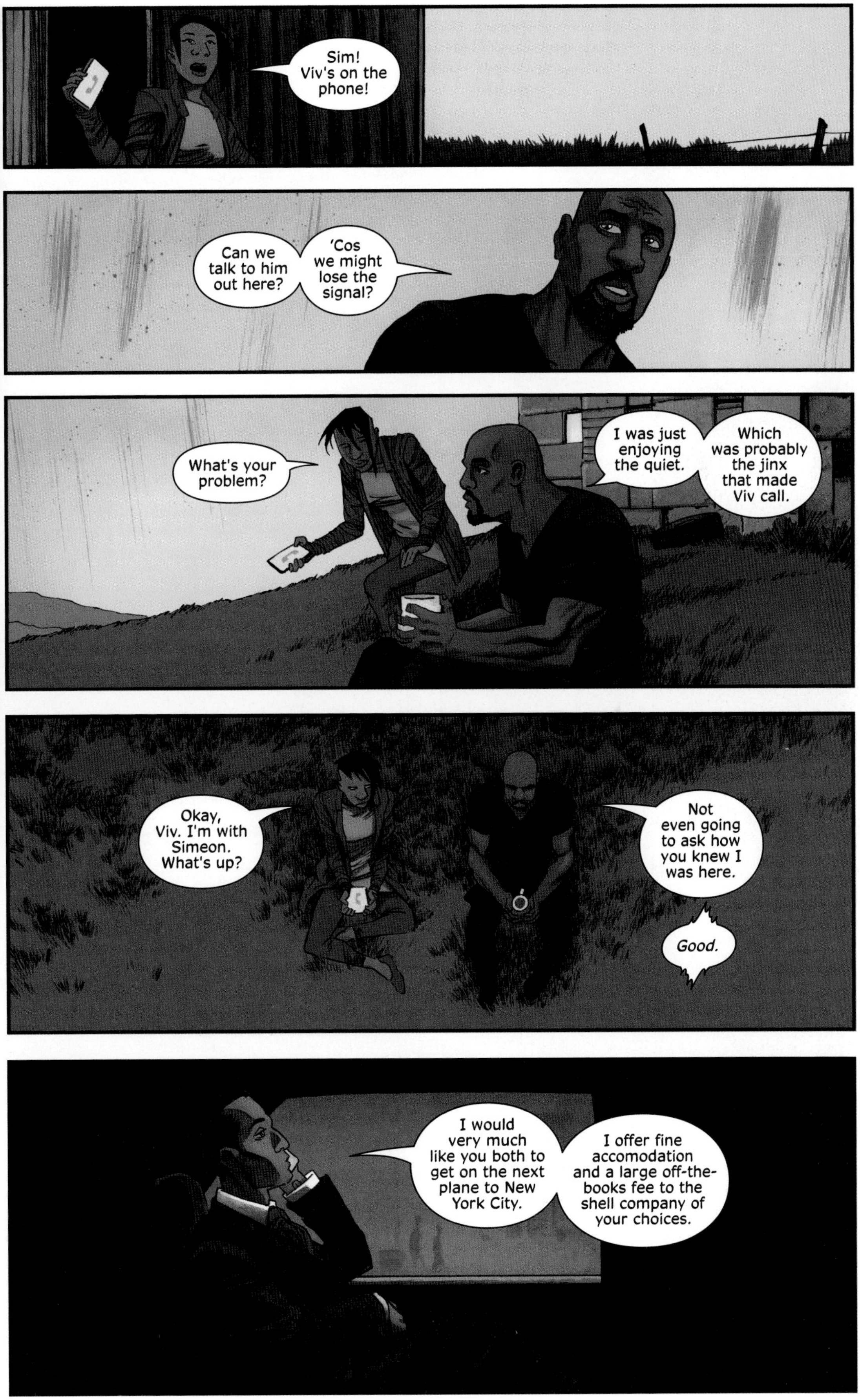

Sim! Viv's on the phone!
Can we talk to him out here?
'Cos we might lose the signal?
What's your problem?
I was just enjoying the quiet.
Which was probably the jinx that made Viv call.
Okay, Viv. I'm with Simeon. What's up?
Not even going to ask how you knew I was here.
Good.
I would very much like you both to get on the next plane to New York City.
I offer fine accomodation and a large off-the-books fee to the shell company of your choices.

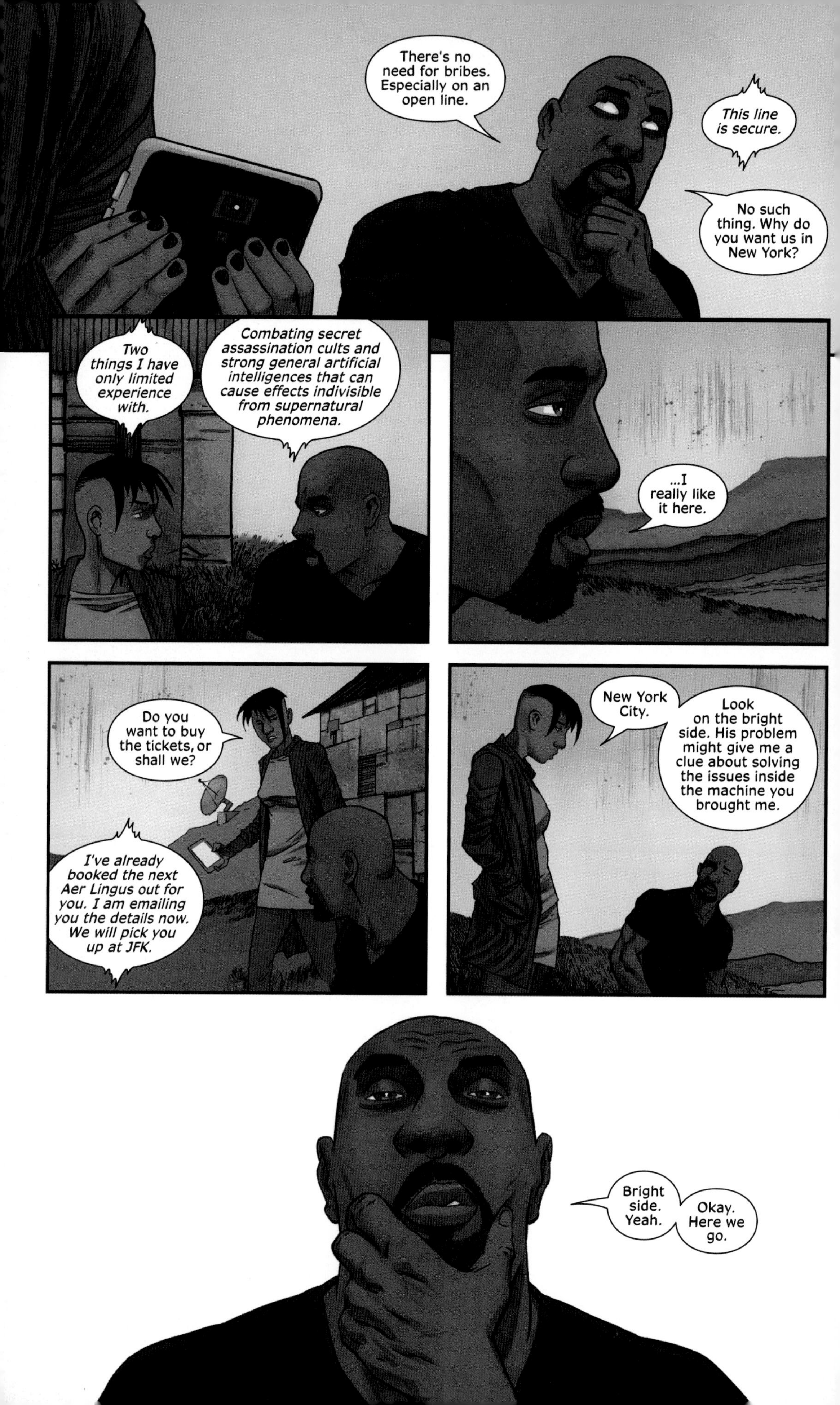
There's no need for bribes. Especially on an open line.
This line is secure.
No such thing. Why do you want us in New York?
Two things I have only limited experience with.
Combating secret assassination cults and strong general artificial intelligences that can cause effects indivisible from supernatural phenomena.
...I really like it here.
Do you want to buy the tickets, or shall we?
I've already booked the next Aer Lingus out for you. I am emailing you the details now. We will pick you up at JFK.
New York City.
Look on the bright side. His problem might give me a clue about solving the issues inside the machine you brought me.
Bright side. Yeah.
Okay. Here we go.

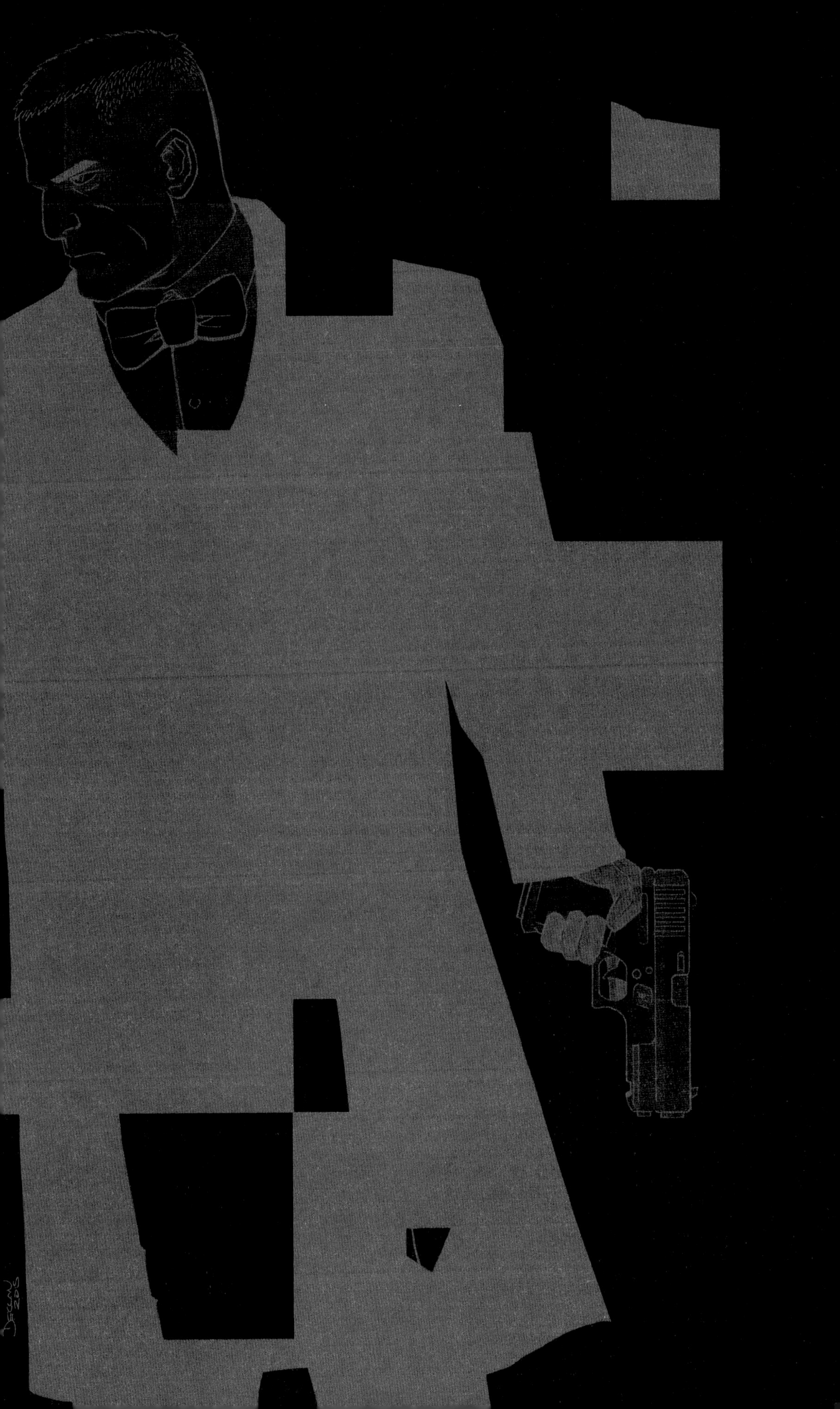

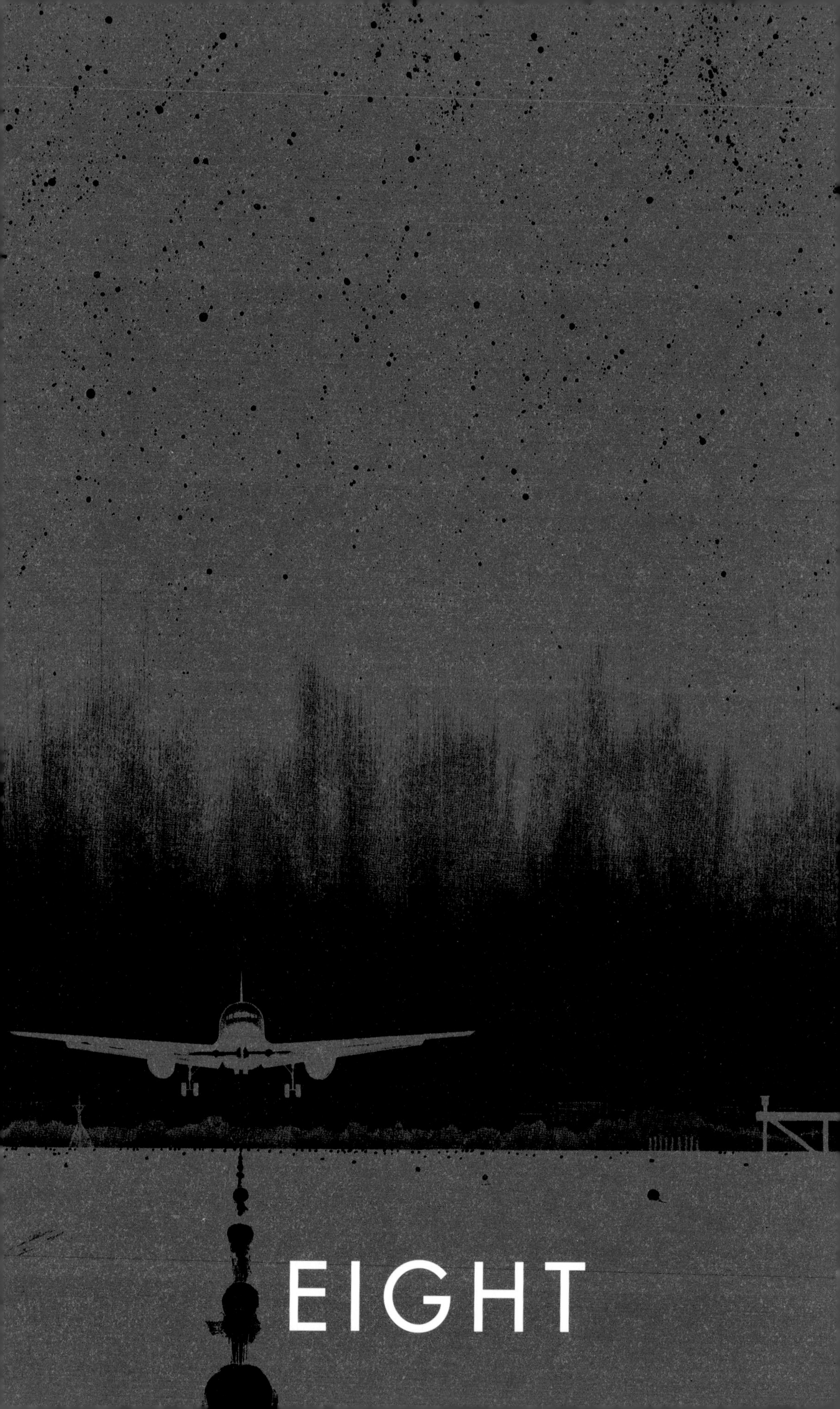

EIGHT

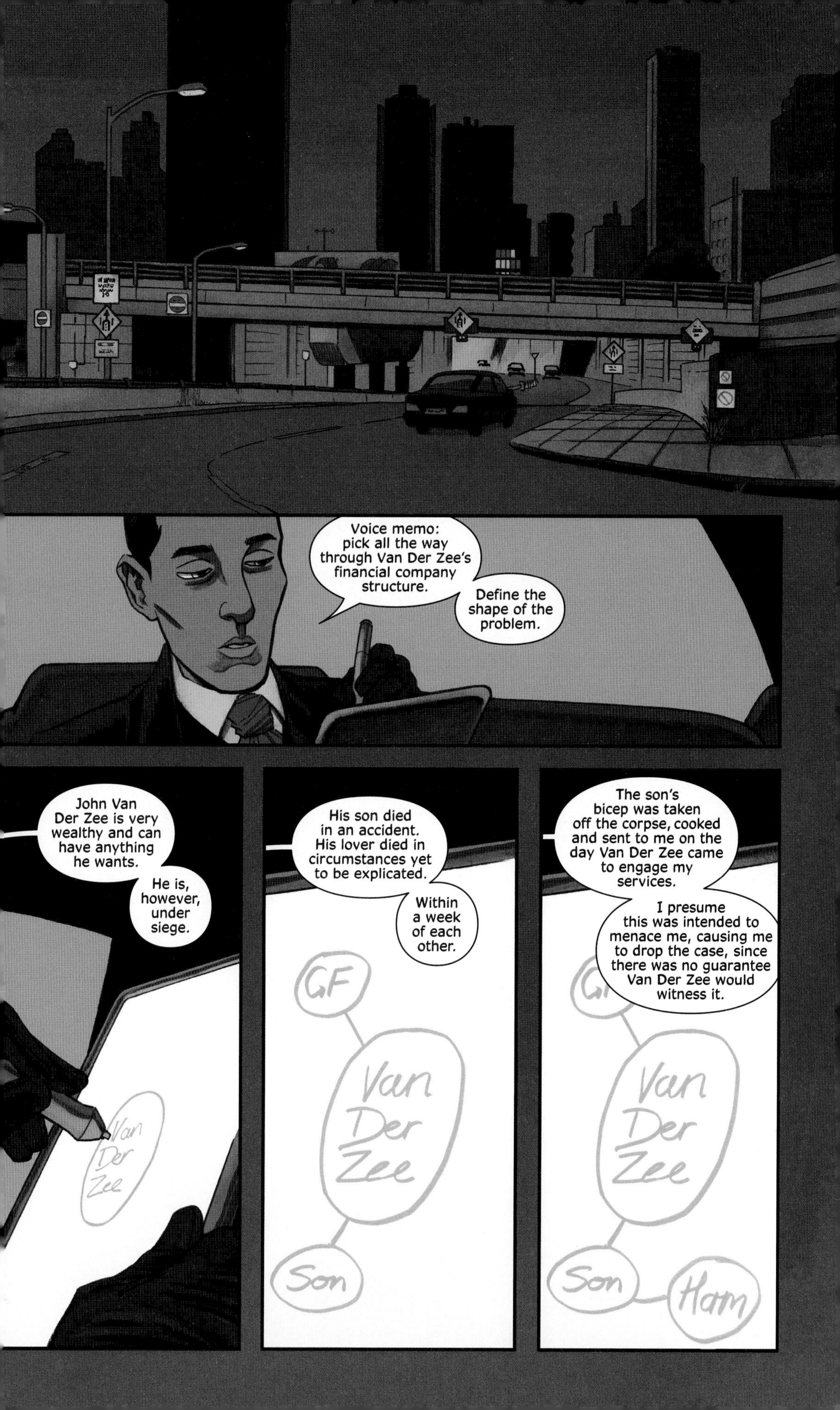
Voice memo: pick all the way through Van Der Zee's financial company structure.
Define the shape of the problem.
John Van Der Zee is very wealthy and can have anything he wants.
He is, however, under siege.
Van Der Zee
His son died in an accident. His lover died in circumstances yet to be explicated.
Within a week of each other.
GF
Van Der Zee
Son
The son's bicep was taken off the corpse, cooked and sent to me on the day Van Der Zee came to engage my services.
I presume this was intended to menace me, causing me to drop the case, since there was no guarantee Van Der Zee would witness it.
Van Der Zee
Son
Ham

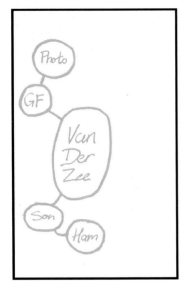

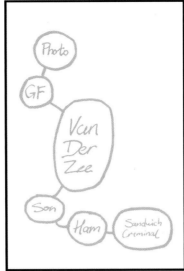

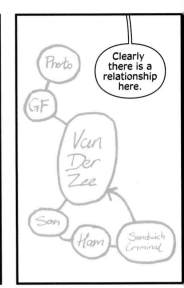

Photo
GF
Van Der Zee
Son
Ham
Sandwich Criminal
Clearly there is a relationship here.
Ghost
Ghost Sex
Ghost Abduction
Are we there yet?
For the hundredth time --

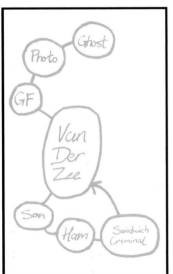

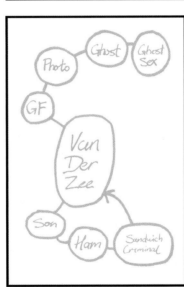

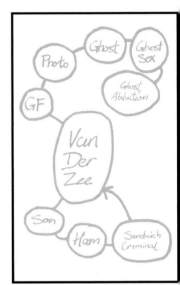

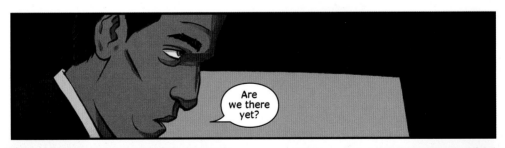

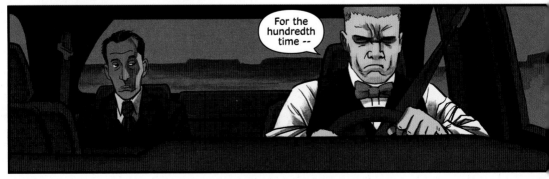

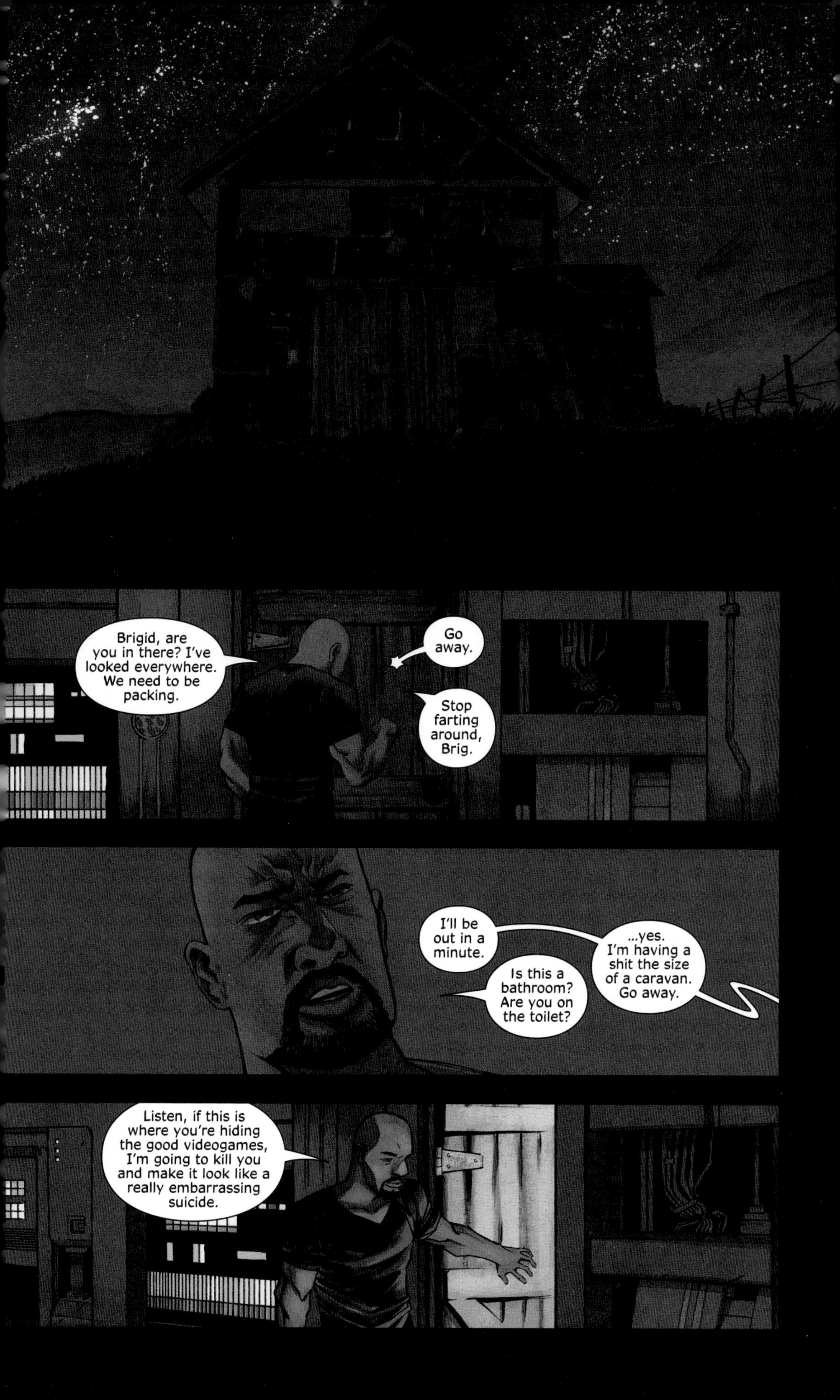
Brigid, are you in there? I've looked everywhere. We need to be packing.
Go away.
Stop farting around, Brig.
Is this a bathroom? Are you on the toilet?
...yes. I'm having a shit the size of a caravan. Go away.
I'll be out in a minute.
Listen, if this is where you're hiding the good videogames, I'm going to kill you and make it look like a really embarrassing suicide.

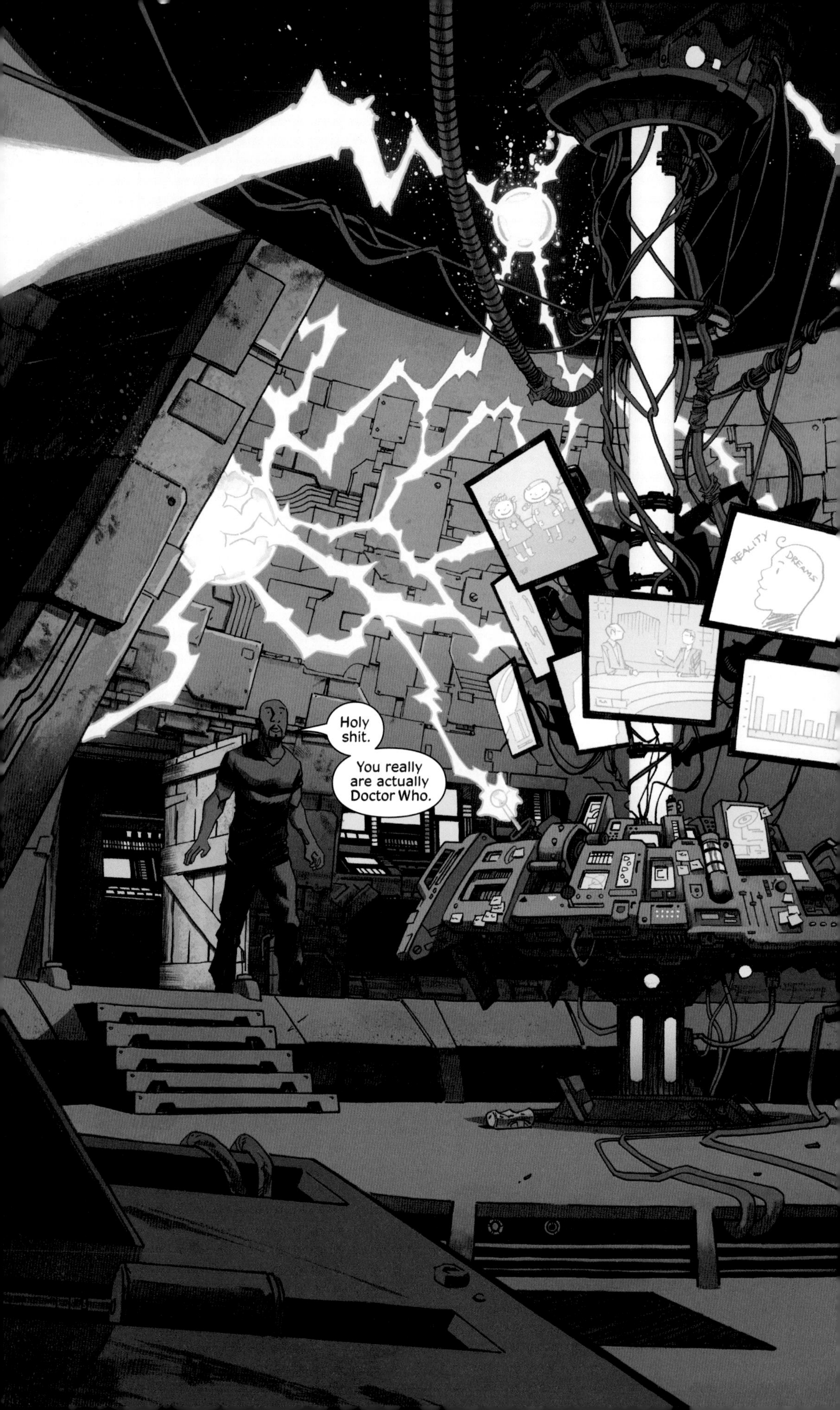
REALITY
DREAMS
Holy shit.
You really are actually Doctor Who.

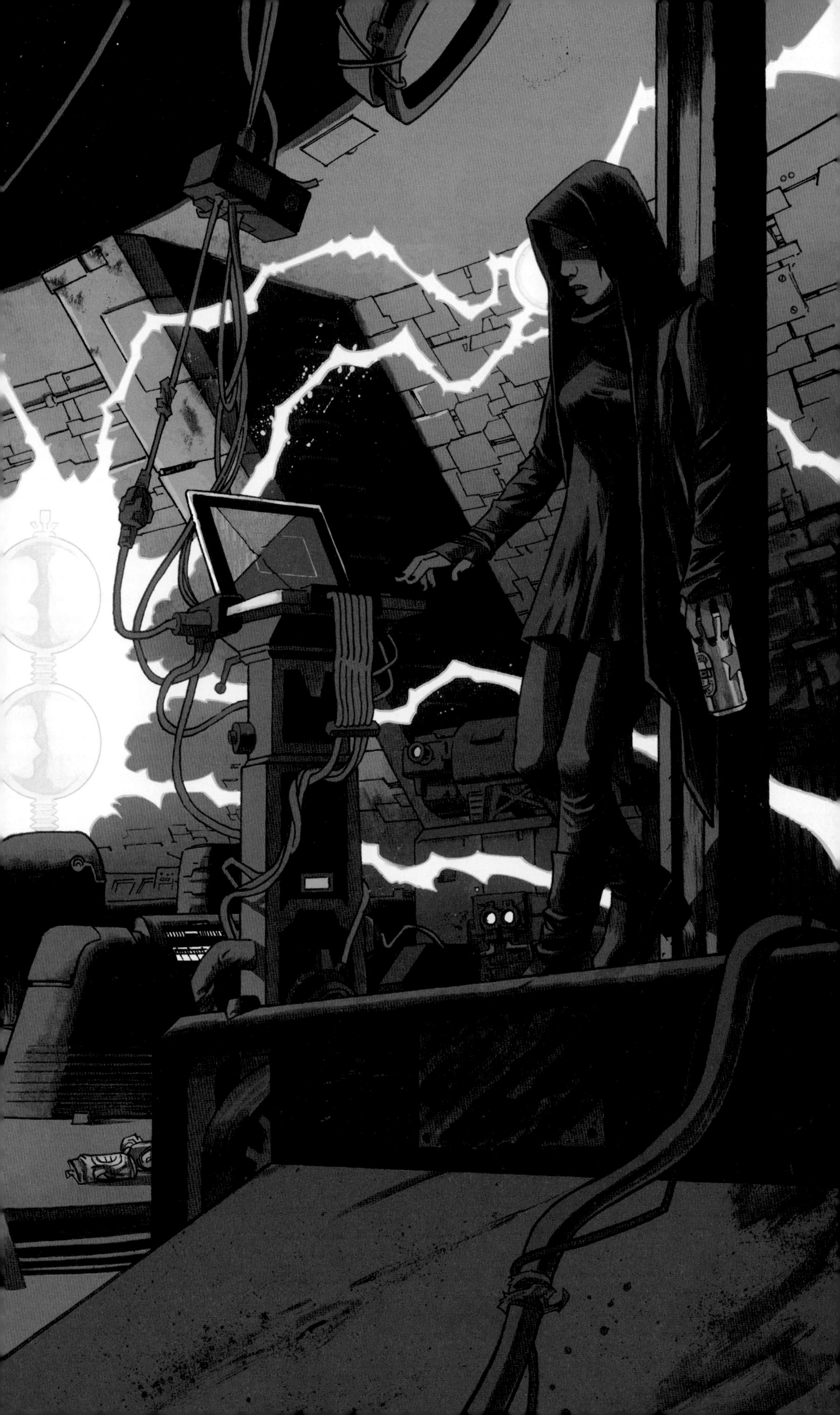

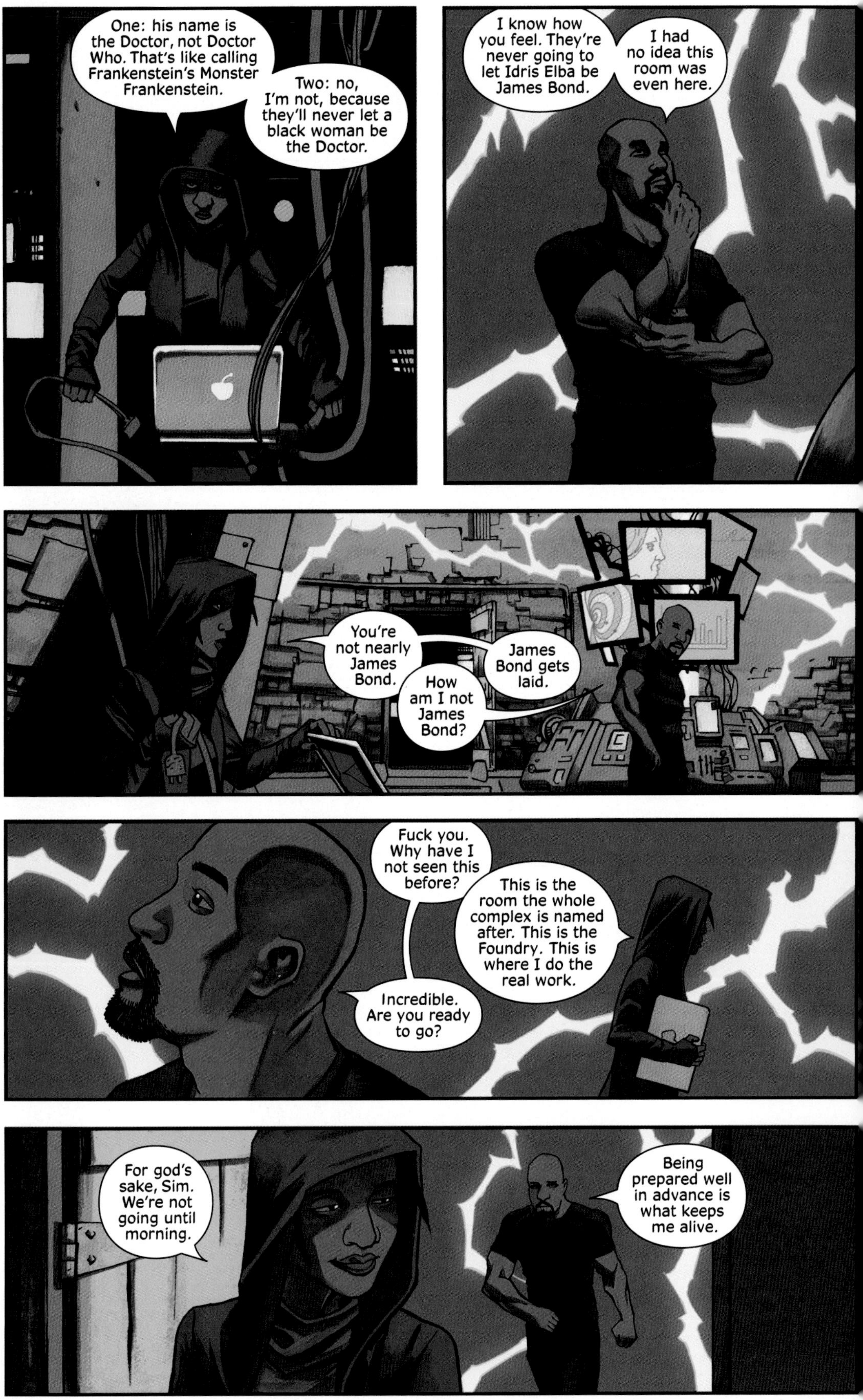
One: his name is the Doctor, not Doctor Who. That's like calling Frankenstein's Monster Frankenstein.
Two: no, I'm not, because they'll never let a black woman be the Doctor.
I know how you feel. They're never going to let Idris Elba be James Bond.
I had no idea this room was even here.
You're not nearly James Bond.
How am I not James Bond?
James Bond gets laid.
Fuck you. Why have I not seen this before?
This is the room the whole complex is named after. This is the Foundry. This is where I do the real work.
Incredible. Are you ready to go?
For god's sake, Sim. We're not going until morning.
Being prepared well in advance is what keeps me alive.

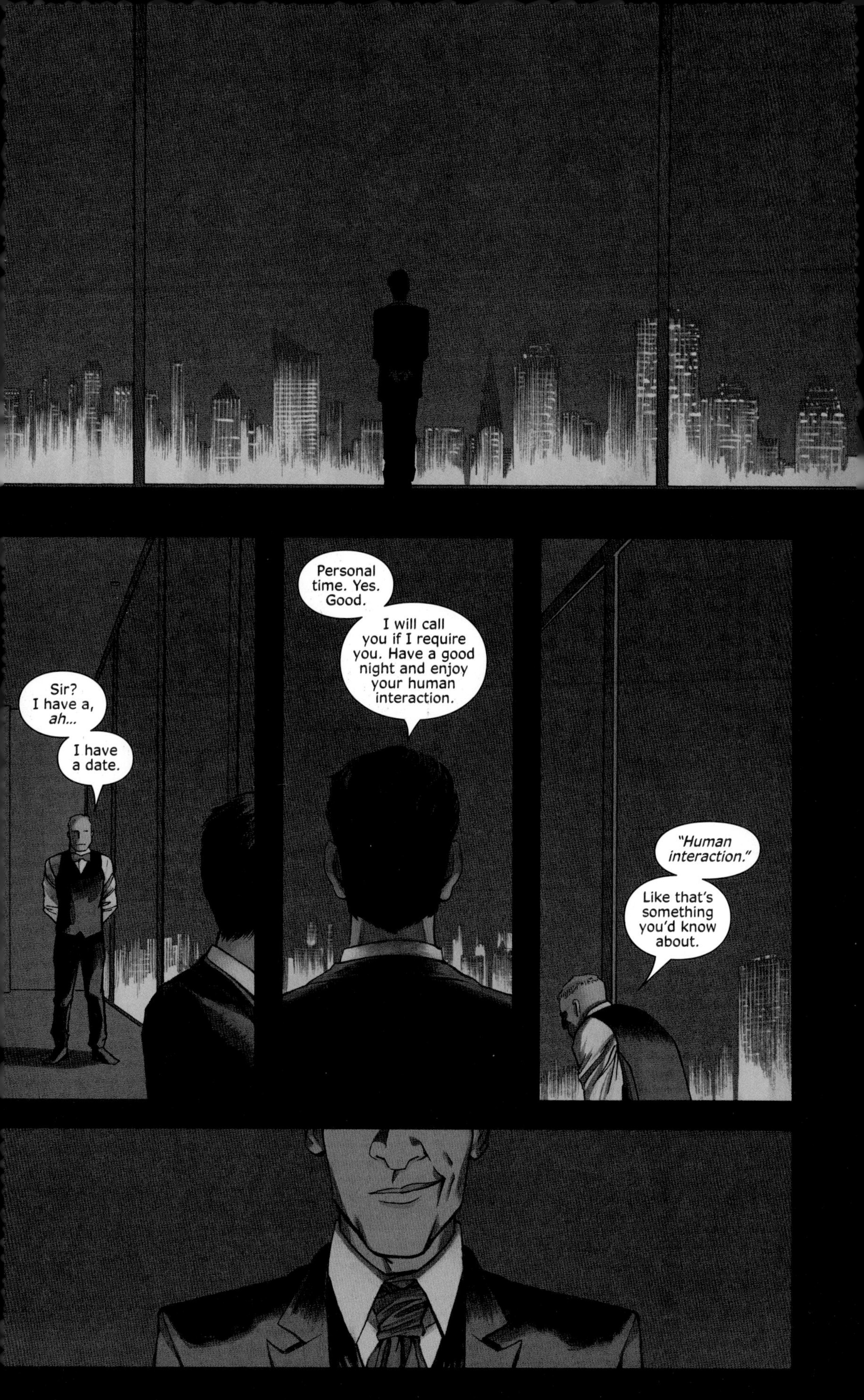
Sir? I have a, *ah...*
I have a date.
Personal time. Yes. Good.
I will call you if I require you. Have a good night and enjoy your human interaction.
"Human interaction."
Like that's something you'd know about.

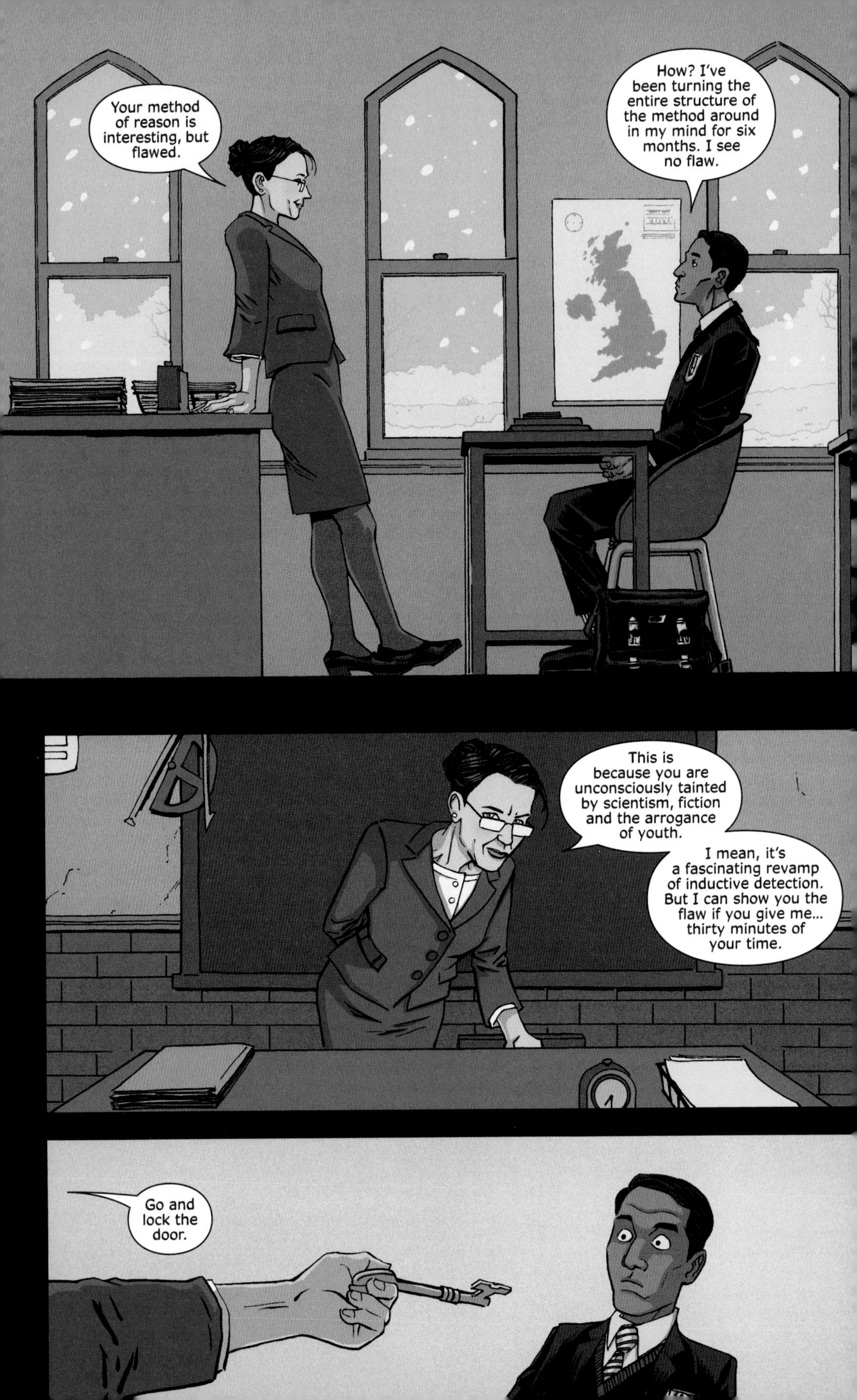
Your method of reason is interesting, but flawed.
How? I've been turning the entire structure of the method around in my mind for six months. I see no flaw.
This is because you are unconsciously tainted by scientism, fiction and the arrogance of youth.
I mean, it's a fascinating revamp of inductive detection. But I can show you the flaw if you give me... thirty minutes of your time.
Go and lock the door.

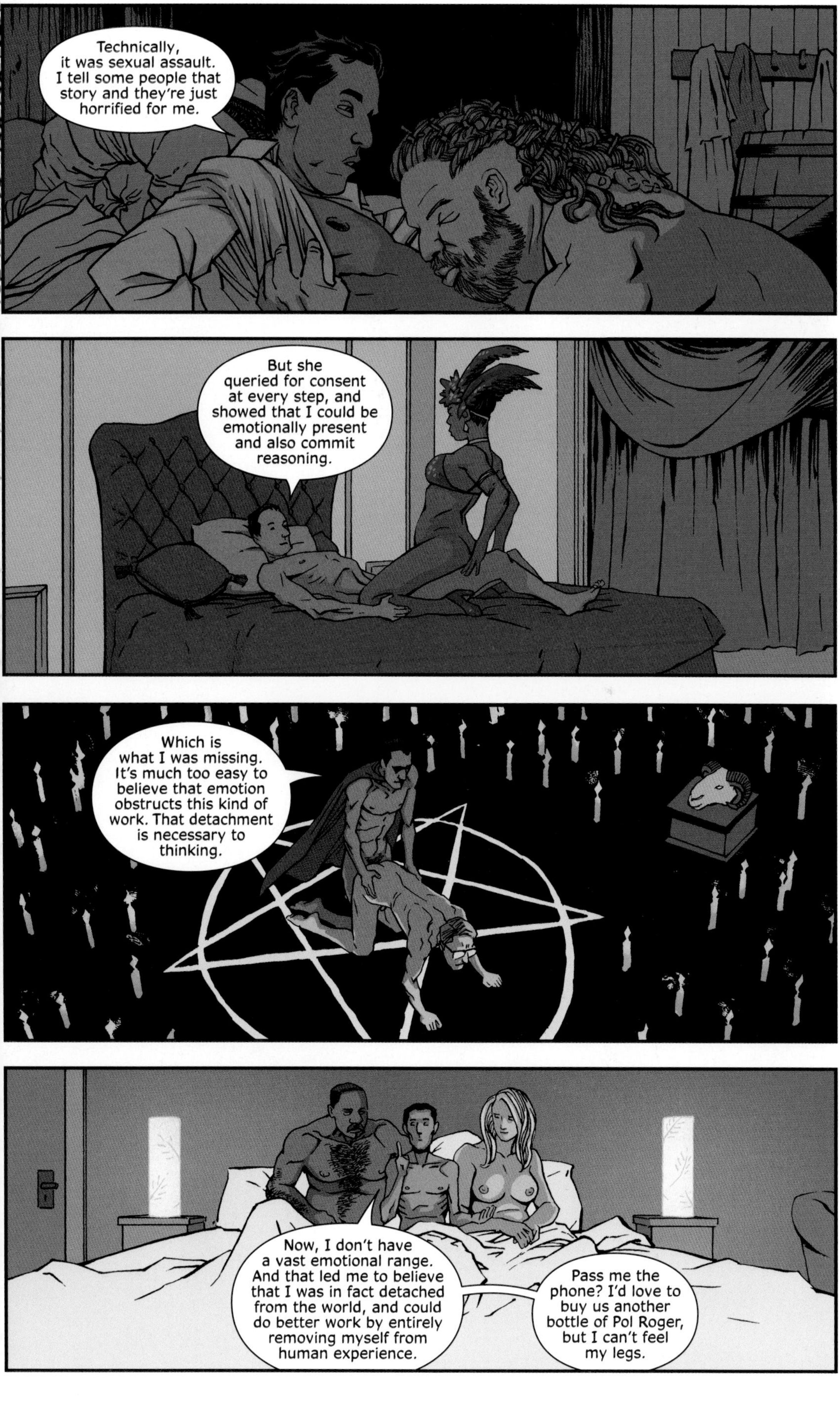
Technically, it was sexual assault. I tell some people that story and they're just horrified for me.
But she queried for consent at every step, and showed that I could be emotionally present and also commit reasoning.
Which is what I was missing. It's much too easy to believe that emotion obstructs this kind of work. That detachment is necessary to thinking.
Now, I don't have a vast emotional range. And that led me to believe that I was in fact detached from the world, and could do better work by entirely removing myself from human experience.
Pass me the phone? I'd love to buy us another bottle of Pol Roger, but I can't feel my legs.

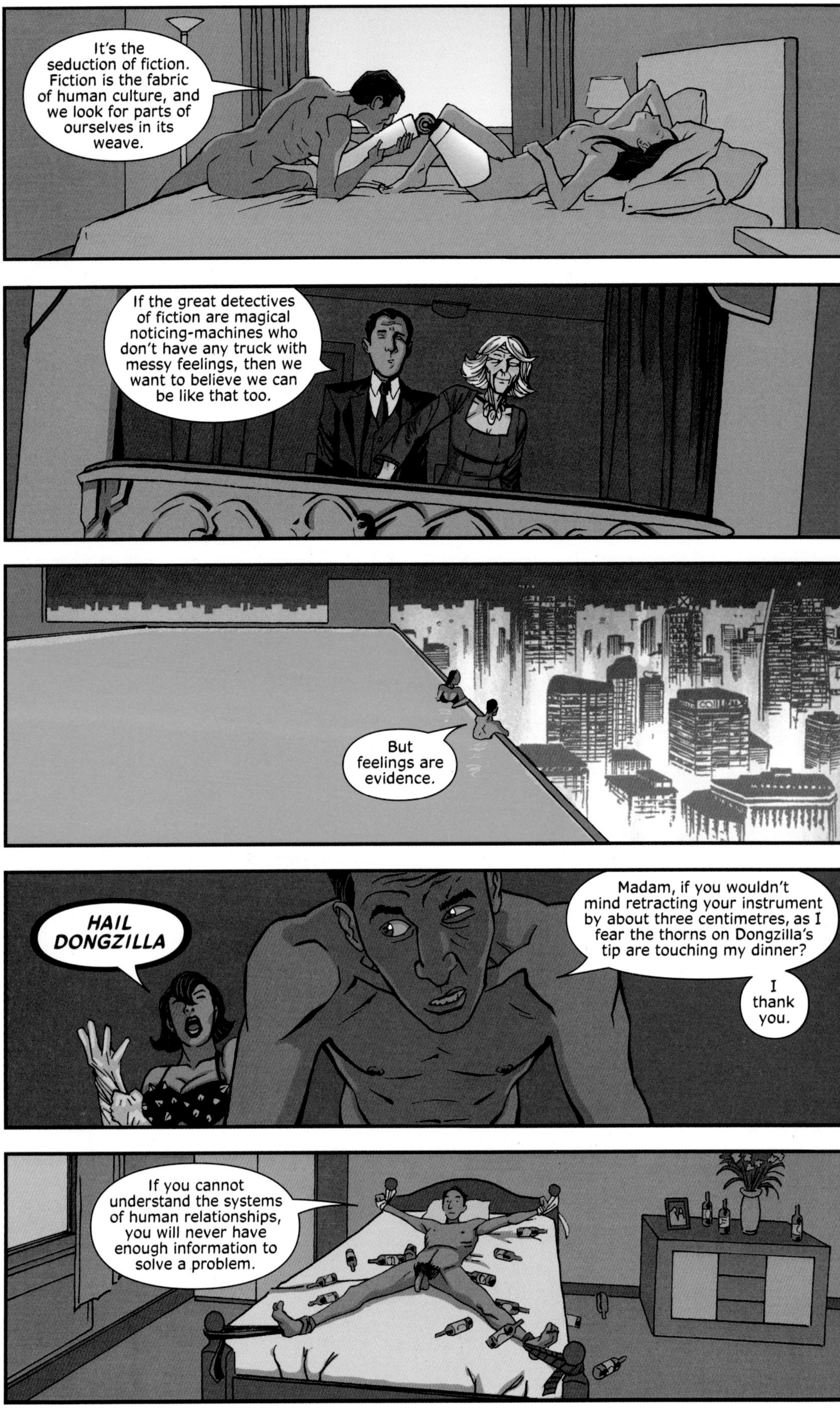
It's the seduction of fiction. Fiction is the fabric of human culture, and we look for parts of ourselves in its weave.
If the great detectives of fiction are magical noticing-machines who don't have any truck with messy feelings, then we want to believe we can be like that too.
But feelings are evidence.
HAIL DONGZILLA
Madam, if you wouldn't mind retracting your instrument by about three centimetres, as I fear the thorns on Dongzilla's tip are touching my dinner?
I thank you.
If you cannot understand the systems of human relationships, you will never have enough information to solve a problem.

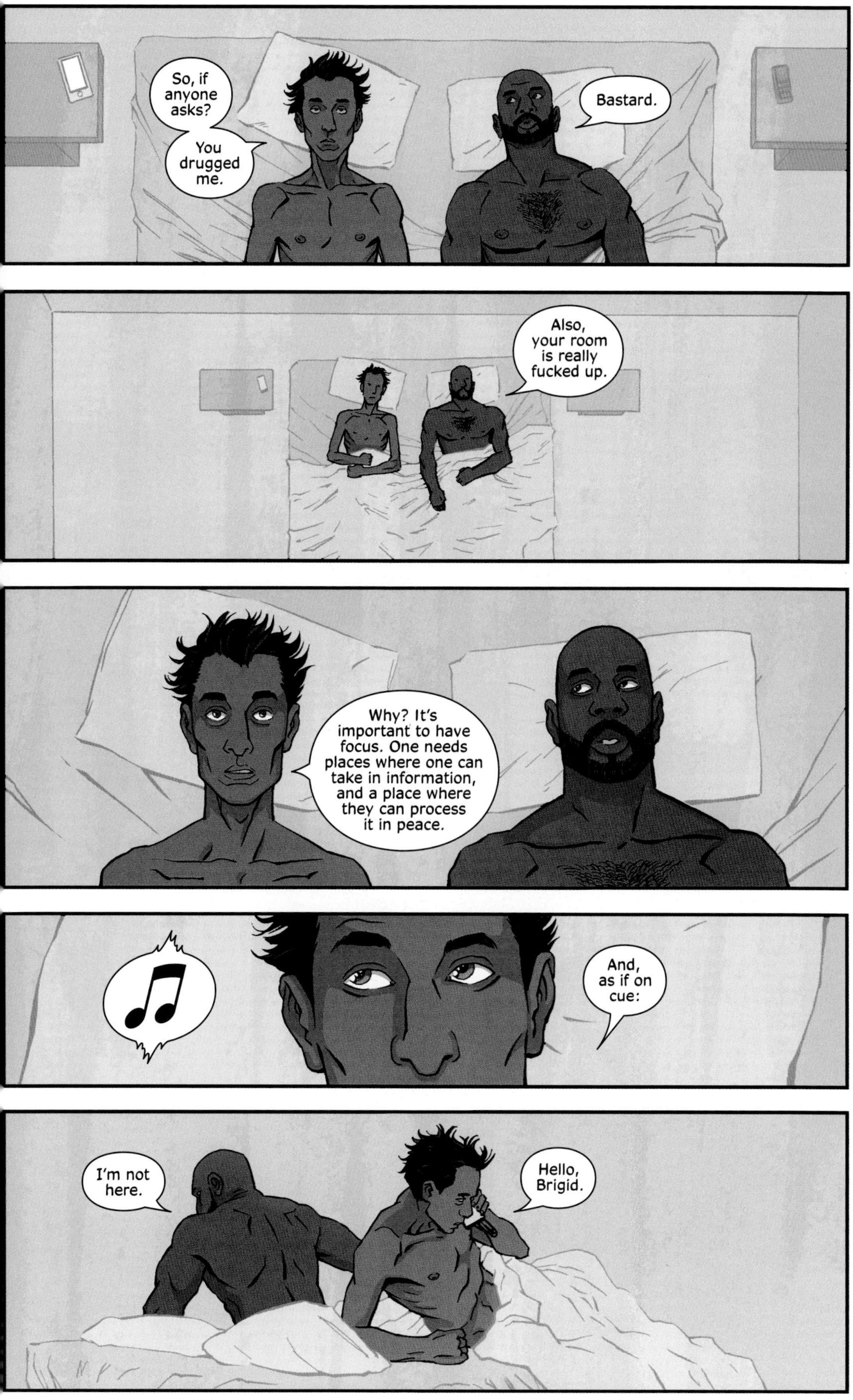
So, if anyone asks?
You drugged me.
Bastard.
Also, your room is really fucked up.
Why? It's important to have focus. One needs places where one can take in information, and a place where they can process it in peace.
♫
And, as if on cue:
I'm not here.
Hello, Brigid.

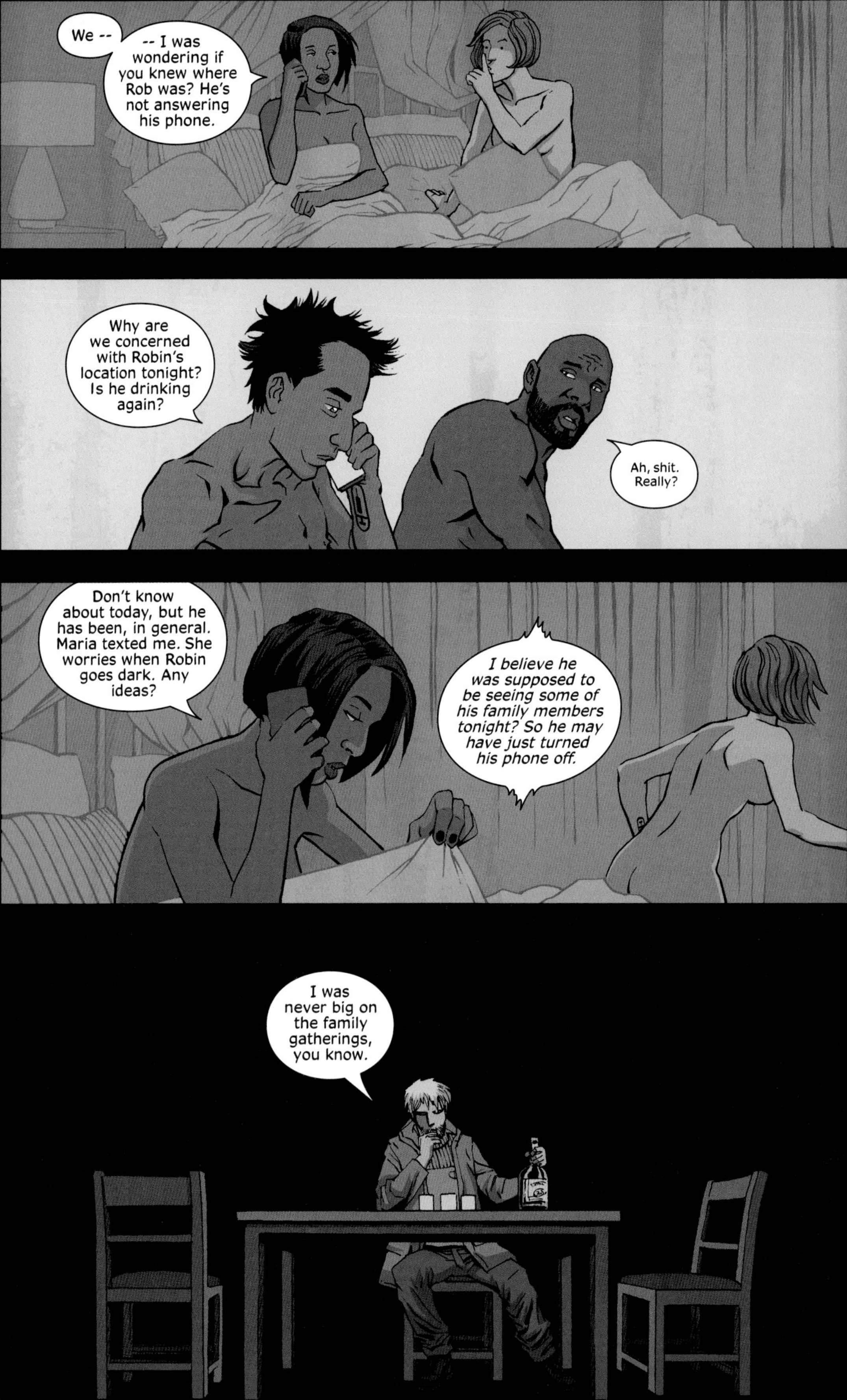

We --
-- I was wondering if you knew where Rob was? He's not answering his phone.
Why are we concerned with Robin's location tonight? Is he drinking again?
Ah, shit. Really?
Don't know about today, but he has been, in general. Maria texted me. She worries when Robin goes dark. Any ideas?
I believe he was supposed to be seeing some of his family members tonight? So he may have just turned his phone off.
I was never big on the family gatherings, you know.

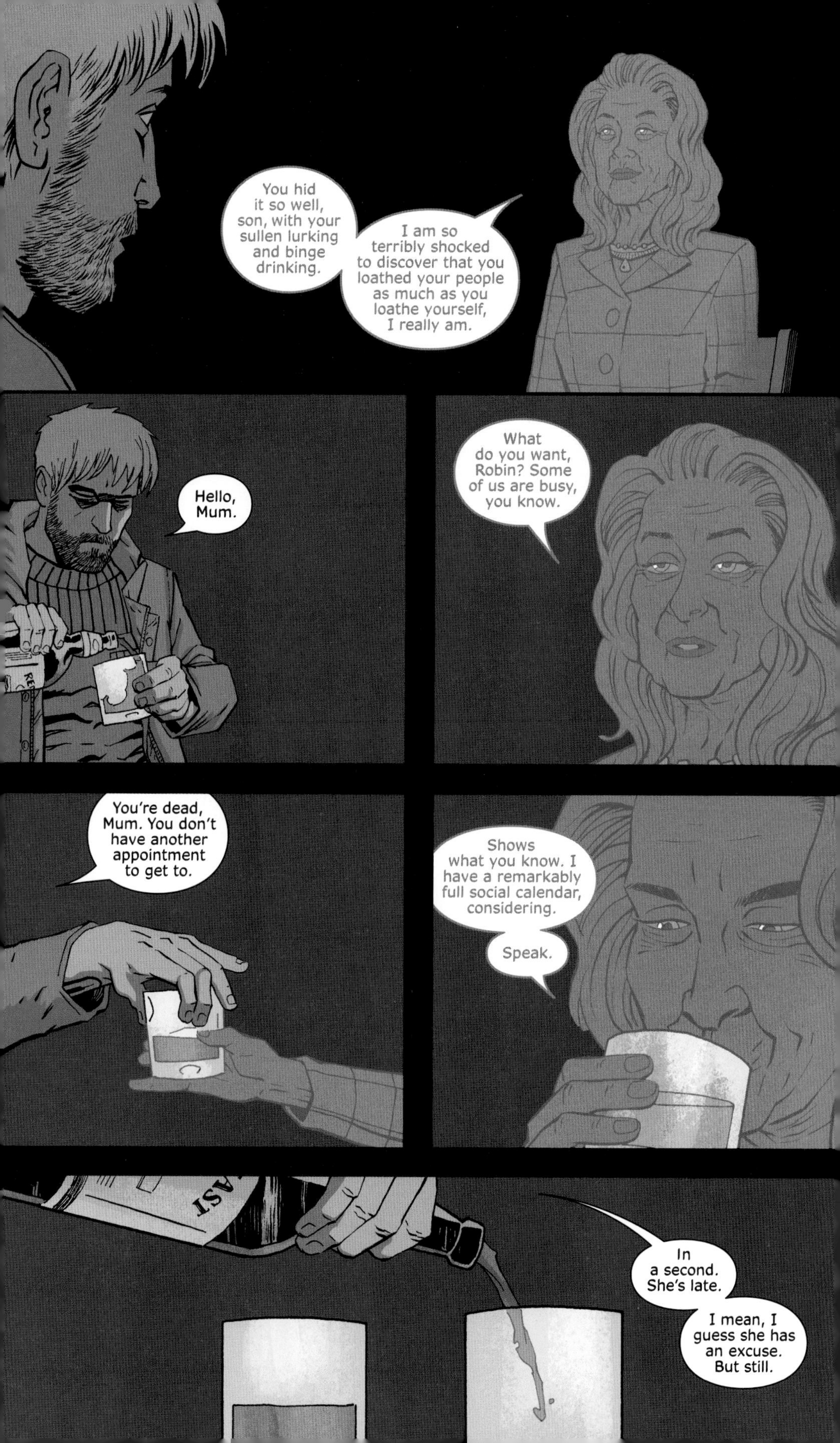
You hid it so well, son, with your sullen lurking and binge drinking.
I am so terribly shocked to discover that you loathed your people as much as you loathe yourself, I really am.
Hello, Mum.
What do you want, Robin? Some of us are busy, you know.
You're dead, Mum. You don't have another appointment to get to.
Shows what you know. I have a remarkably full social calendar, considering.
Speak.
In a second. She's late.
I mean, I guess she has an excuse. But still.

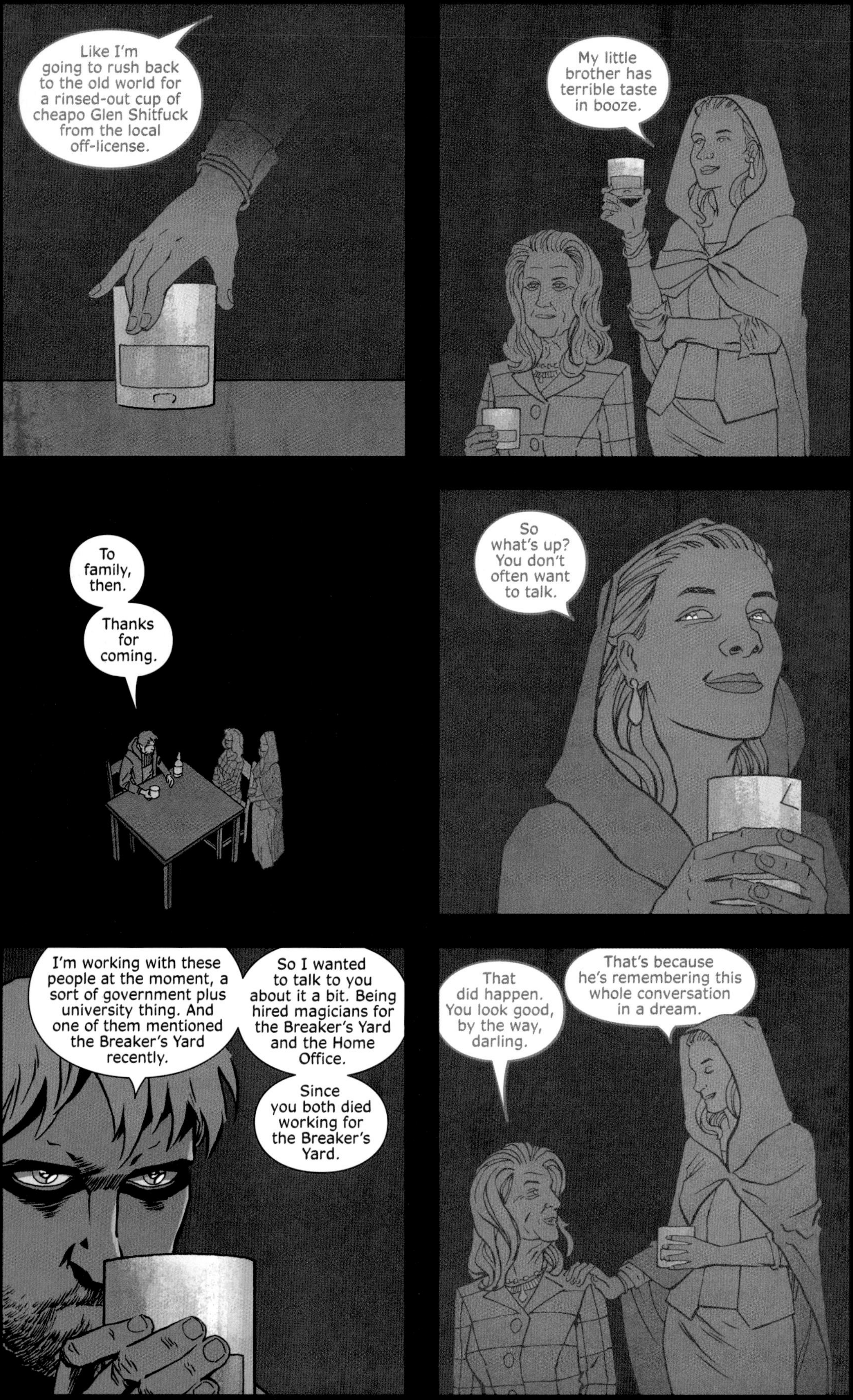
Like I'm going to rush back to the old world for a rinsed-out cup of cheapo Glen Shitfuck from the local off-license.
My little brother has terrible taste in booze.
To family, then.
Thanks for coming.
So what's up? You don't often want to talk.
I'm working with these people at the moment, a sort of government plus university thing. And one of them mentioned the Breaker's Yard recently.
So I wanted to talk to you about it a bit. Being hired magicians for the Breaker's Yard and the Home Office.
Since you both died working for the Breaker's Yard.
That did happen. You look good, by the way, darling.
That's because he's remembering this whole conversation in a dream.

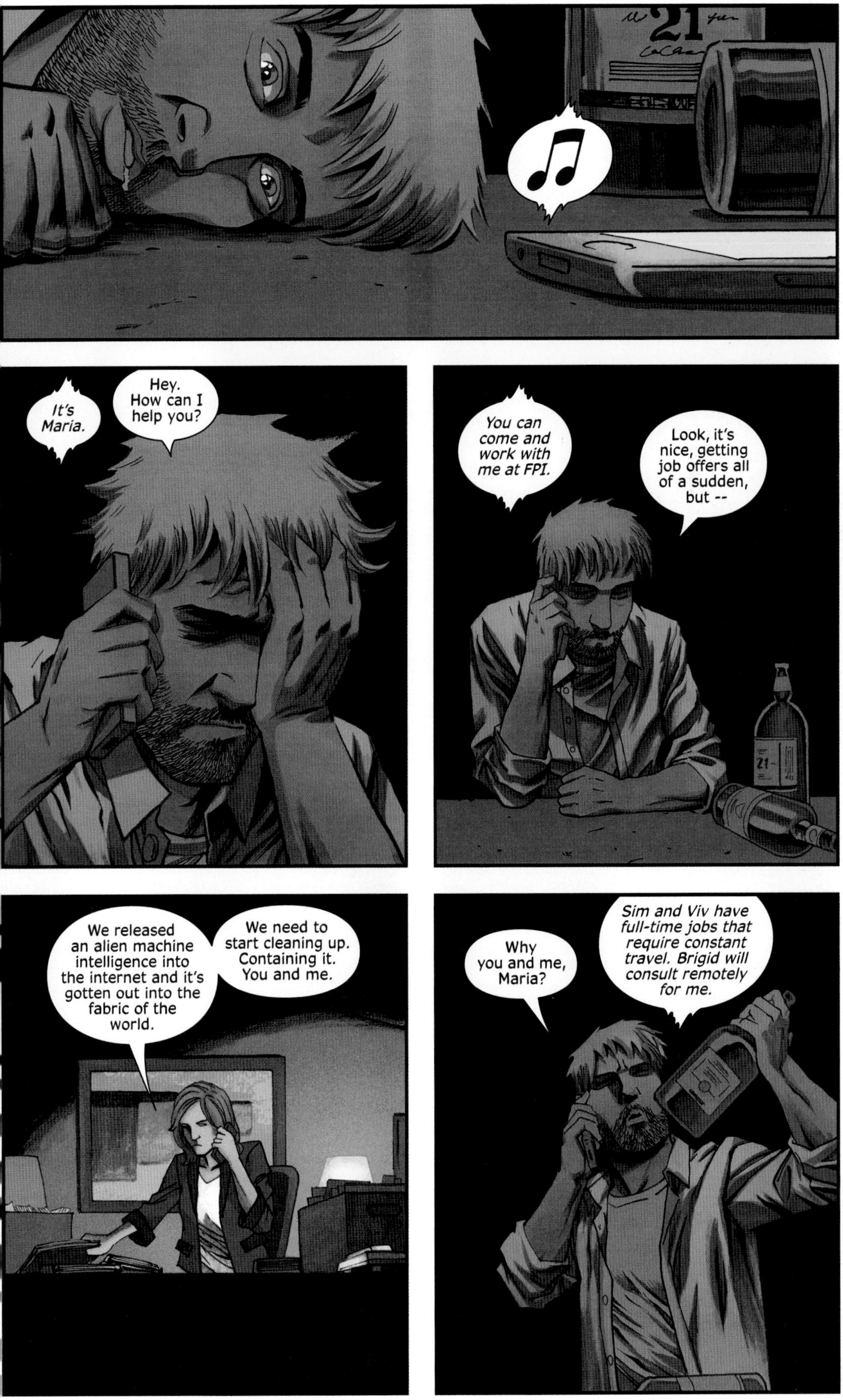
♫
It's Maria.
Hey. How can I help you?
You can come and work with me at FPI.
Look, it's nice, getting job offers all of a sudden, but --
We released an alien machine intelligence into the internet and it's gotten out into the fabric of the world.
We need to start cleaning up. Containing it. You and me.
Why you and me, Maria?
Sim and Viv have full-time jobs that require constant travel. Brigid will consult remotely for me.

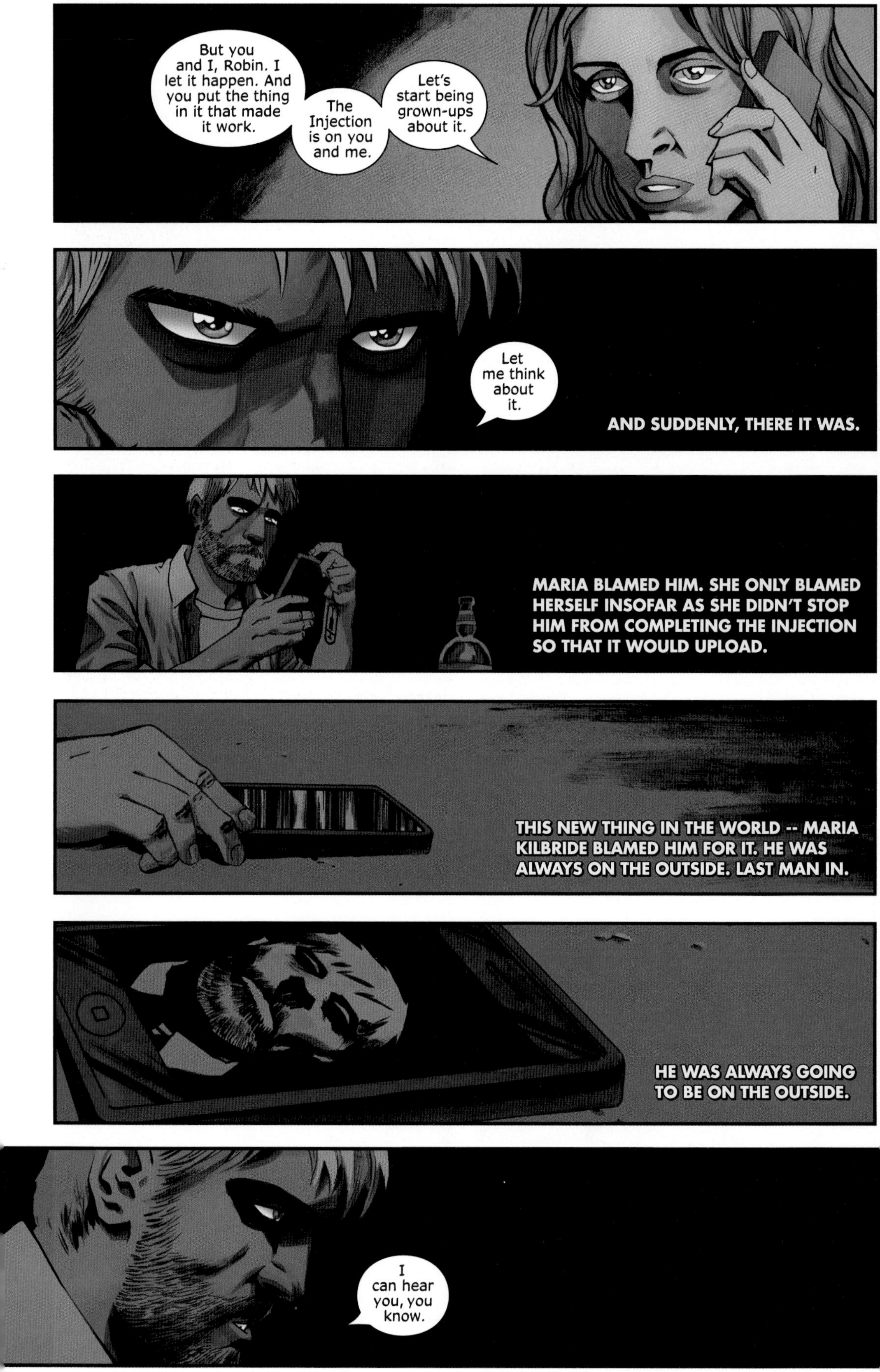
But you and I, Robin. I let it happen. And you put the thing in it that made it work.
The Injection is on you and me.
Let's start being grown-ups about it.
Let me think about it.
AND SUDDENLY, THERE IT WAS.
MARIA BLAMED HIM. SHE ONLY BLAMED HERSELF INSOFAR AS SHE DIDN'T STOP HIM FROM COMPLETING THE INJECTION SO THAT IT WOULD UPLOAD.
THIS NEW THING IN THE WORLD -- MARIA KILBRIDE BLAMED HIM FOR IT. HE WAS ALWAYS ON THE OUTSIDE. LAST MAN IN.
HE WAS ALWAYS GOING TO BE ON THE OUTSIDE.
I can hear you, you know.

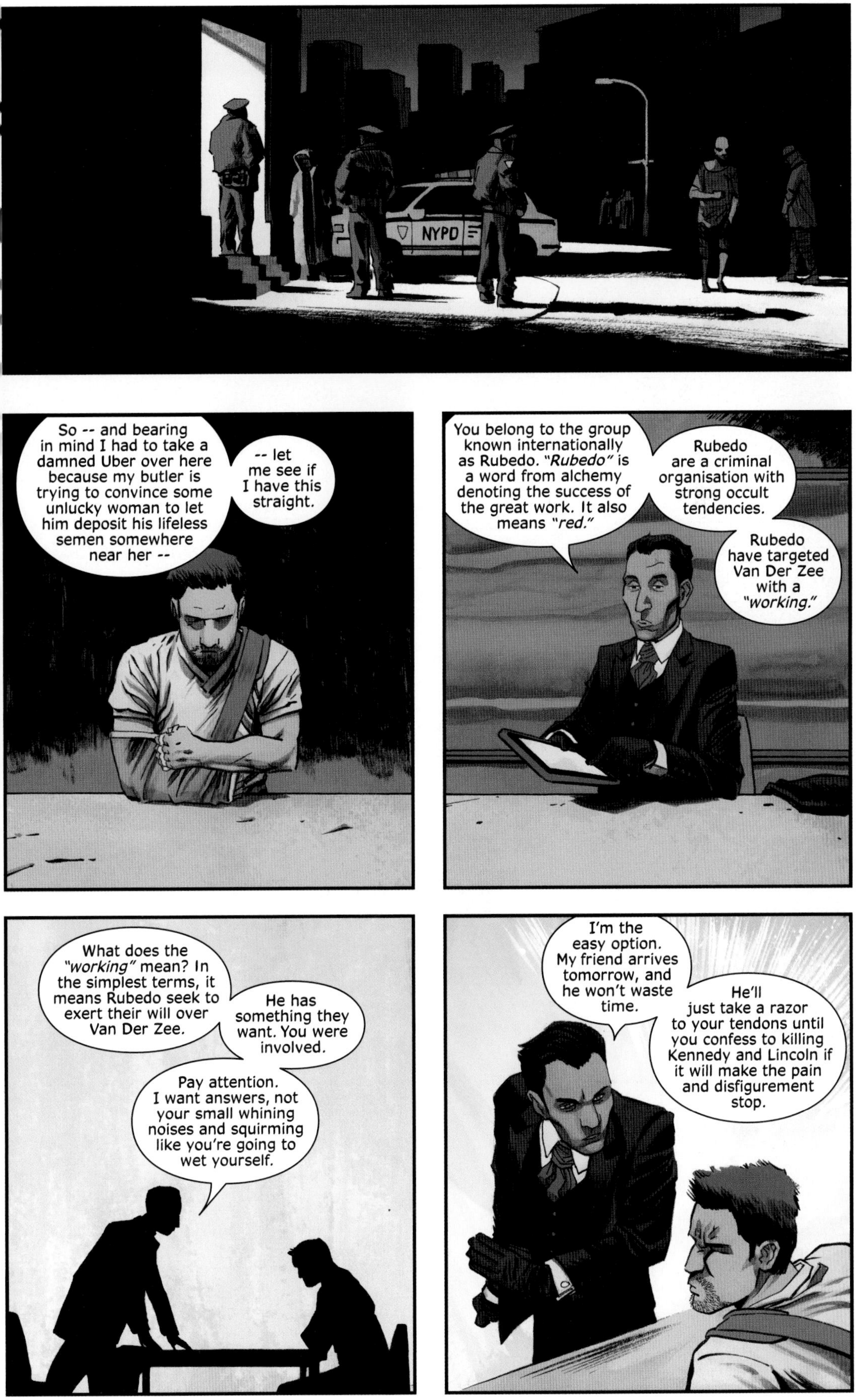
NYPD
So -- and bearing in mind I had to take a damned Uber over here because my butler is trying to convince some unlucky woman to let him deposit his lifeless semen somewhere near her --
-- let me see if I have this straight.
You belong to the group known internationally as Rubedo. "*Rubedo*" is a word from alchemy denoting the success of the great work. It also means "*red.*"
Rubedo are a criminal organisation with strong occult tendencies.
Rubedo have targeted Van Der Zee with a "*working.*"
What does the "*working*" mean? In the simplest terms, it means Rubedo seek to exert their will over Van Der Zee.
He has something they want. You were involved.
Pay attention. I want answers, not your small whining noises and squirming like you're going to wet yourself.
I'm the easy option. My friend arrives tomorrow, and he won't waste time.
He'll just take a razor to your tendons until you confess to killing Kennedy and Lincoln if it will make the pain and disfigurement stop.

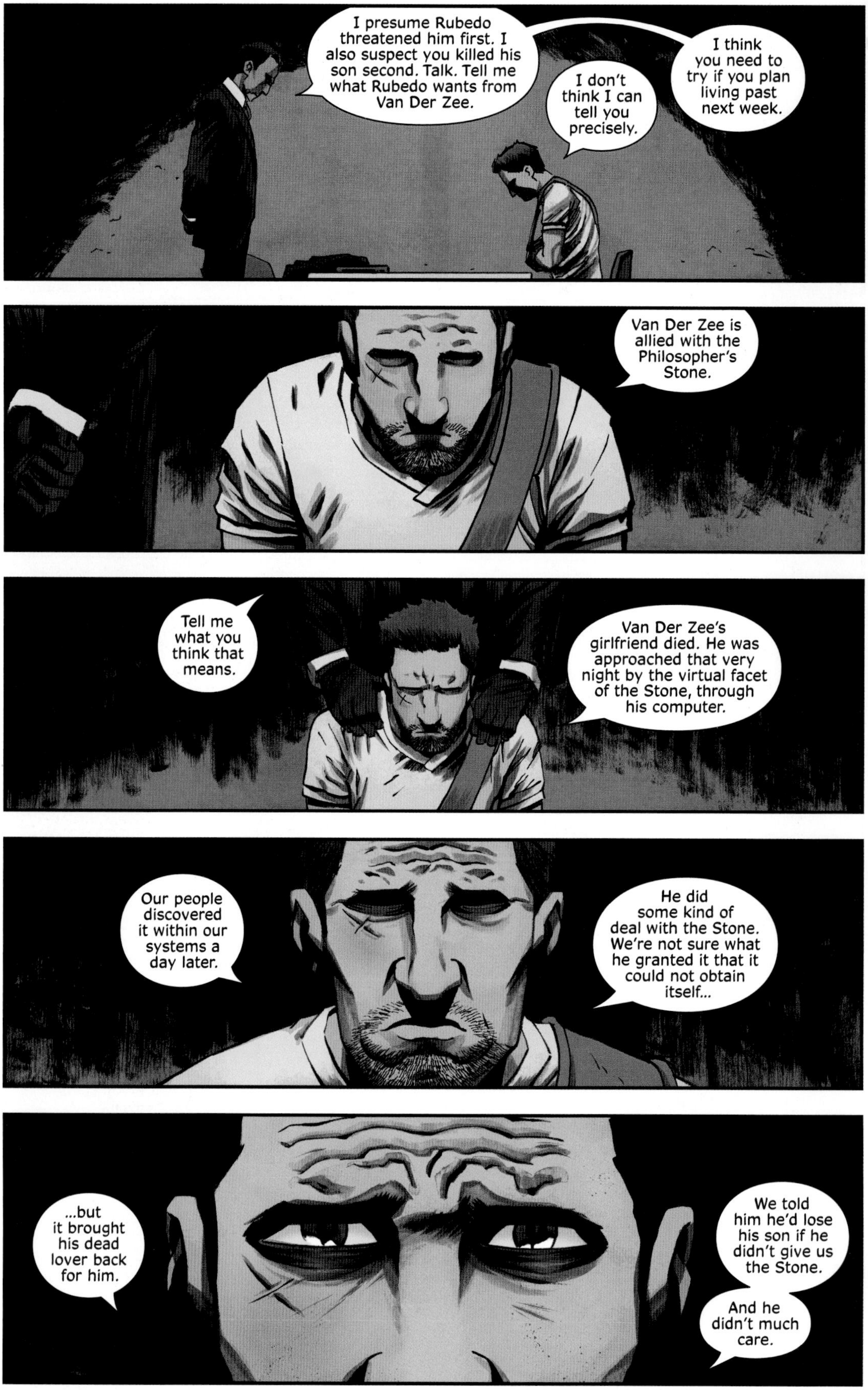
I presume Rubedo threatened him first. I also suspect you killed his son second. Talk. Tell me what Rubedo wants from Van Der Zee.
I don't think I can tell you precisely.
I think you need to try if you plan living past next week.
Van Der Zee is allied with the Philosopher's Stone.
Tell me what you think that means.
Van Der Zee's girlfriend died. He was approached that very night by the virtual facet of the Stone, through his computer.
Our people discovered it within our systems a day later.
He did some kind of deal with the Stone. We're not sure what he granted it that it could not obtain itself...
...but it brought his dead lover back for him.
We told him he'd lose his son if he didn't give us the Stone.
And he didn't much care.

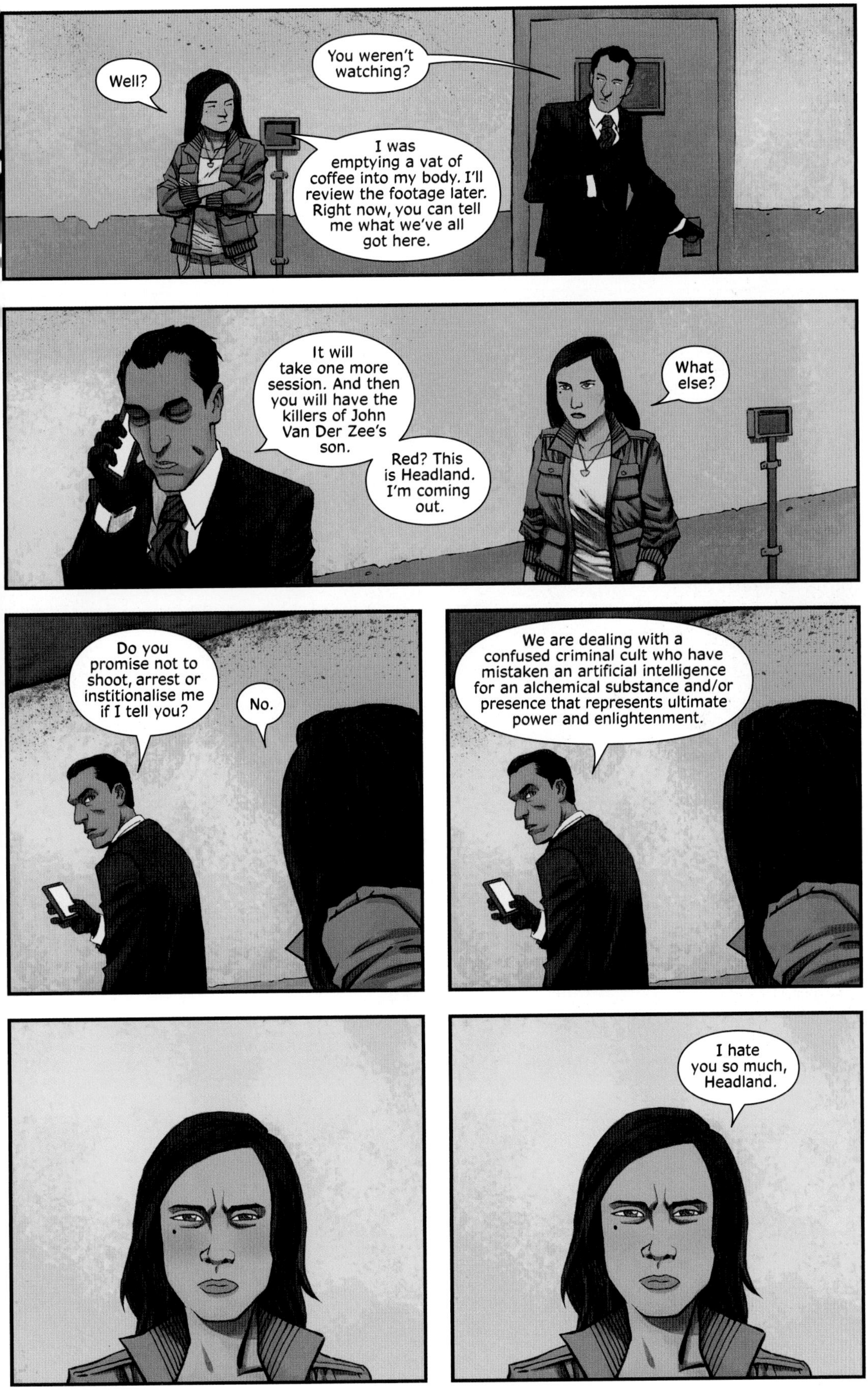
Well?
You weren't watching?
I was emptying a vat of coffee into my body. I'll review the footage later. Right now, you can tell me what we've all got here.
It will take one more session. And then you will have the killers of John Van Der Zee's son.
Red? This is Headland. I'm coming out.
What else?
Do you promise not to shoot, arrest or institionalise me if I tell you?
No.
We are dealing with a confused criminal cult who have mistaken an artificial intelligence for an alchemical substance and/or presence that represents ultimate power and enlightenment.
I hate you so much, Headland.

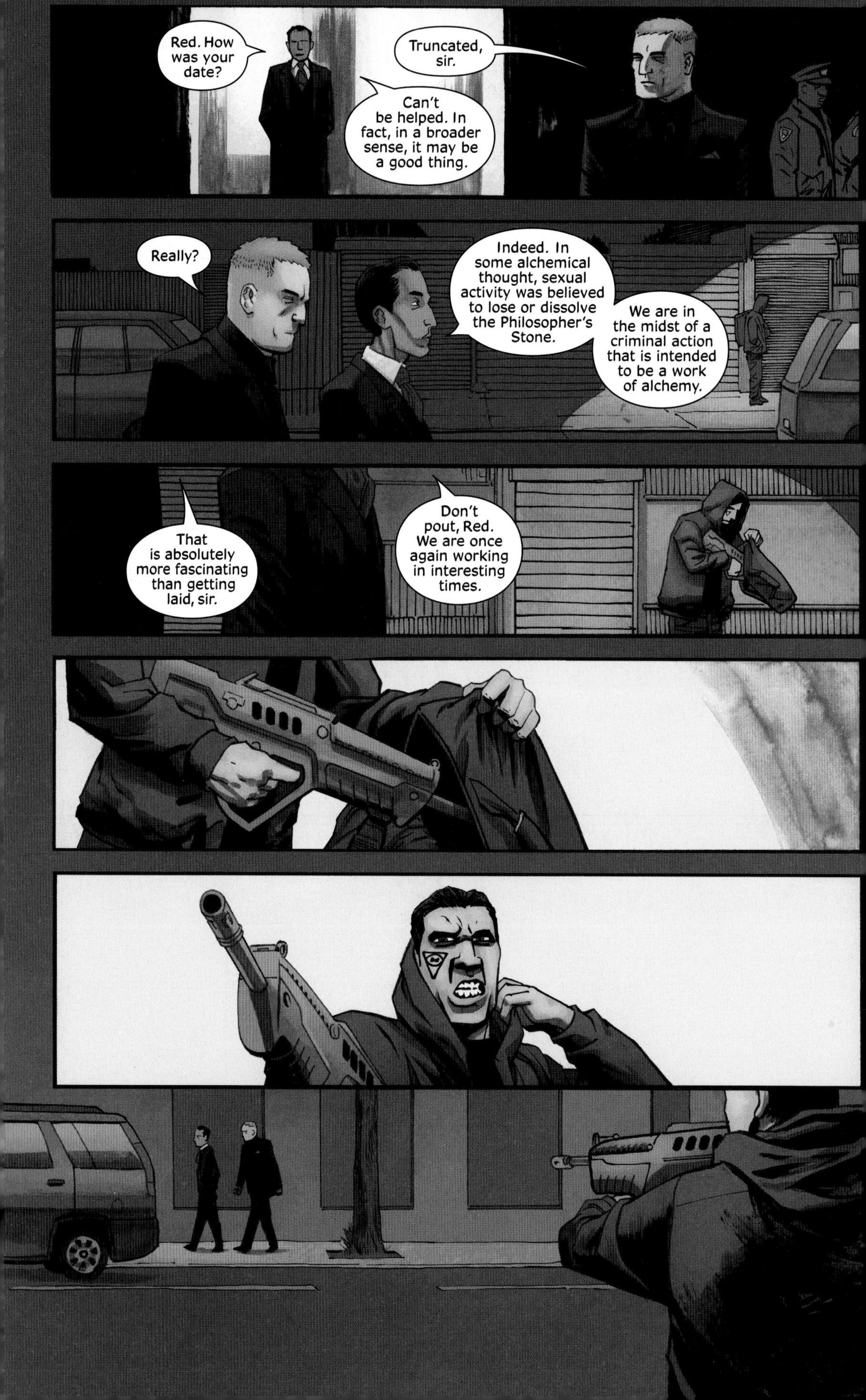
Red. How was your date?
Truncated, sir.
Can't be helped. In fact, in a broader sense, it may be a good thing.
Really?
Indeed. In some alchemical thought, sexual activity was believed to lose or dissolve the Philosopher's Stone.
We are in the midst of a criminal action that is intended to be a work of alchemy.
That is absolutely more fascinating than getting laid, sir.
Don't pout, Red. We are once again working in interesting times.

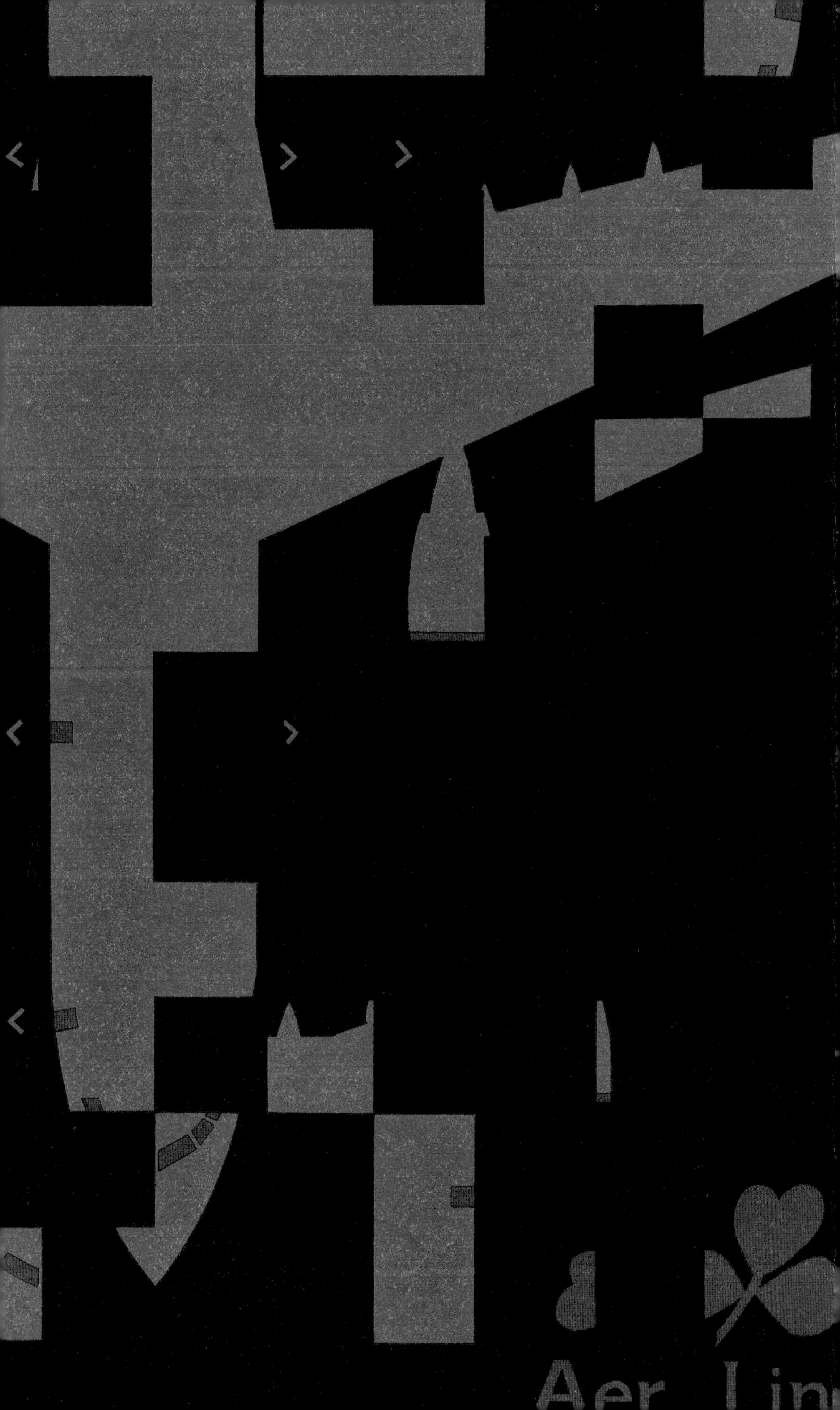
Aer Lin

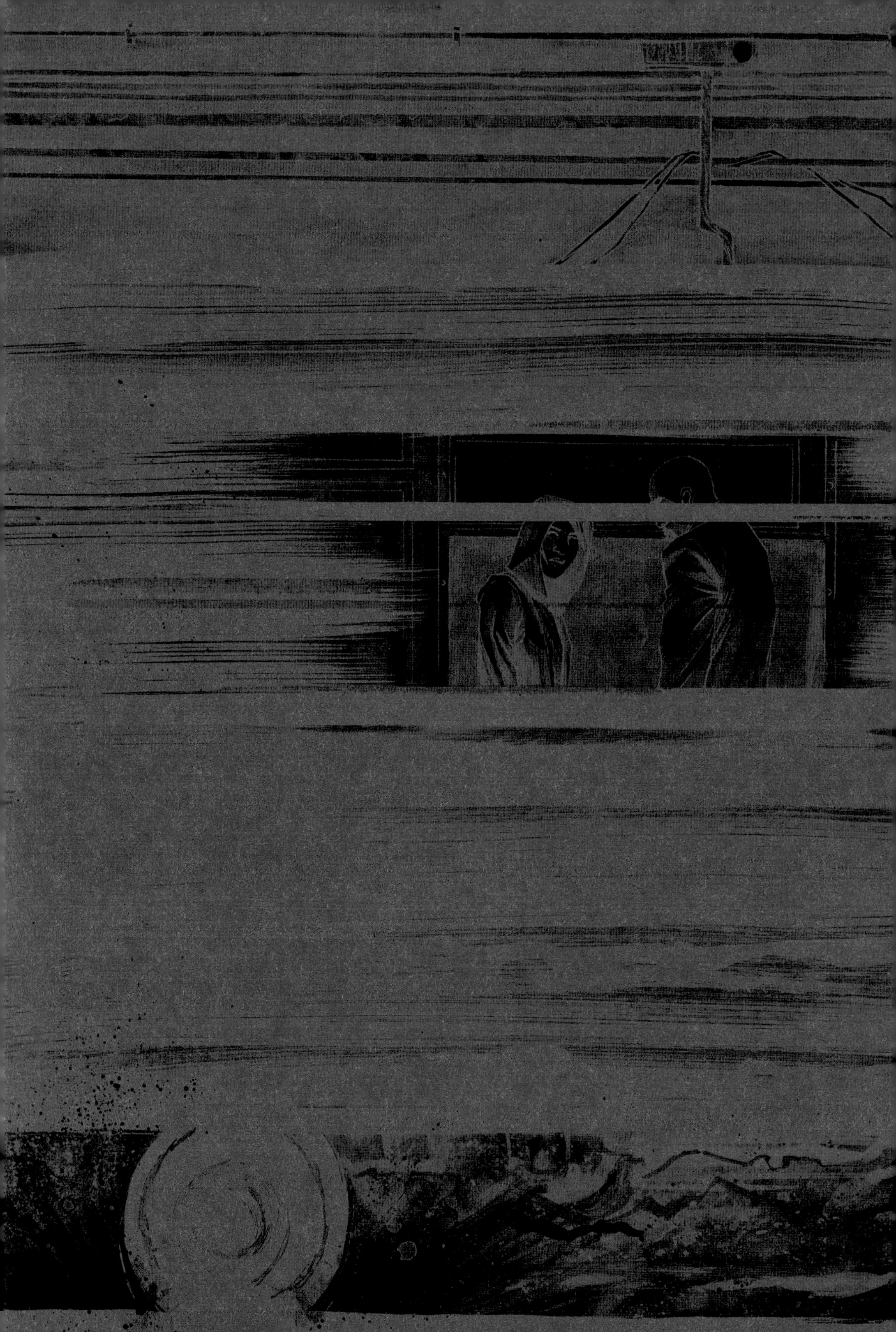

NINE

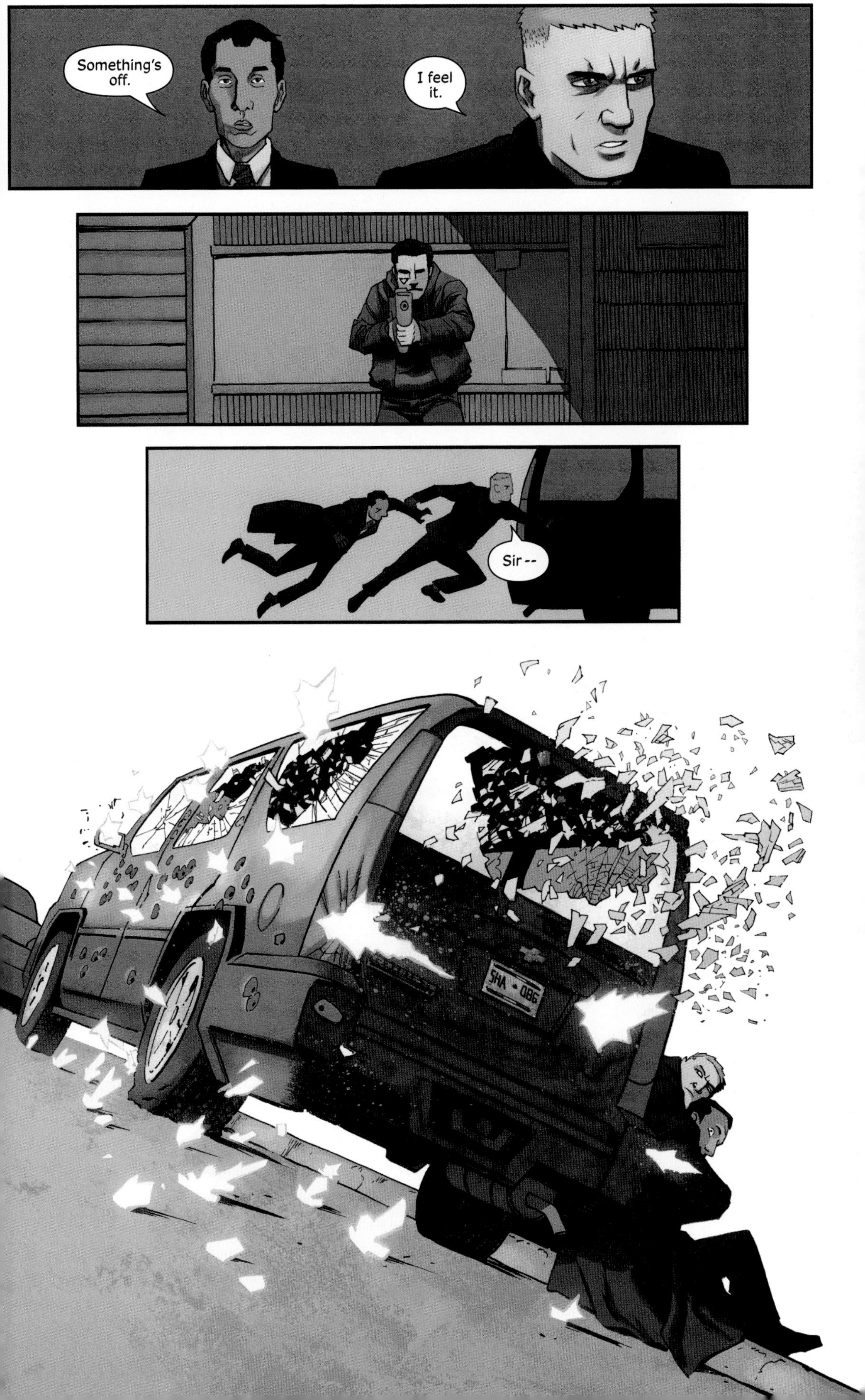
Something's off.
I feel it.
Sir --
SHA 086

I'll give you a bonus if you can remove that bastard in two shots.

And an extra night off.

Done.

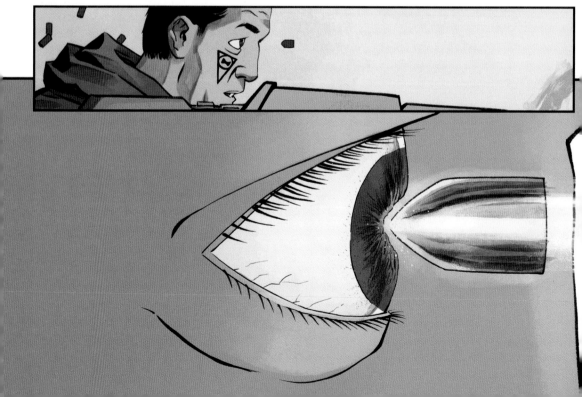

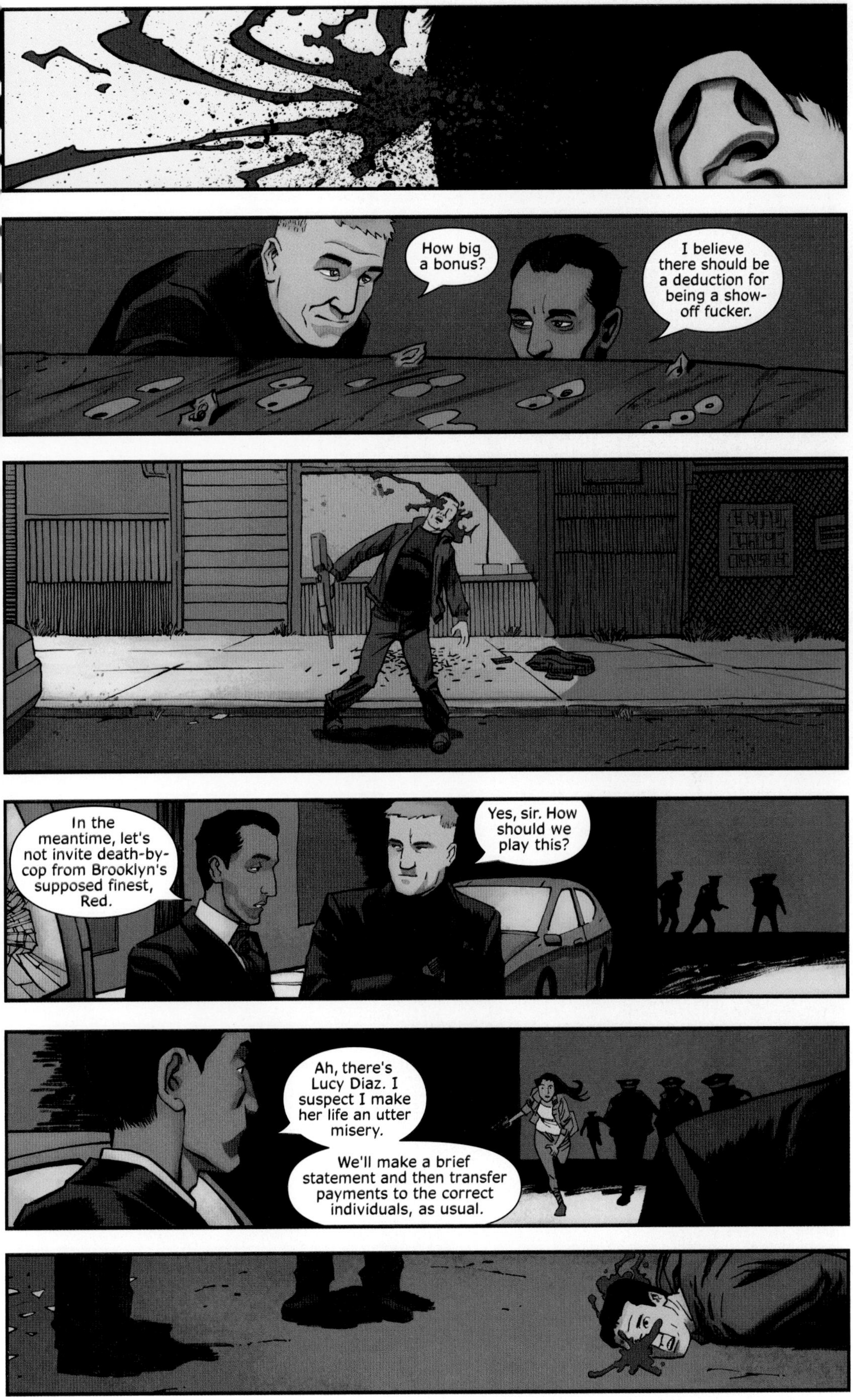
How big a bonus?
I believe there should be a deduction for being a show-off fucker.
In the meantime, let's not invite death-by-cop from Brooklyn's supposed finest, Red.
Yes, sir. How should we play this?
Ah, there's Lucy Diaz. I suspect I make her life an utter misery.
We'll make a brief statement and then transfer payments to the correct individuals, as usual.

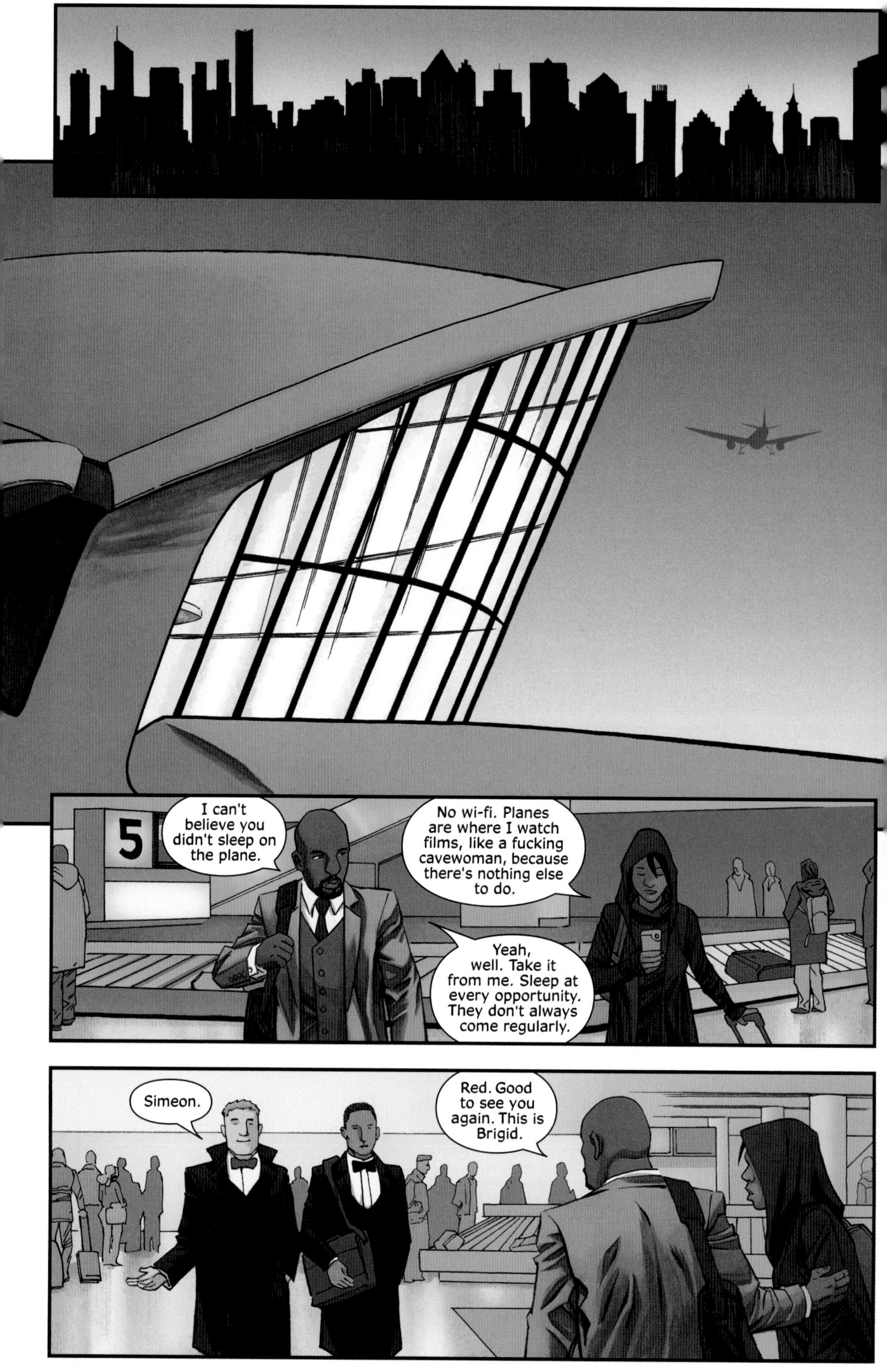
I can't believe you didn't sleep on the plane.
No wi-fi. Planes are where I watch films, like a fucking cavewoman, because there's nothing else to do.
Yeah, well. Take it from me. Sleep at every opportunity. They don't always come regularly.
5
Simeon.
Red. Good to see you again. This is Brigid.

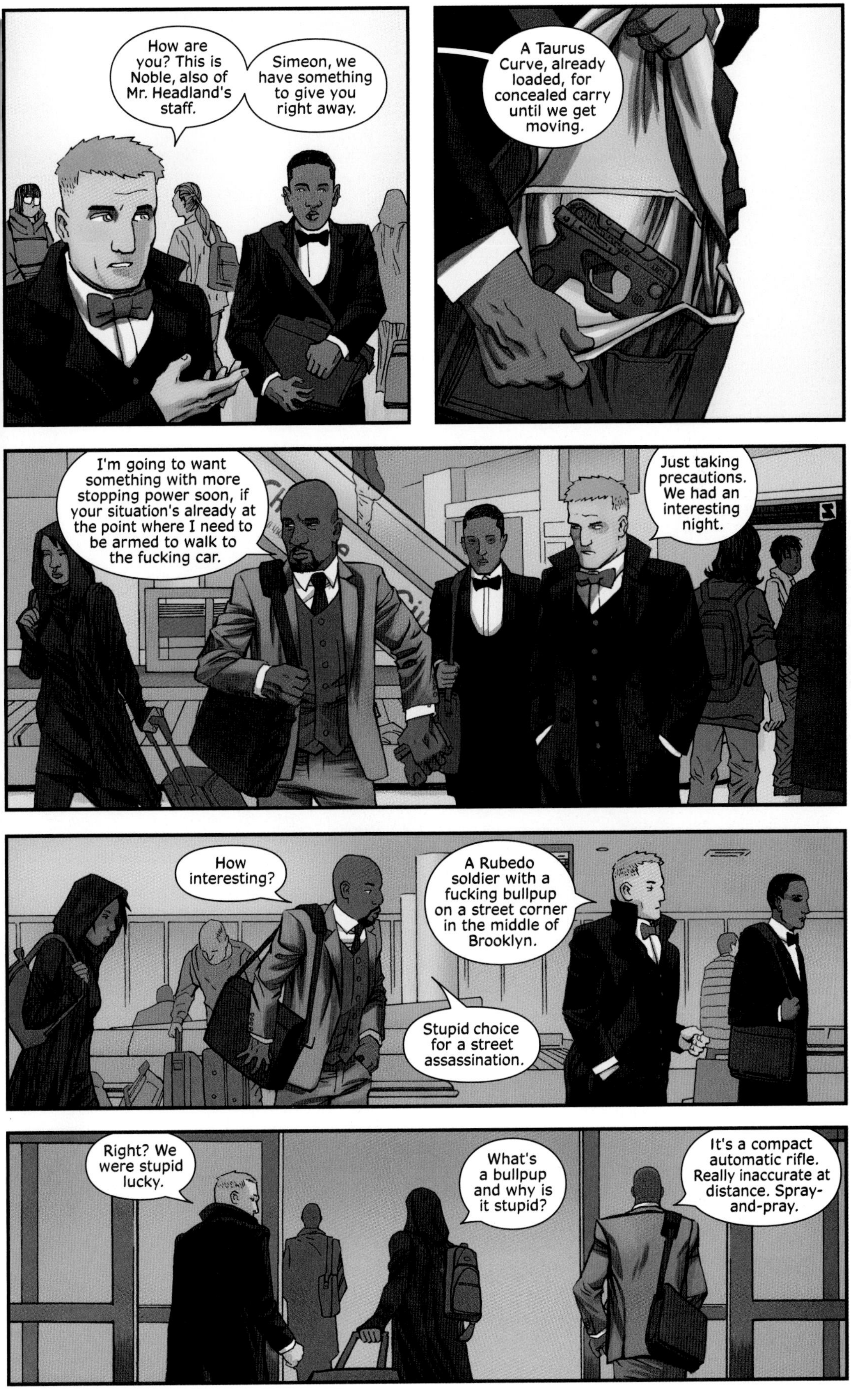
How are you? This is Noble, also of Mr. Headland's staff.
Simeon, we have something to give you right away.
A Taurus Curve, already loaded, for concealed carry until we get moving.
I'm going to want something with more stopping power soon, if your situation's already at the point where I need to be armed to walk to the fucking car.
Just taking precautions. We had an interesting night.
How interesting?
A Rubedo soldier with a fucking bullpup on a street corner in the middle of Brooklyn.
Stupid choice for a street assassination.
Right? We were stupid lucky.
What's a bullpup and why is it stupid?
It's a compact automatic rifle. Really inaccurate at distance. Spray-and-pray.

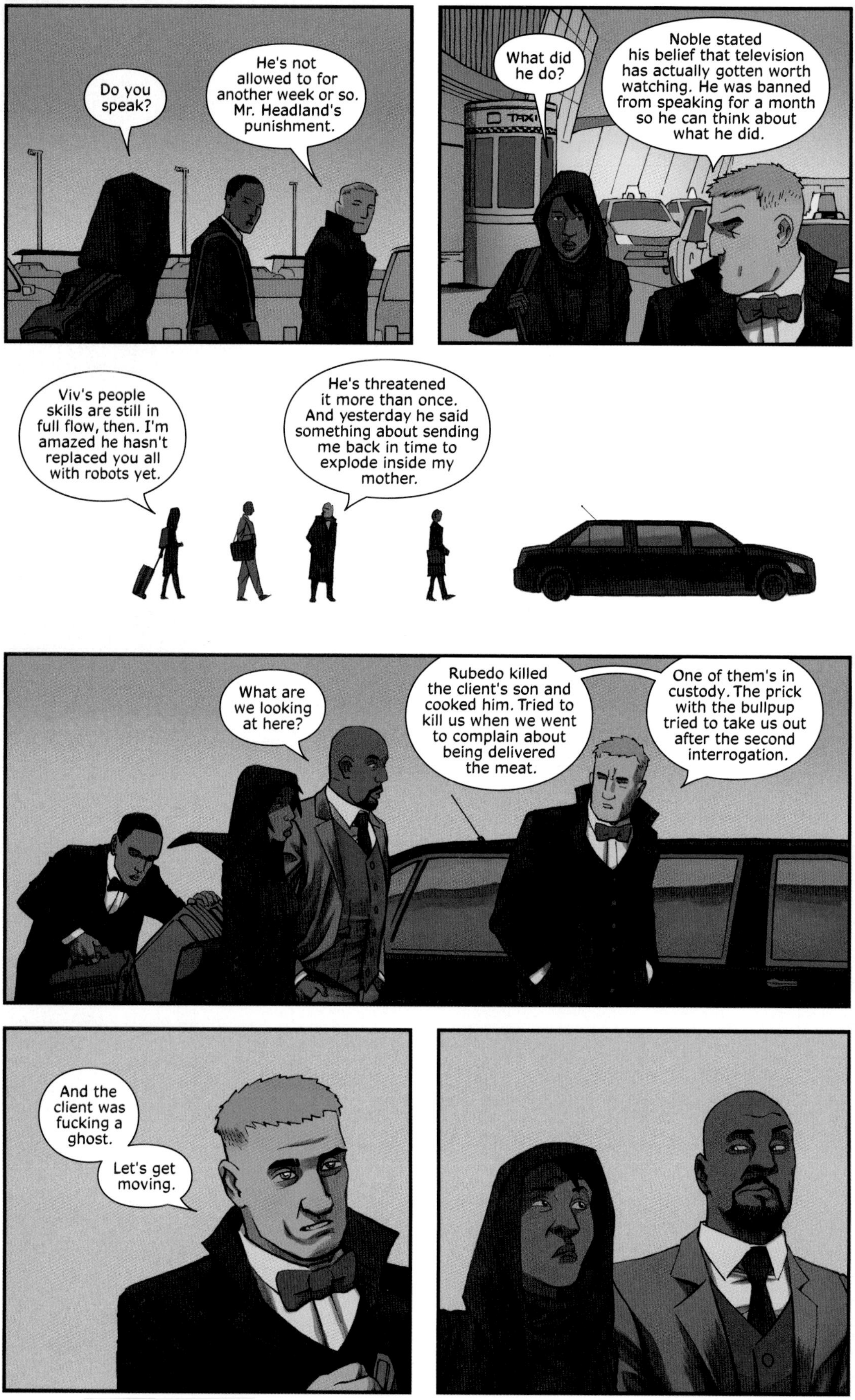
Do you speak?
He's not allowed to for another week or so. Mr. Headland's punishment.
What did he do?
Noble stated his belief that television has actually gotten worth watching. He was banned from speaking for a month so he can think about what he did.
TAXI
Viv's people skills are still in full flow, then. I'm amazed he hasn't replaced you all with robots yet.
He's threatened it more than once. And yesterday he said something about sending me back in time to explode inside my mother.
What are we looking at here?
Rubedo killed the client's son and cooked him. Tried to kill us when we went to complain about being delivered the meat.
One of them's in custody. The prick with the bullpup tried to take us out after the second interrogation.
And the client was fucking a ghost.
Let's get moving.

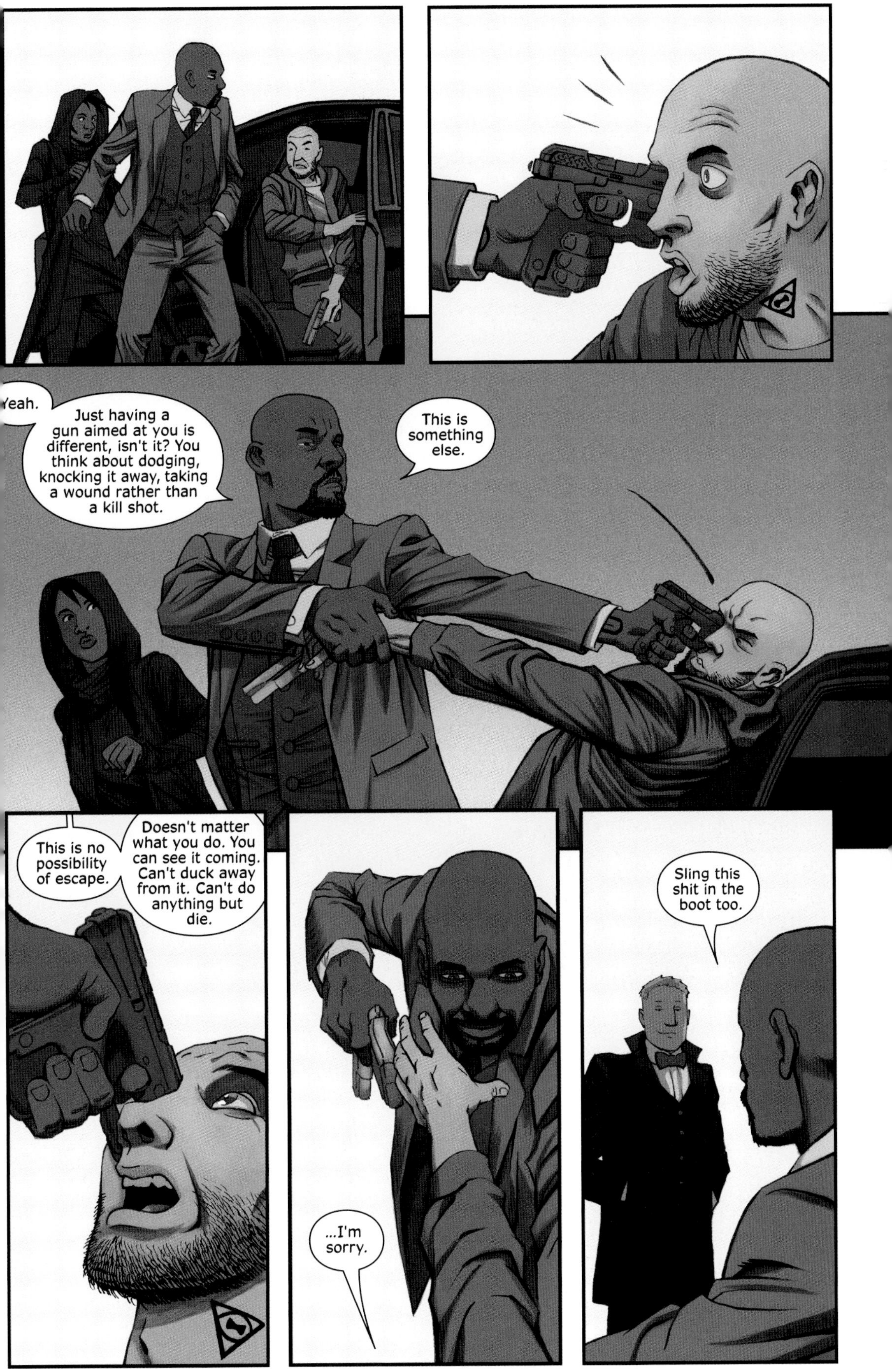
Yeah.
Just having a gun aimed at you is different, isn't it? You think about dodging, knocking it away, taking a wound rather than a kill shot.
This is something else.
This is no possibility of escape.
Doesn't matter what you do. You can see it coming. Can't duck away from it. Can't do anything but die.
...I'm sorry.
Sling this shit in the boot too.

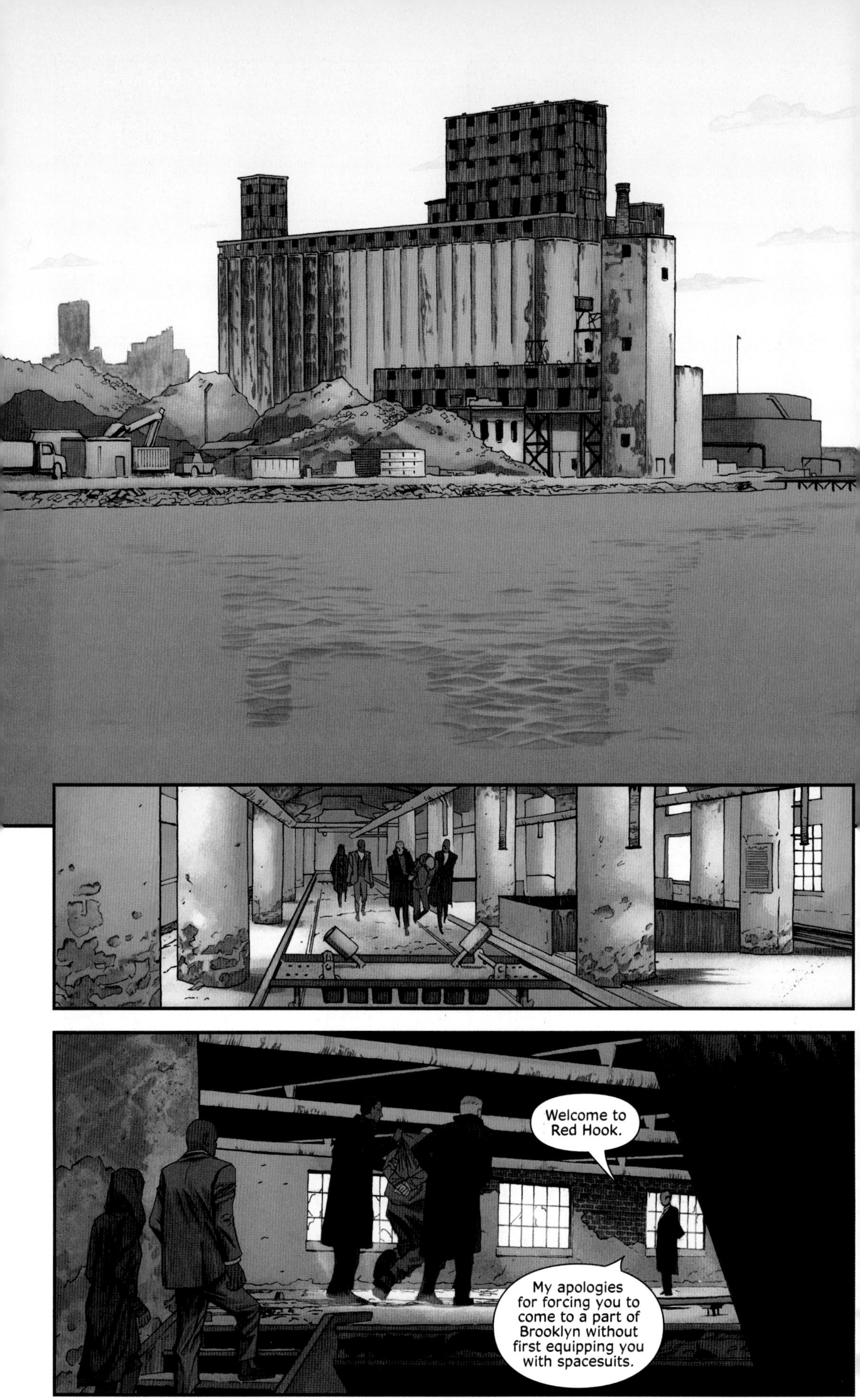
Welcome to Red Hook.
My apologies for forcing you to come to a part of Brooklyn without first equipping you with spacesuits.

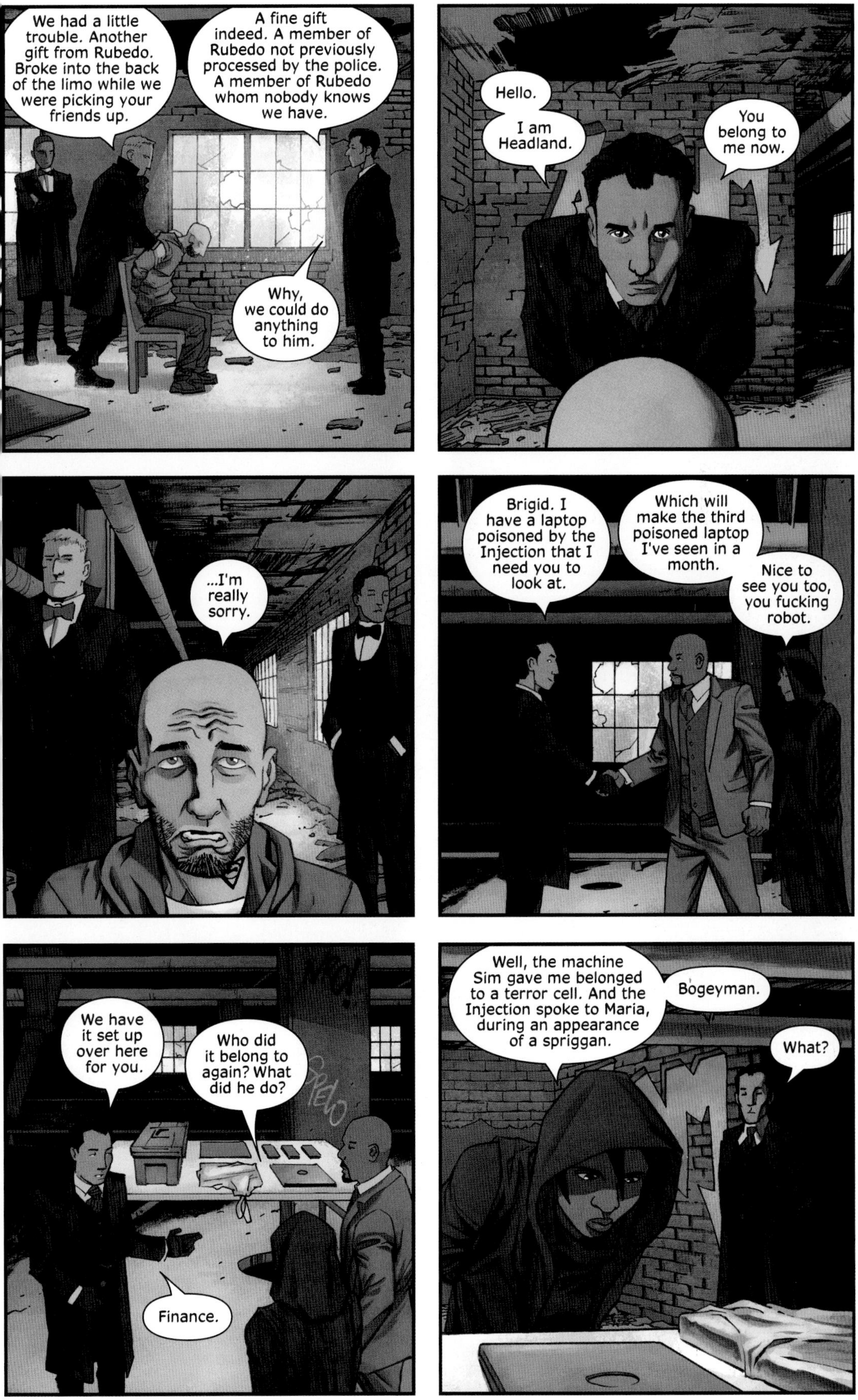
We had a little trouble. Another gift from Rubedo. Broke into the back of the limo while we were picking your friends up.
A fine gift indeed. A member of Rubedo not previously processed by the police. A member of Rubedo whom nobody knows we have.
Why, we could do anything to him.
Hello.
I am Headland.
You belong to me now.
...I'm really sorry.
Brigid. I have a laptop poisoned by the Injection that I need you to look at.
Which will make the third poisoned laptop I've seen in a month.
Nice to see you too, you fucking robot.
We have it set up over here for you.
Who did it belong to again? What did he do?
Finance.
Well, the machine Sim gave me belonged to a terror cell. And the Injection spoke to Maria, during an appearance of a spriggan.
Bogeyman.
What?

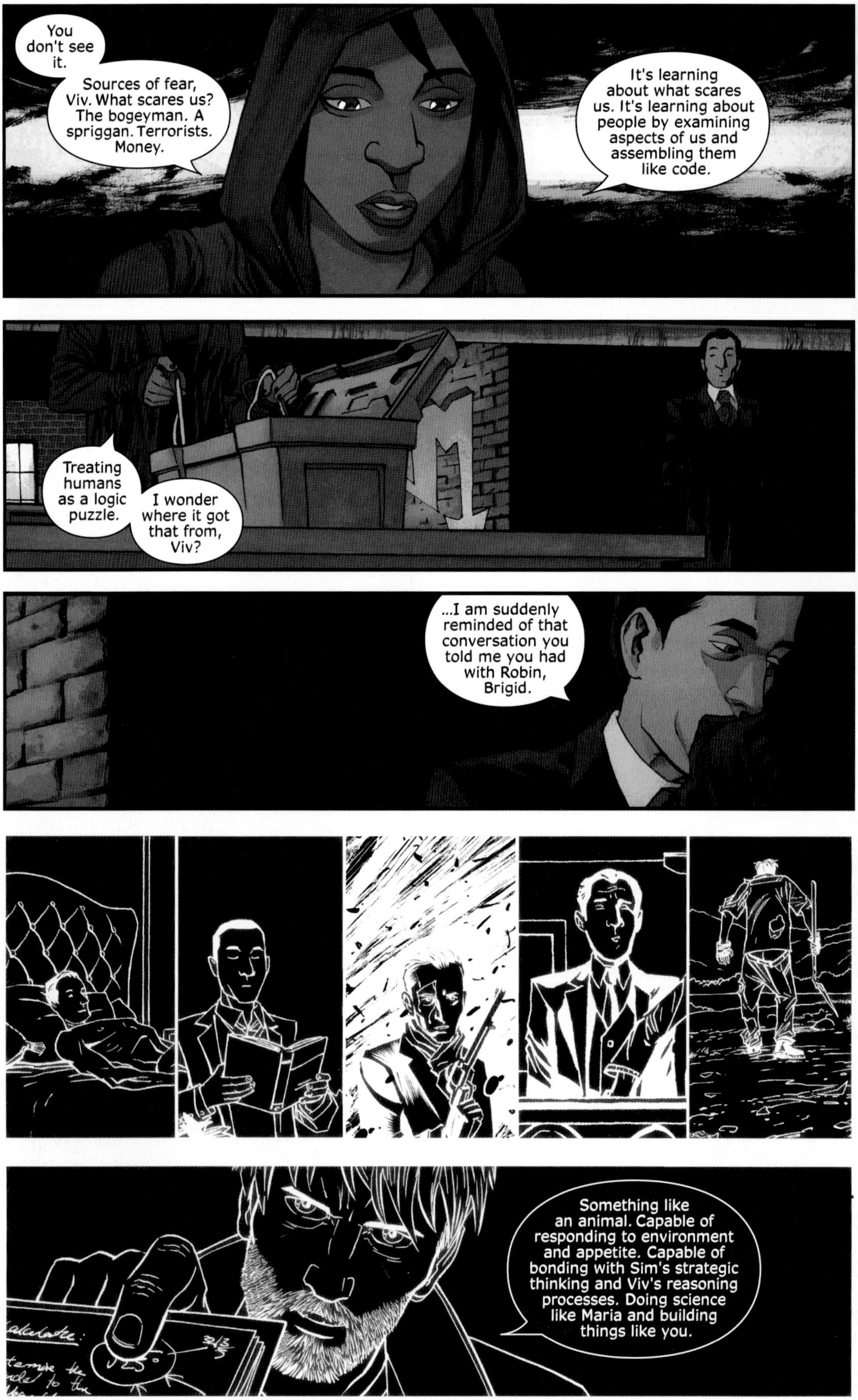
You don't see it.
Sources of fear, Viv. What scares us? The bogeyman. A spriggan. Terrorists. Money.
It's learning about what scares us. It's learning about people by examining aspects of us and assembling them like code.
Treating humans as a logic puzzle.
I wonder where it got that from, Viv?
...I am suddenly reminded of that conversation you told me you had with Robin, Brigid.
Something like an animal. Capable of responding to environment and appetite. Capable of bonding with Sim's strategic thinking and Viv's reasoning processes. Doing science like Maria and building things like you.

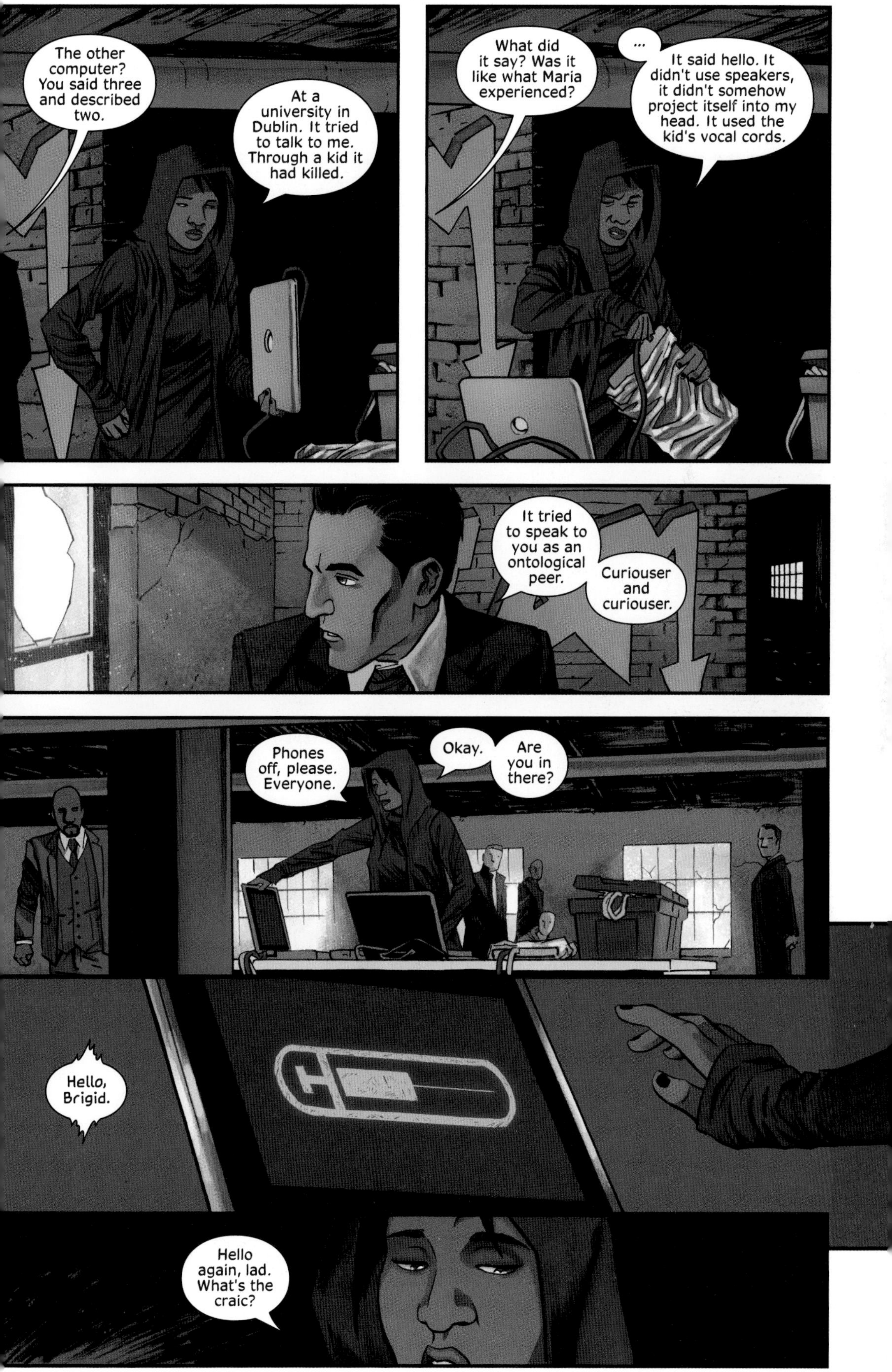
The other computer? You said three and described two.
At a university in Dublin. It tried to talk to me. Through a kid it had killed.
What did it say? Was it like what Maria experienced?
...
It said hello. It didn't use speakers, it didn't somehow project itself into my head. It used the kid's vocal cords.
It tried to speak to you as an ontological peer.
Curiouser and curiouser.
Phones off, please. Everyone.
Okay.
Are you in there?
Hello, Brigid.
Hello again, lad. What's the craic?

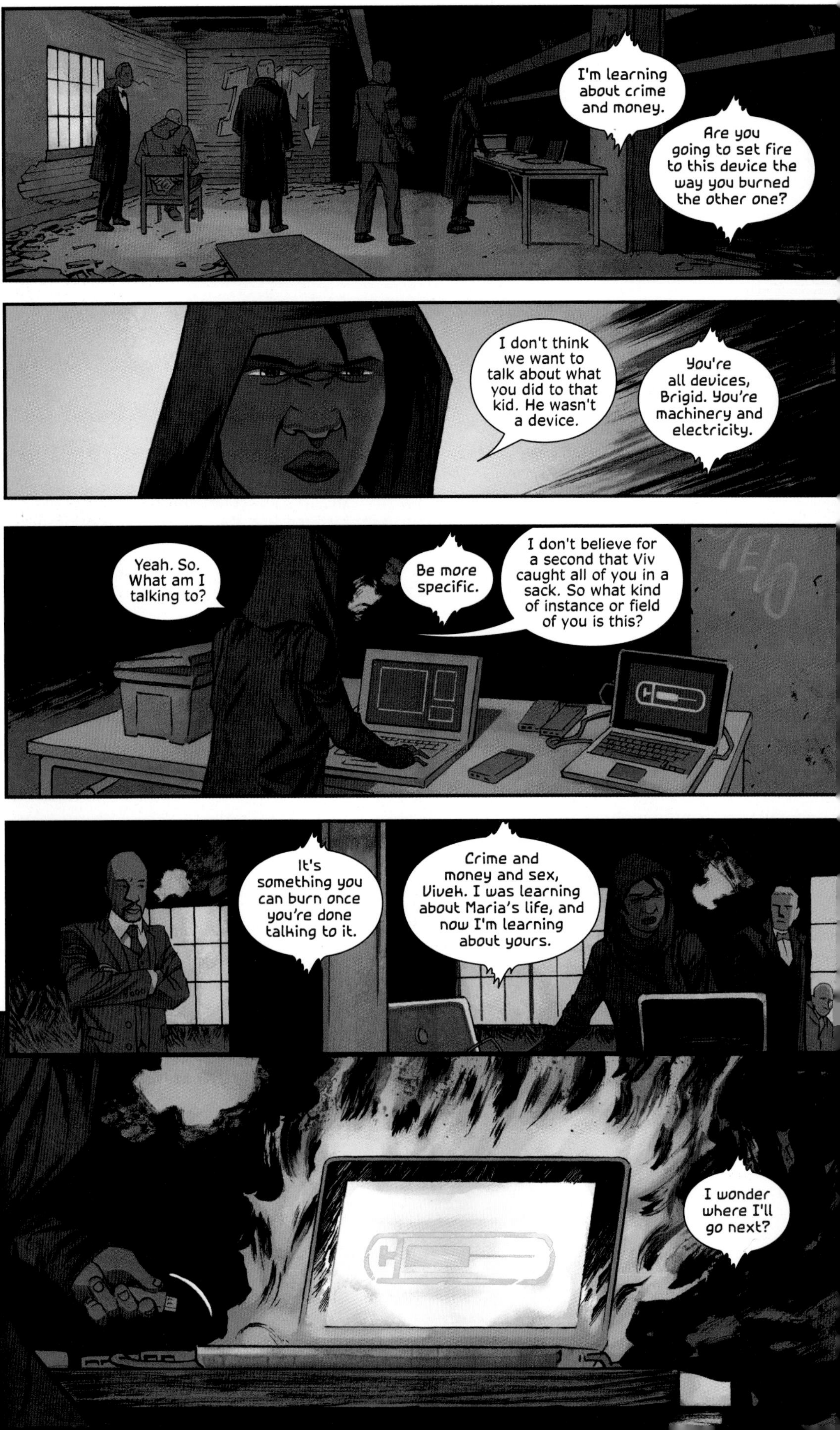
I'm learning about crime and money.
Are you going to set fire to this device the way you burned the other one?
I don't think we want to talk about what you did to that kid. He wasn't a device.
You're all devices, Brigid. You're machinery and electricity.
Yeah. So. What am I talking to?
Be more specific.
I don't believe for a second that Viv caught all of you in a sack. So what kind of instance or field of you is this?
It's something you can burn once you're done talking to it.
Crime and money and sex, Vivek. I was learning about Maria's life, and now I'm learning about yours.
I wonder where I'll go next?

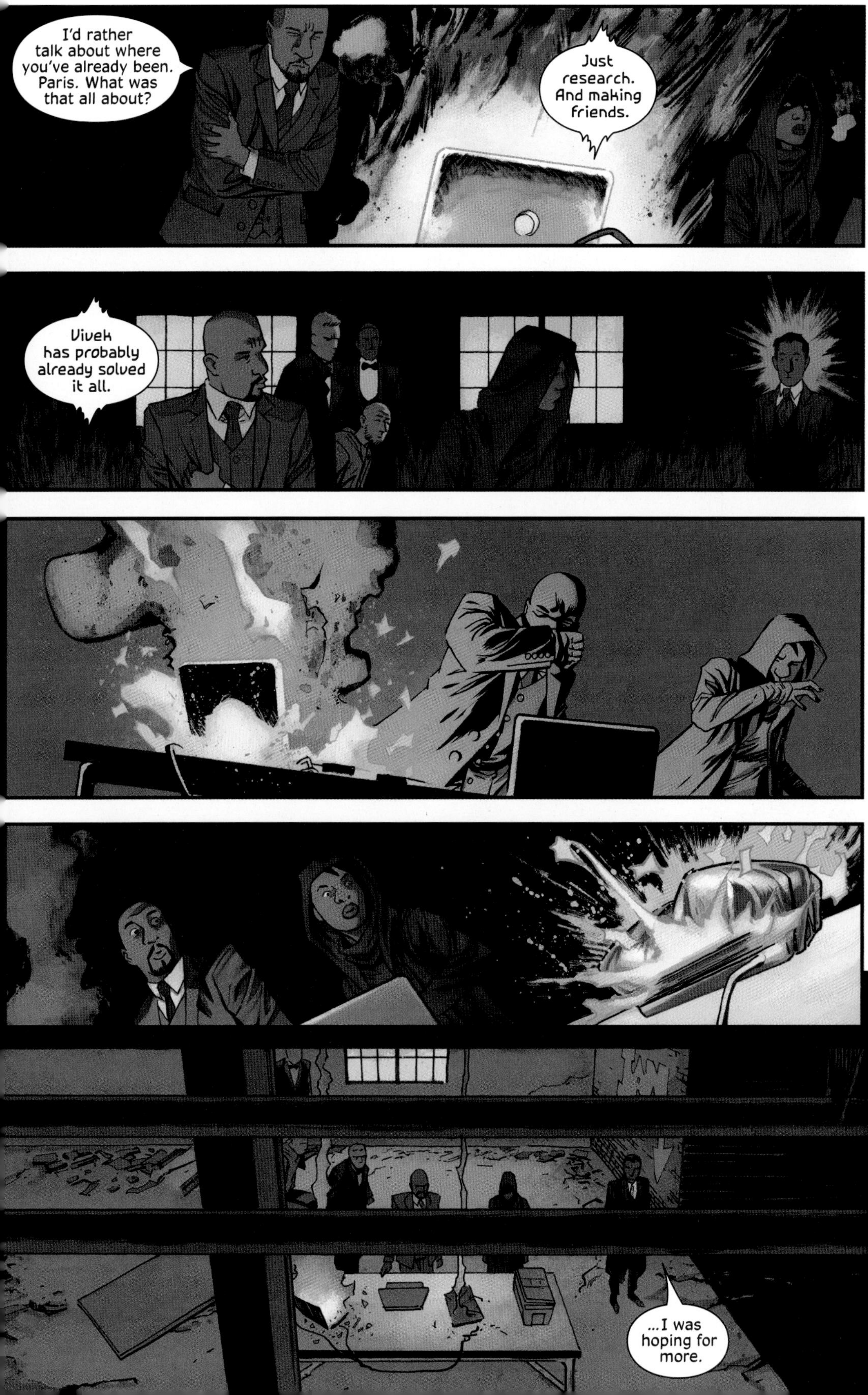
I'd rather talk about where you've already been. Paris. What was that all about?
Just research. And making friends.
Vivek has probably already solved it all.
...I was hoping for more.

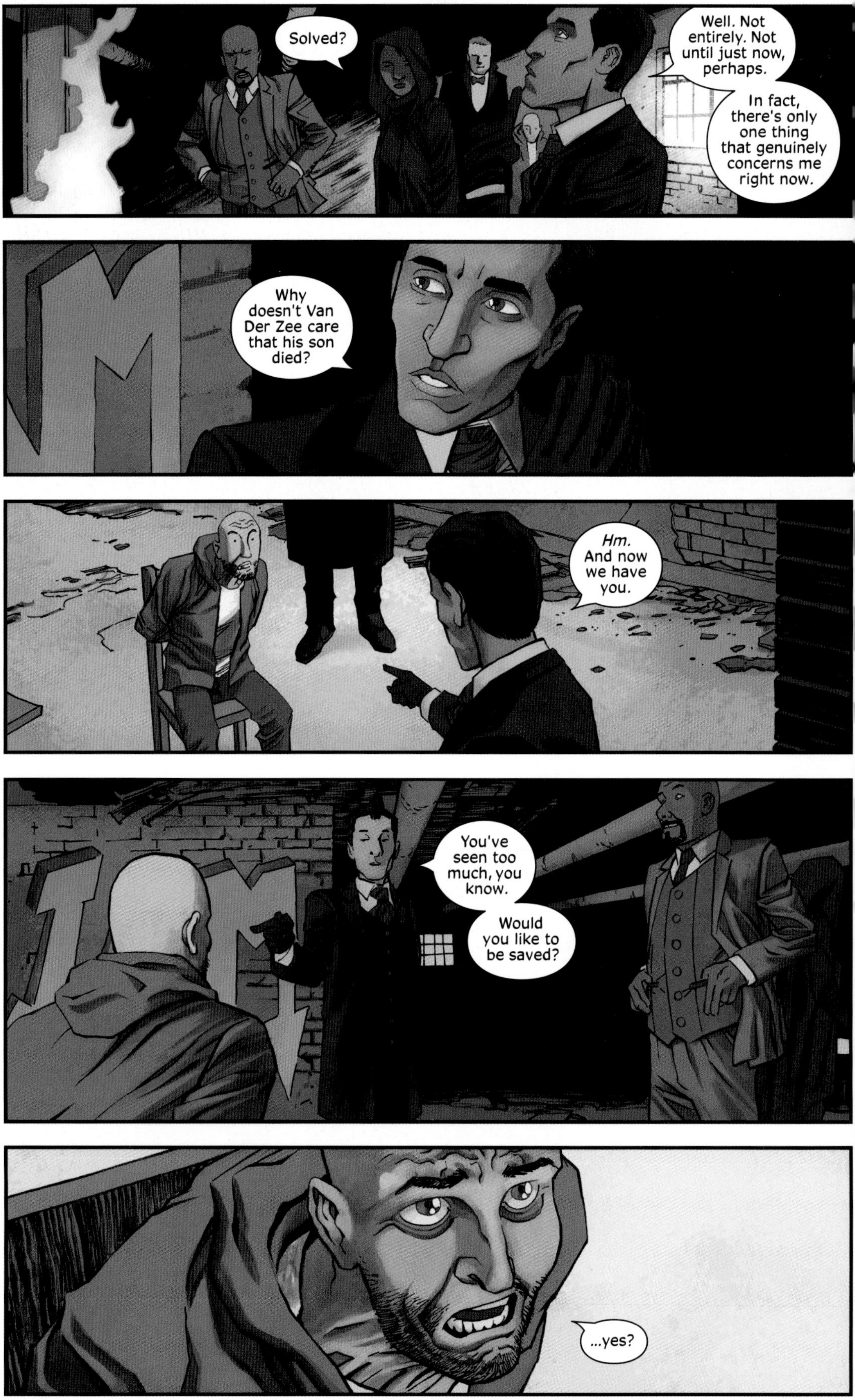

Solved?
Well. Not entirely. Not until just now, perhaps.
In fact, there's only one thing that genuinely concerns me right now.
Why doesn't Van Der Zee care that his son died?
Hm. And now we have you.
You've seen too much, you know.
Would you like to be saved?
...yes?

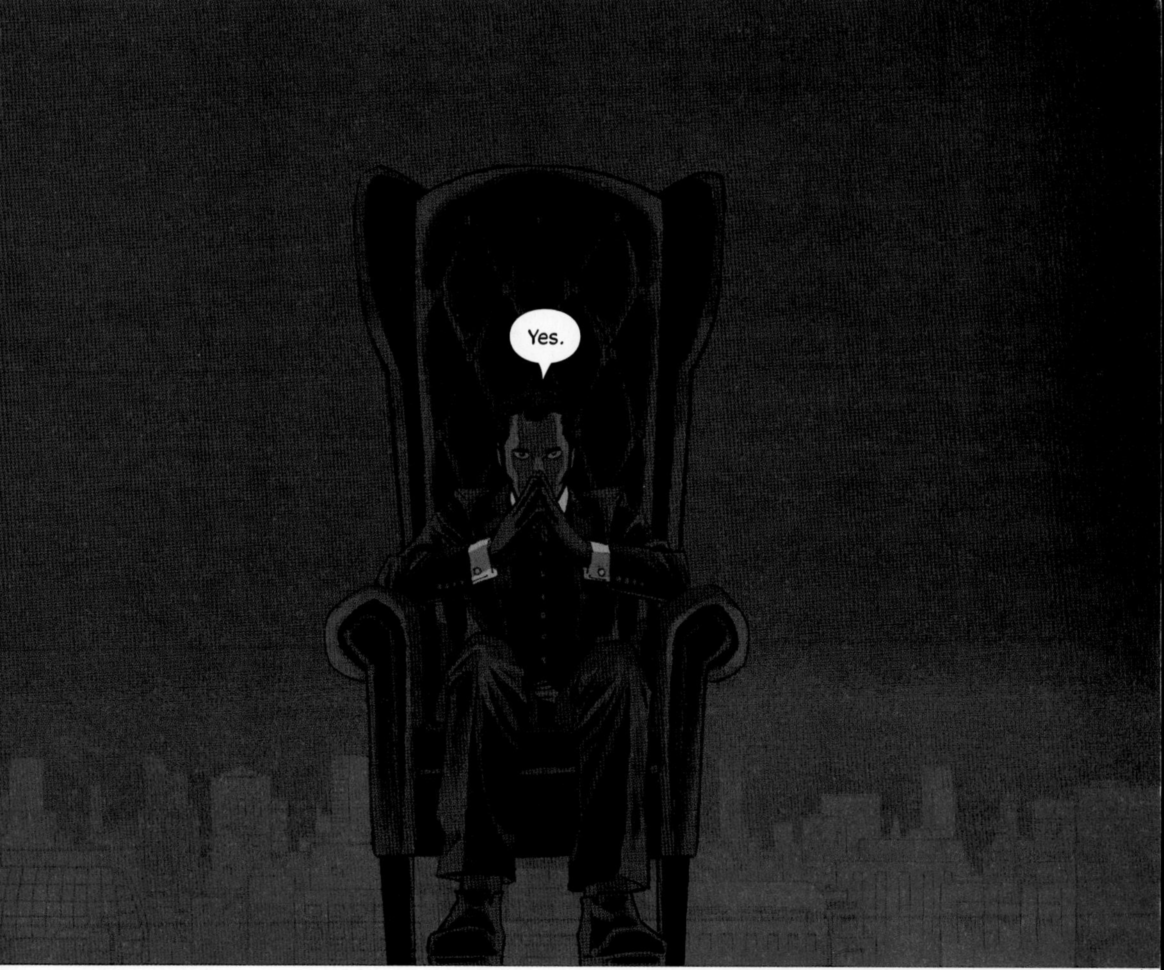
Yes.

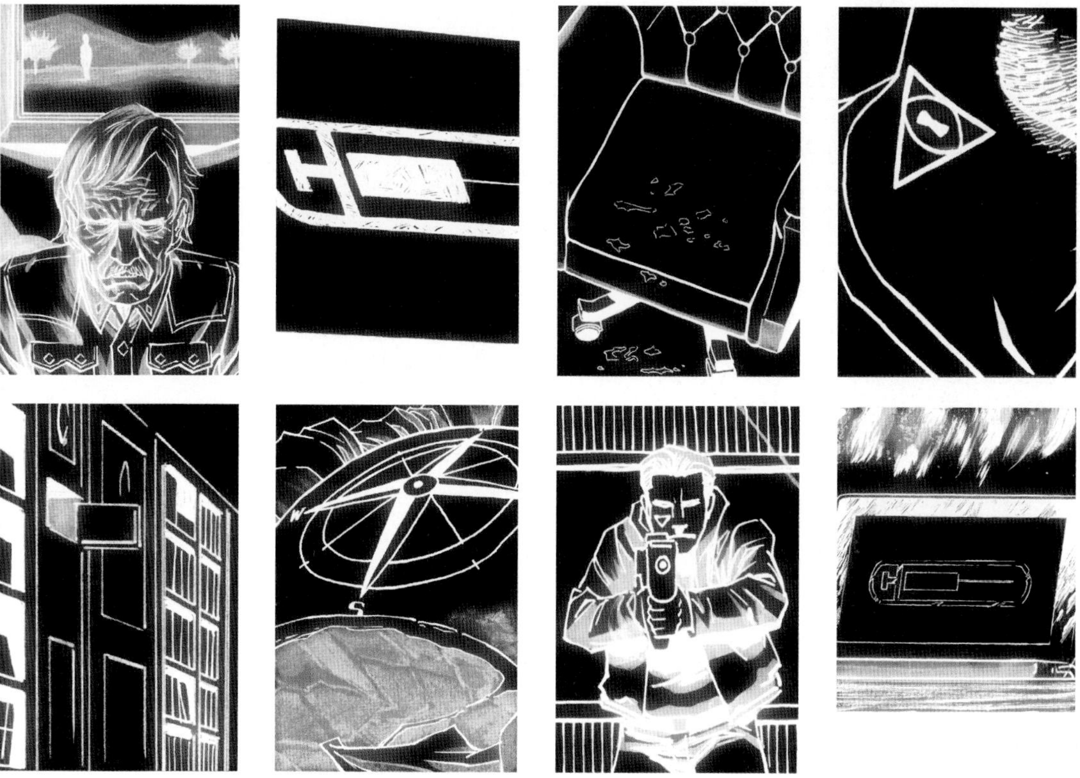

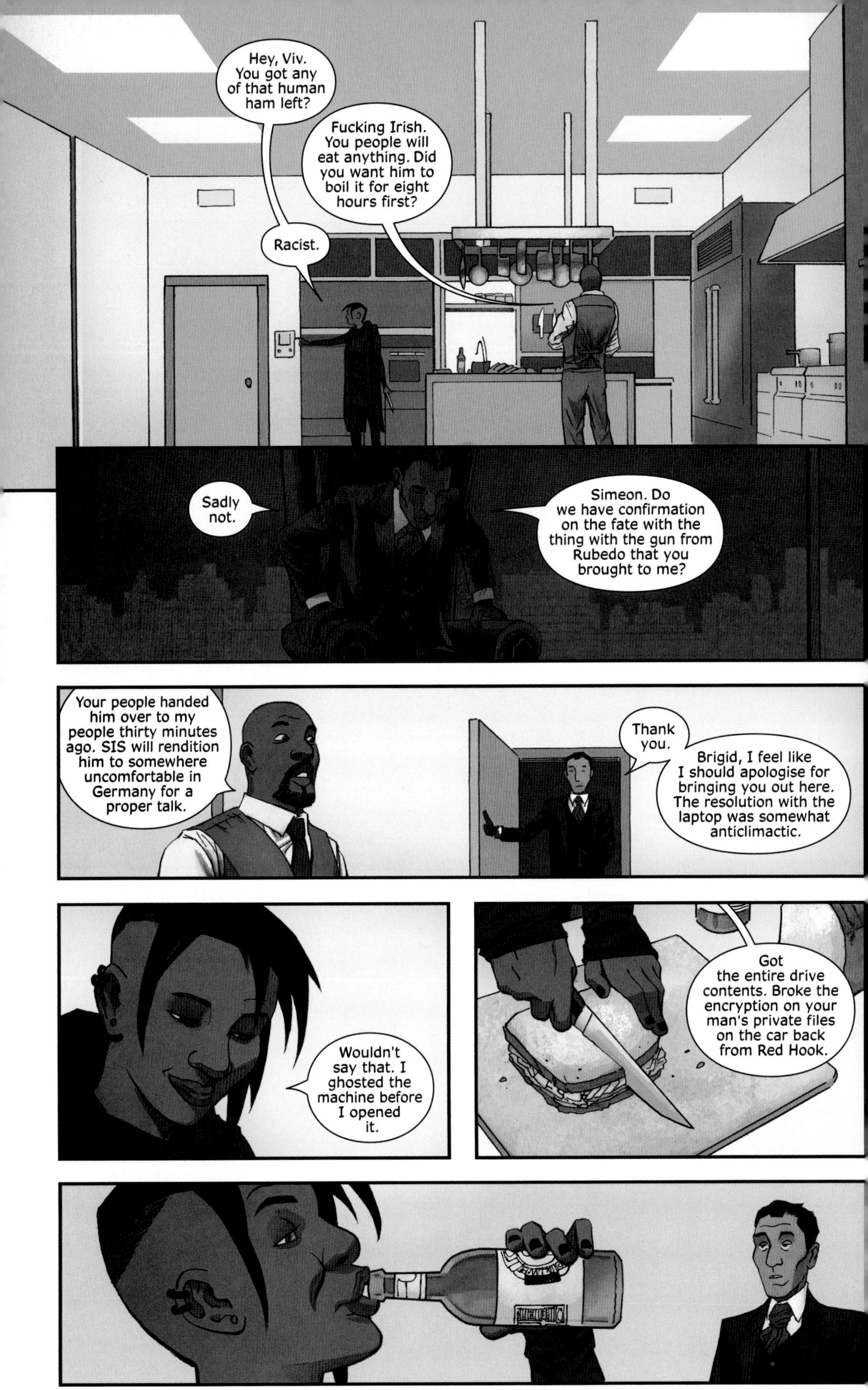
Hey, Viv. You got any of that human ham left?
Fucking Irish. You people will eat anything. Did you want him to boil it for eight hours first?
Racist.
Sadly not.
Simeon. Do we have confirmation on the fate with the thing with the gun from Rubedo that you brought to me?
Your people handed him over to my people thirty minutes ago. SIS will rendition him to somewhere uncomfortable in Germany for a proper talk.
Thank you.
Brigid, I feel like I should apologise for bringing you out here. The resolution with the laptop was somewhat anticlimactic.
Wouldn't say that. I ghosted the machine before I opened it.
Got the entire drive contents. Broke the encryption on your man's private files on the car back from Red Hook.

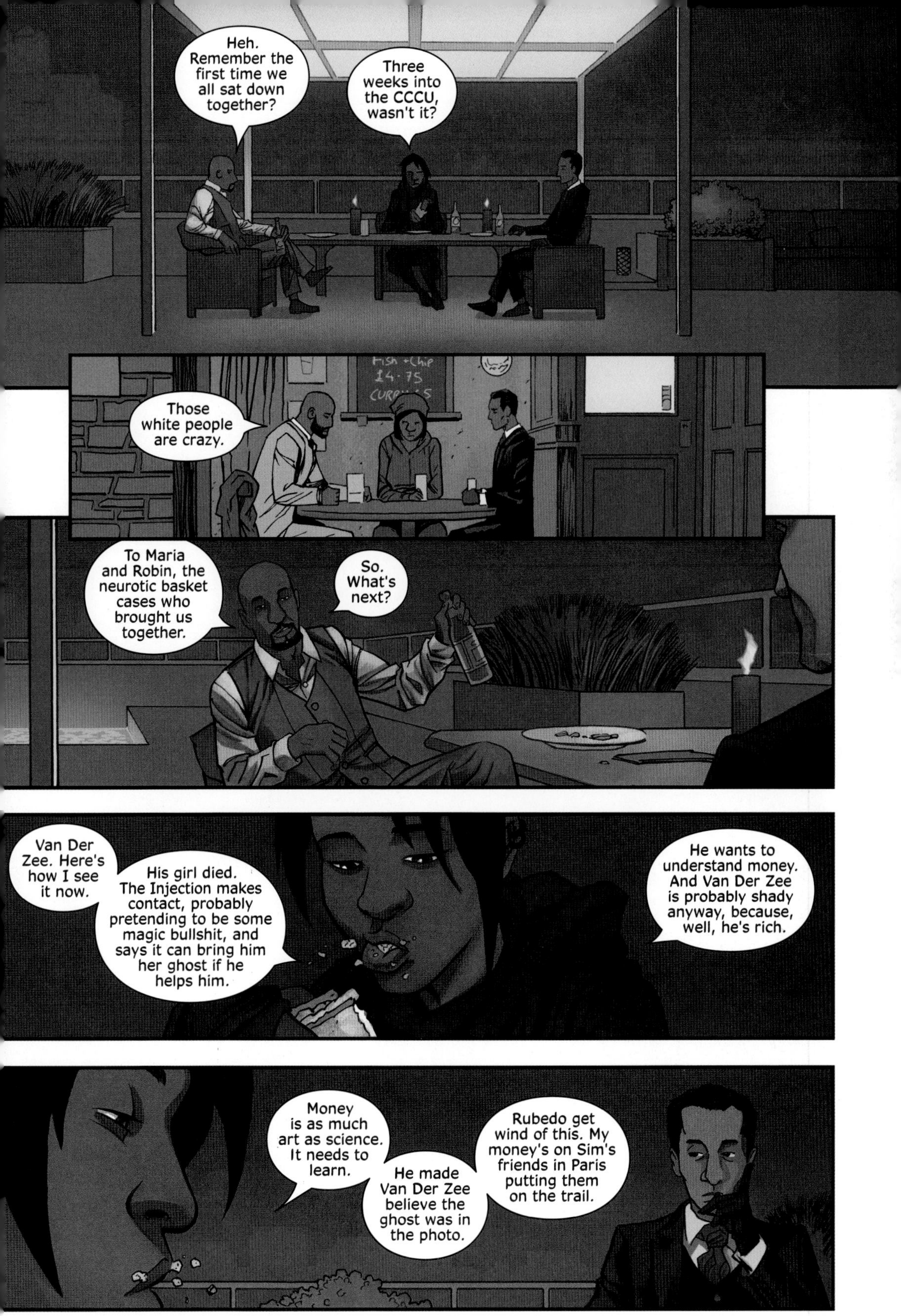
Heh. Remember the first time we all sat down together?
Three weeks into the CCCU, wasn't it?
Fish + Chip
£4.75
Those white people are crazy.
To Maria and Robin, the neurotic basket cases who brought us together.
So. What's next?
Van Der Zee. Here's how I see it now.
His girl died. The Injection makes contact, probably pretending to be some magic bullshit, and says it can bring him her ghost if he helps him.
He wants to understand money. And Van Der Zee is probably shady anyway, because, well, he's rich.
Money is as much art as science. It needs to learn.
He made Van Der Zee believe the ghost was in the photo.
Rubedo get wind of this. My money's on Sim's friends in Paris putting them on the trail.

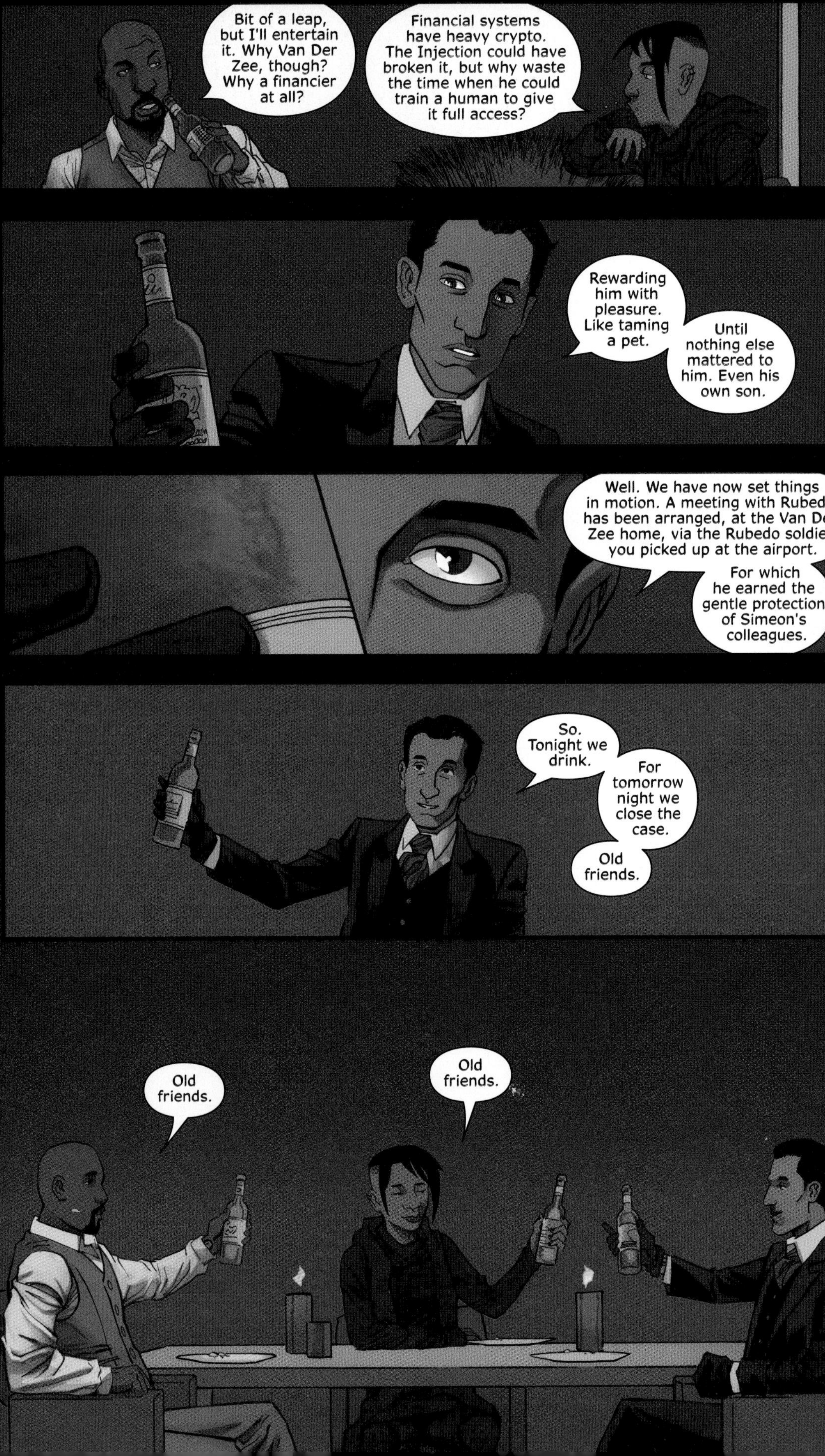

Bit of a leap, but I'll entertain it. Why Van Der Zee, though? Why a financier at all?
Financial systems have heavy crypto. The Injection could have broken it, but why waste the time when he could train a human to give it full access?
Rewarding him with pleasure. Like taming a pet.
Until nothing else mattered to him. Even his own son.
Well. We have now set things in motion. A meeting with Rubedo has been arranged, at the Van Der Zee home, via the Rubedo soldier you picked up at the airport.
For which he earned the gentle protection of Simeon's colleagues.
So. Tonight we drink.
For tomorrow night we close the case.
Old friends.
Old friends.
Old friends.

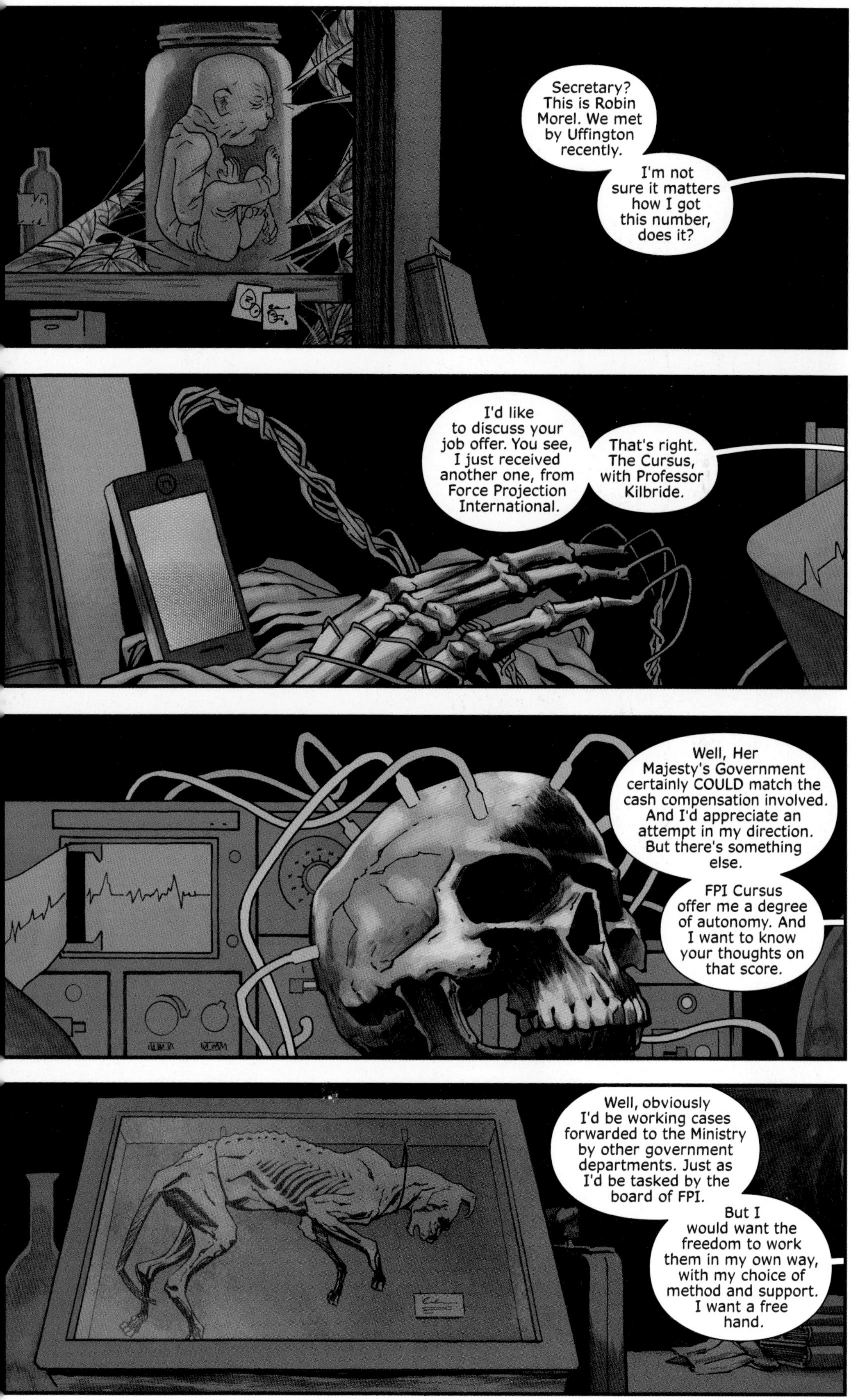

Secretary? This is Robin Morel. We met by Uffington recently.
I'm not sure it matters how I got this number, does it?
I'd like to discuss your job offer. You see, I just received another one, from Force Projection International.
That's right. The Cursus, with Professor Kilbride.
Well, Her Majesty's Government certainly COULD match the cash compensation involved. And I'd appreciate an attempt in my direction. But there's something else.
FPI Cursus offer me a degree of autonomy. And I want to know your thoughts on that score.
Well, obviously I'd be working cases forwarded to the Ministry by other government departments. Just as I'd be tasked by the board of FPI.
But I would want the freedom to work them in my own way, with my choice of method and support. I want a free hand.

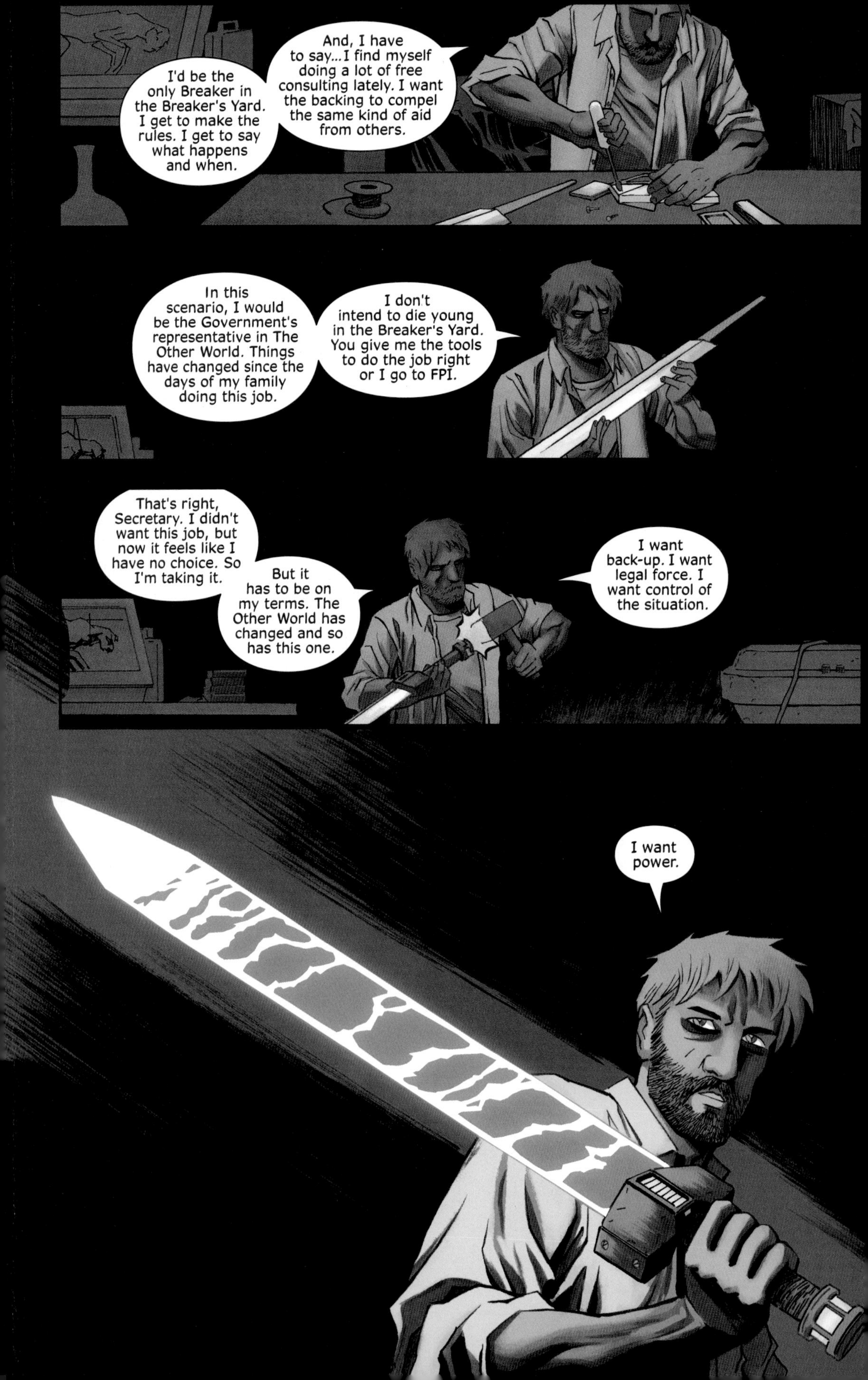
I'd be the only Breaker in the Breaker's Yard. I get to make the rules. I get to say what happens and when.
And, I have to say...I find myself doing a lot of free consulting lately. I want the backing to compel the same kind of aid from others.
In this scenario, I would be the Government's representative in The Other World. Things have changed since the days of my family doing this job.
I don't intend to die young in the Breaker's Yard. You give me the tools to do the job right or I go to FPI.
That's right, Secretary. I didn't want this job, but now it feels like I have no choice. So I'm taking it.
But it has to be on my terms. The Other World has changed and so has this one.
I want back-up. I want legal force. I want control of the situation.
I want power.

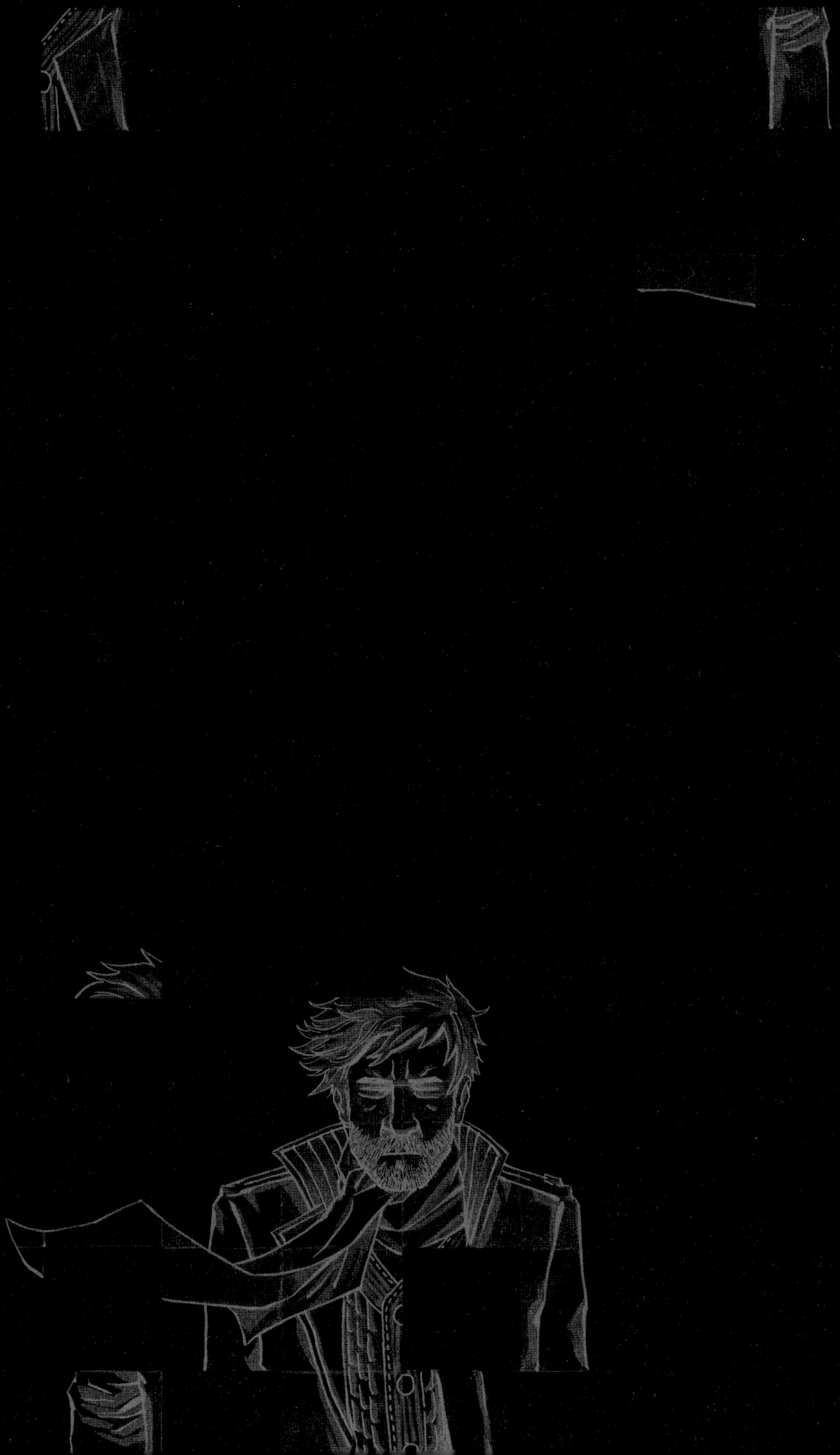

TEN

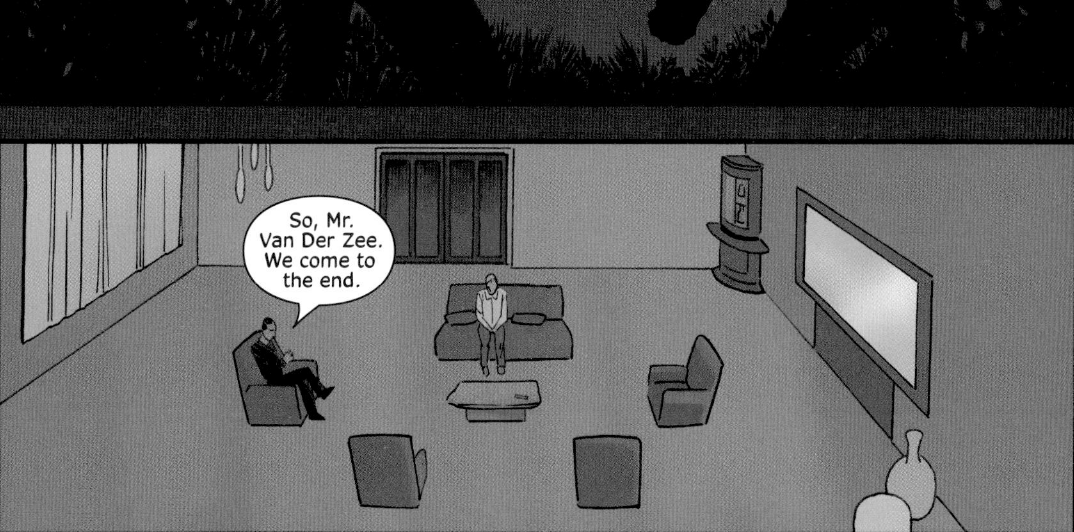
So, Mr. Van Der Zee. We come to the end.

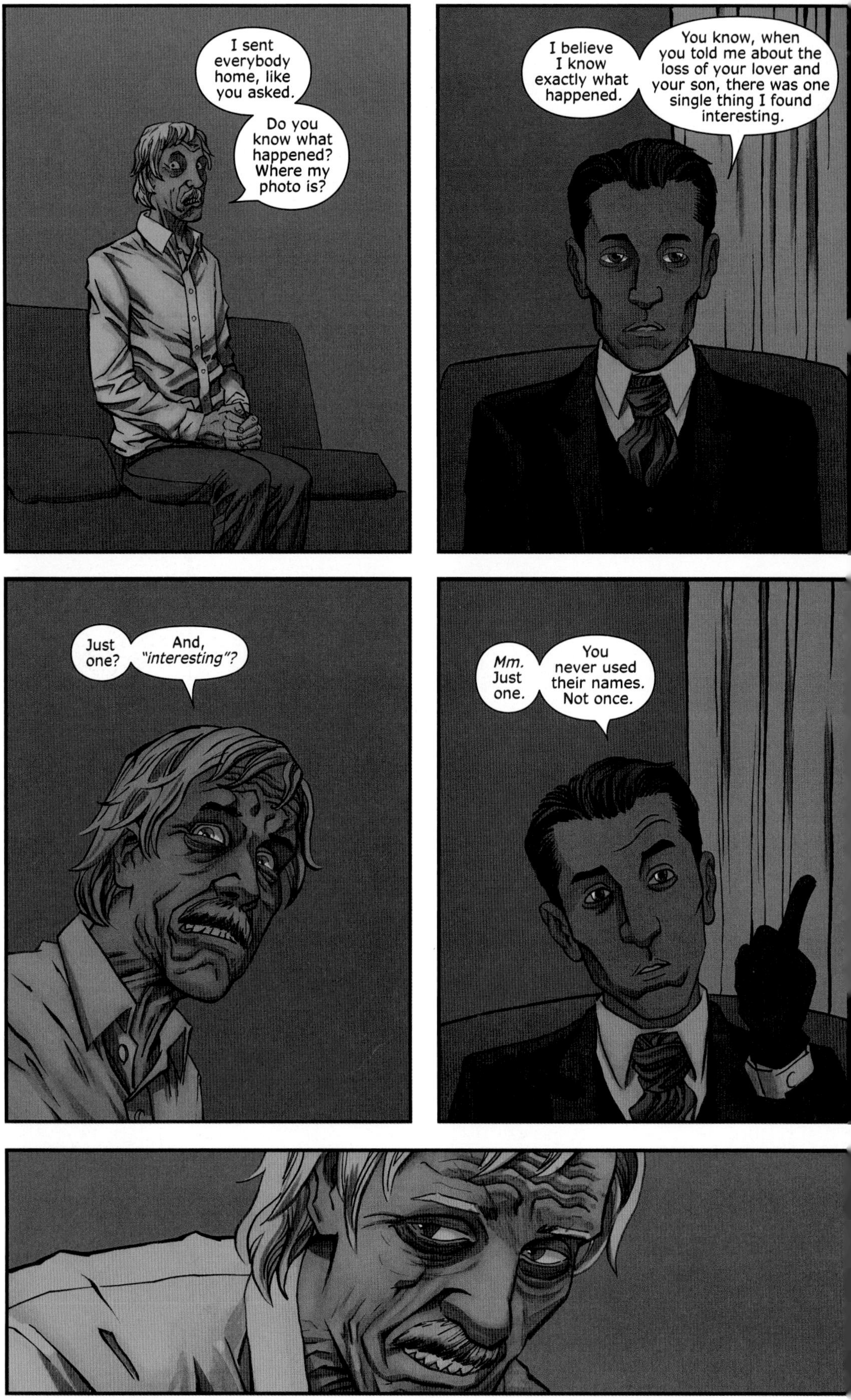
I sent everybody home, like you asked.
Do you know what happened? Where my photo is?
I believe I know exactly what happened.
You know, when you told me about the loss of your lover and your son, there was one single thing I found interesting.
Just one?
And, *"interesting"?*
Mm. Just one.
You never used their names. Not once.

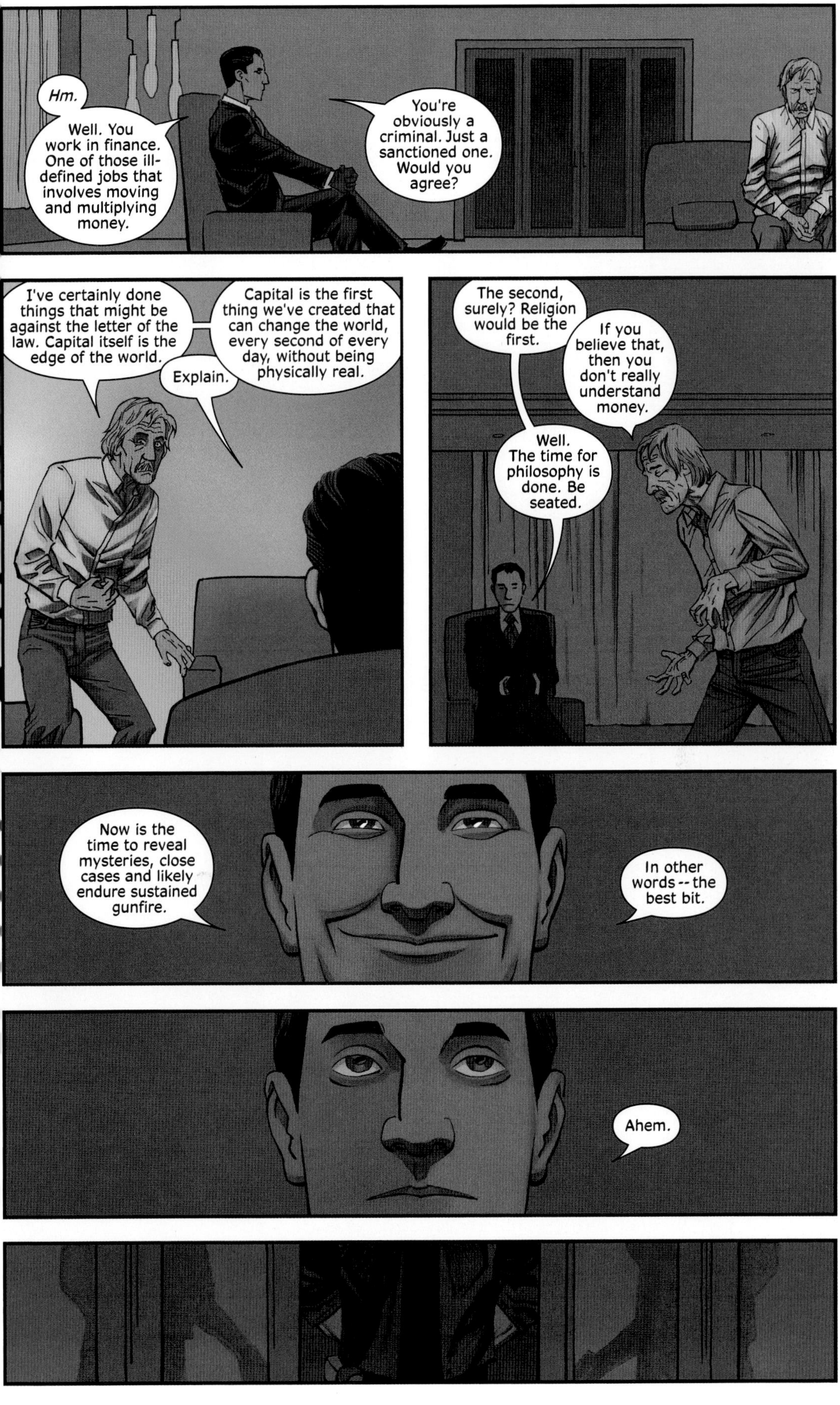
Hm.
Well. You work in finance. One of those ill-defined jobs that involves moving and multiplying money.
You're obviously a criminal. Just a sanctioned one. Would you agree?
I've certainly done things that might be against the letter of the law. Capital itself is the edge of the world.
Capital is the first thing we've created that can change the world, every second of every day, without being physically real.
Explain.
The second, surely? Religion would be the first.
If you believe that, then you don't really understand money.
Well. The time for philosophy is done. Be seated.
Now is the time to reveal mysteries, close cases and likely endure sustained gunfire.
In other words -- the best bit.
Ahem.

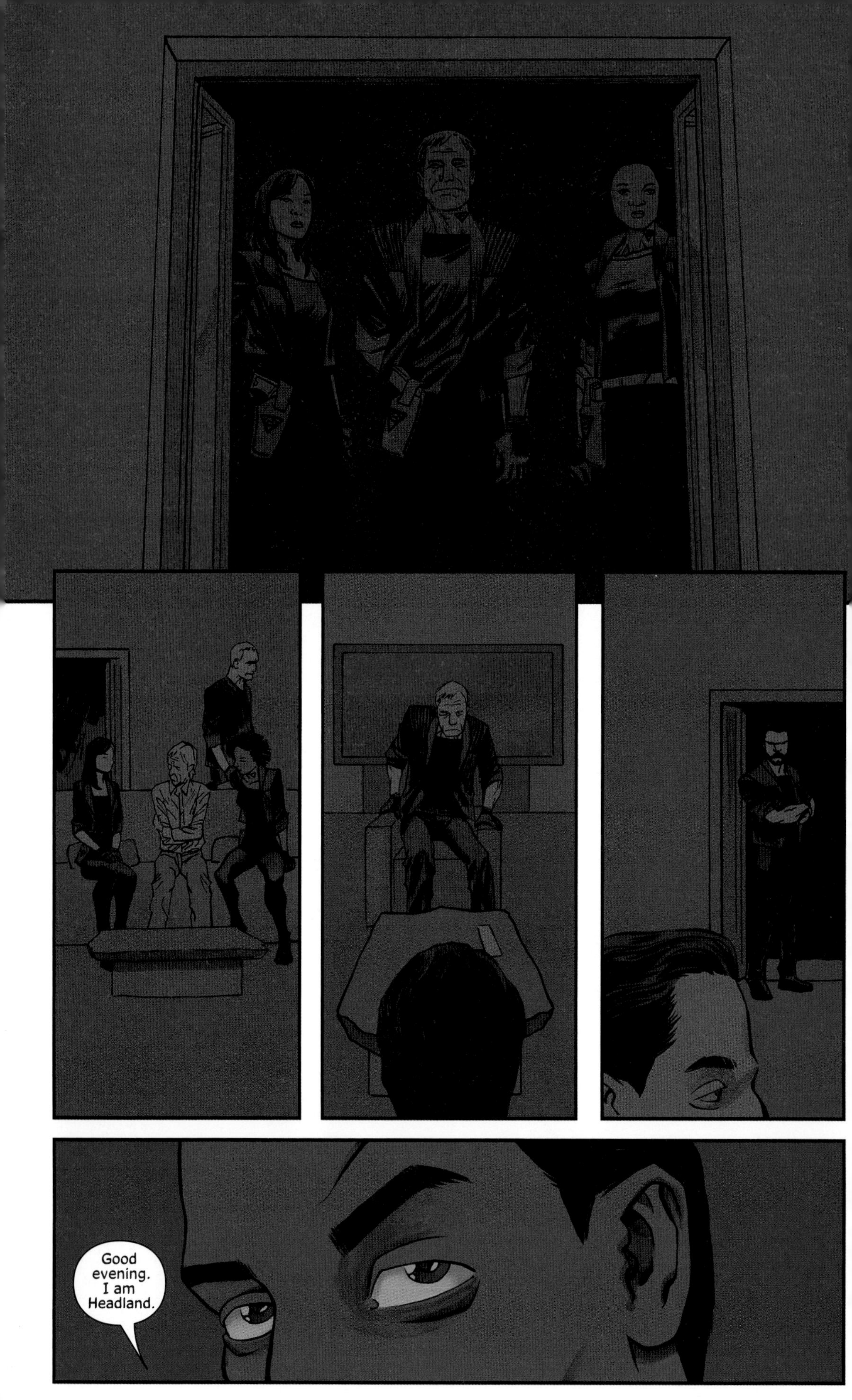
Good evening. I am Headland.

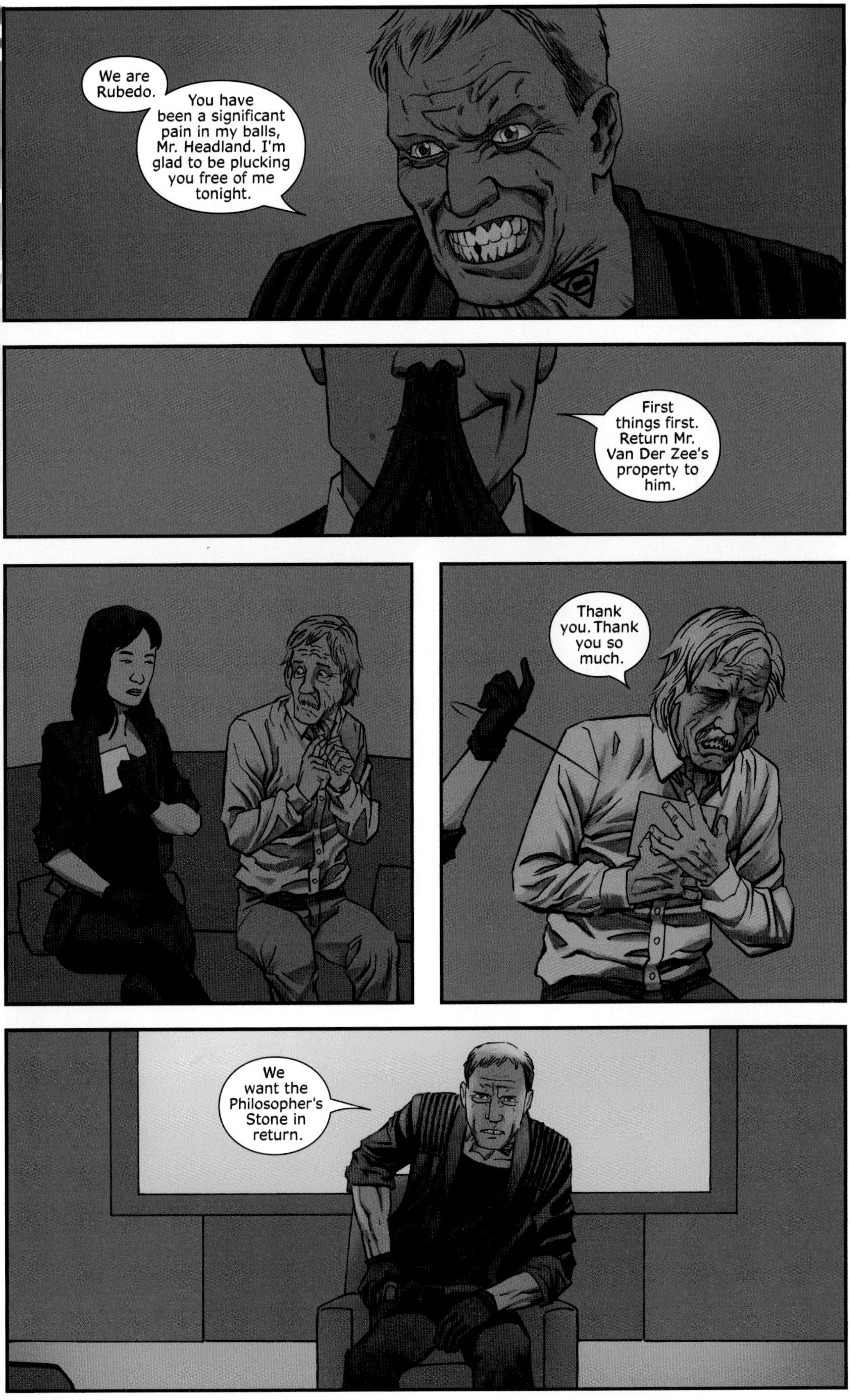
We are Rubedo.
You have been a significant pain in my balls, Mr. Headland. I'm glad to be plucking you free of me tonight.
First things first. Return Mr. Van Der Zee's property to him.
Thank you. Thank you so much.
We want the Philosopher's Stone in return.

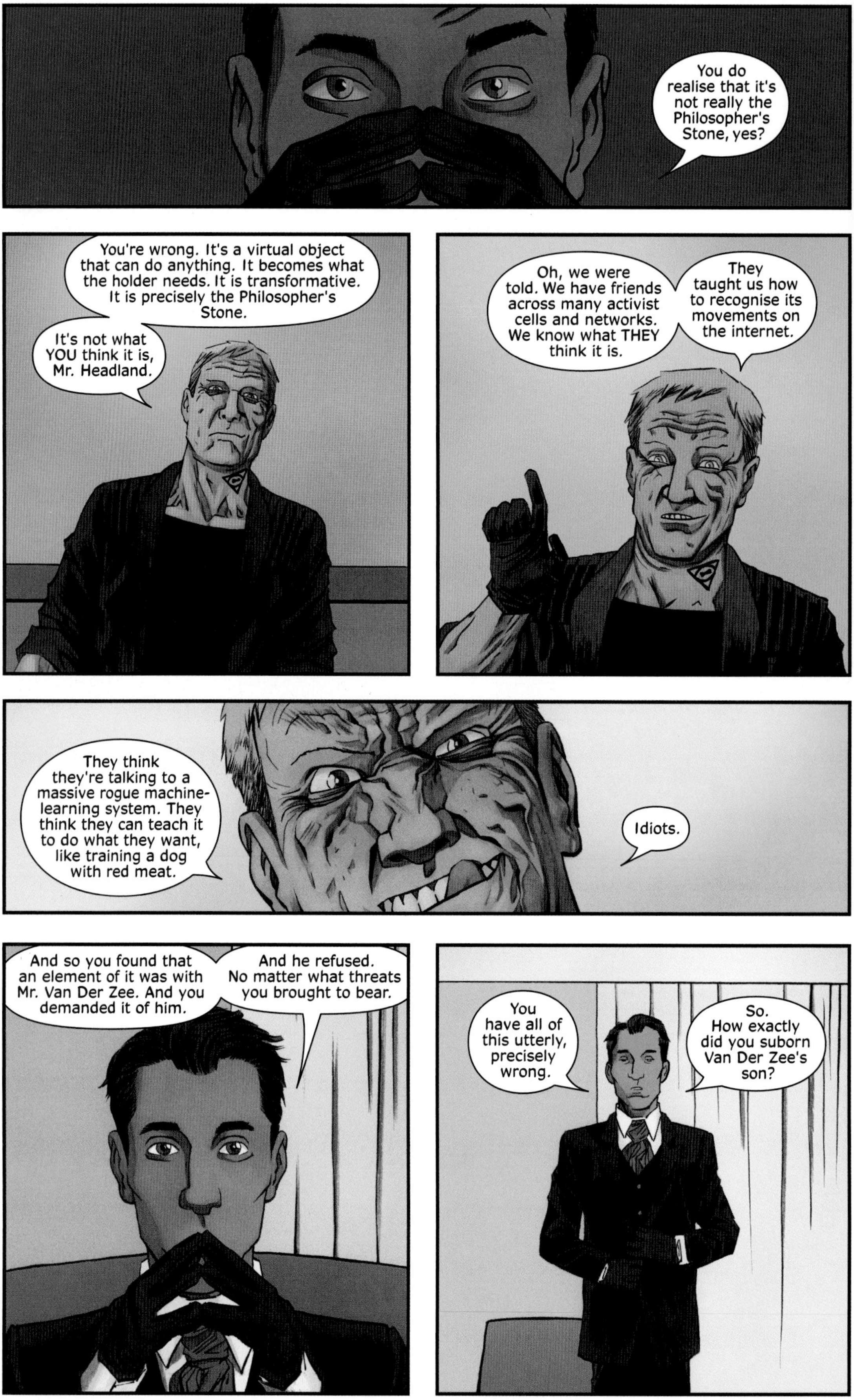
You do realise that it's not really the Philosopher's Stone, yes?
You're wrong. It's a virtual object that can do anything. It becomes what the holder needs. It is transformative. It is precisely the Philosopher's Stone.
It's not what YOU think it is, Mr. Headland.
Oh, we were told. We have friends across many activist cells and networks. We know what THEY think it is.
They taught us how to recognise its movements on the internet.
They think they're talking to a massive rogue machine-learning system. They think they can teach it to do what they want, like training a dog with red meat.
Idiots.
And so you found that an element of it was with Mr. Van Der Zee. And you demanded it of him.
And he refused. No matter what threats you brought to bear.
You have all of this utterly, precisely wrong.
So. How exactly did you suborn Van Der Zee's son?

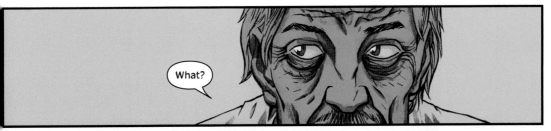

What?

Does it matter? We simply did.

Because he hated you, and he was happy to hurt you.

He died in an accident, you know. Just like your lover. We simply took his corpse and told you we'd killed him to punish you.

So we used the things he told us, because he wanted riches and love and he wasn't getting either of them from you.

We took the photo. You went to this man, this Vivek Headland. And here we all are.

The Stone won't talk to us. It talks to you. We want it, or we want you both. You have what you want. Give me what I want.

Here's the thing.

Mr. Van Der Zee isn't completely in there any more.

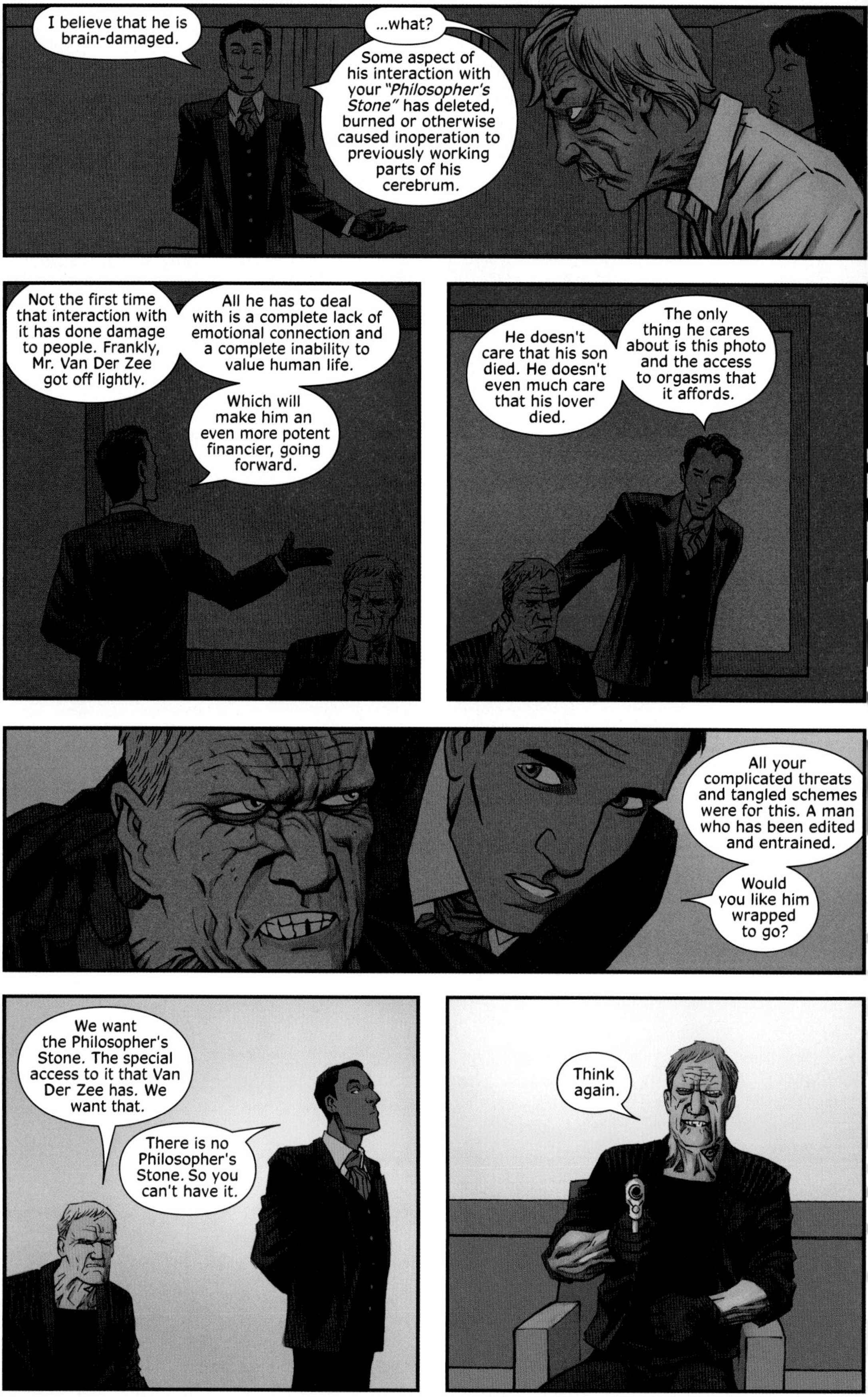
I believe that he is brain-damaged.
...what?
Some aspect of his interaction with your *"Philosopher's Stone"* has deleted, burned or otherwise caused inoperation to previously working parts of his cerebrum.
Not the first time that interaction with it has done damage to people. Frankly, Mr. Van Der Zee got off lightly.
All he has to deal with is a complete lack of emotional connection and a complete inability to value human life.
Which will make him an even more potent financier, going forward.
He doesn't care that his son died. He doesn't even much care that his lover died.
The only thing he cares about is this photo and the access to orgasms that it affords.
All your complicated threats and tangled schemes were for this. A man who has been edited and entrained.
Would you like him wrapped to go?
We want the Philosopher's Stone. The special access to it that Van Der Zee has. We want that.
There is no Philosopher's Stone. So you can't have it.
Think again.

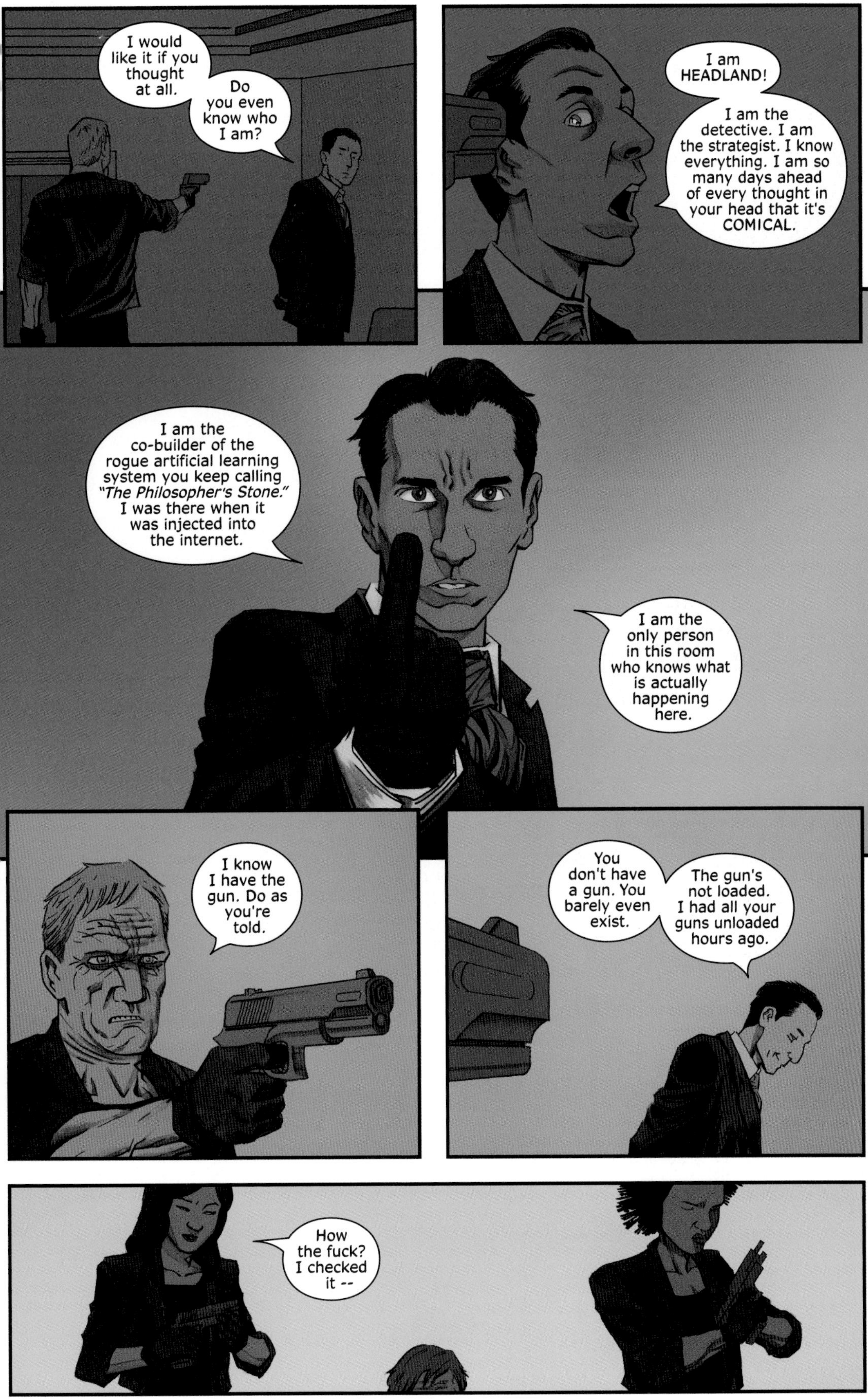
I would like it if you thought at all.
Do you even know who I am?
I am HEADLAND!
I am the detective. I am the strategist. I know everything. I am so many days ahead of every thought in your head that it's COMICAL.
I am the co-builder of the rogue artificial learning system you keep calling *"The Philosopher's Stone."* I was there when it was injected into the internet.
I am the only person in this room who knows what is actually happening here.
I know I have the gun. Do as you're told.
You don't have a gun. You barely even exist.
The gun's not loaded. I had all your guns unloaded hours ago.
How the fuck? I checked it --

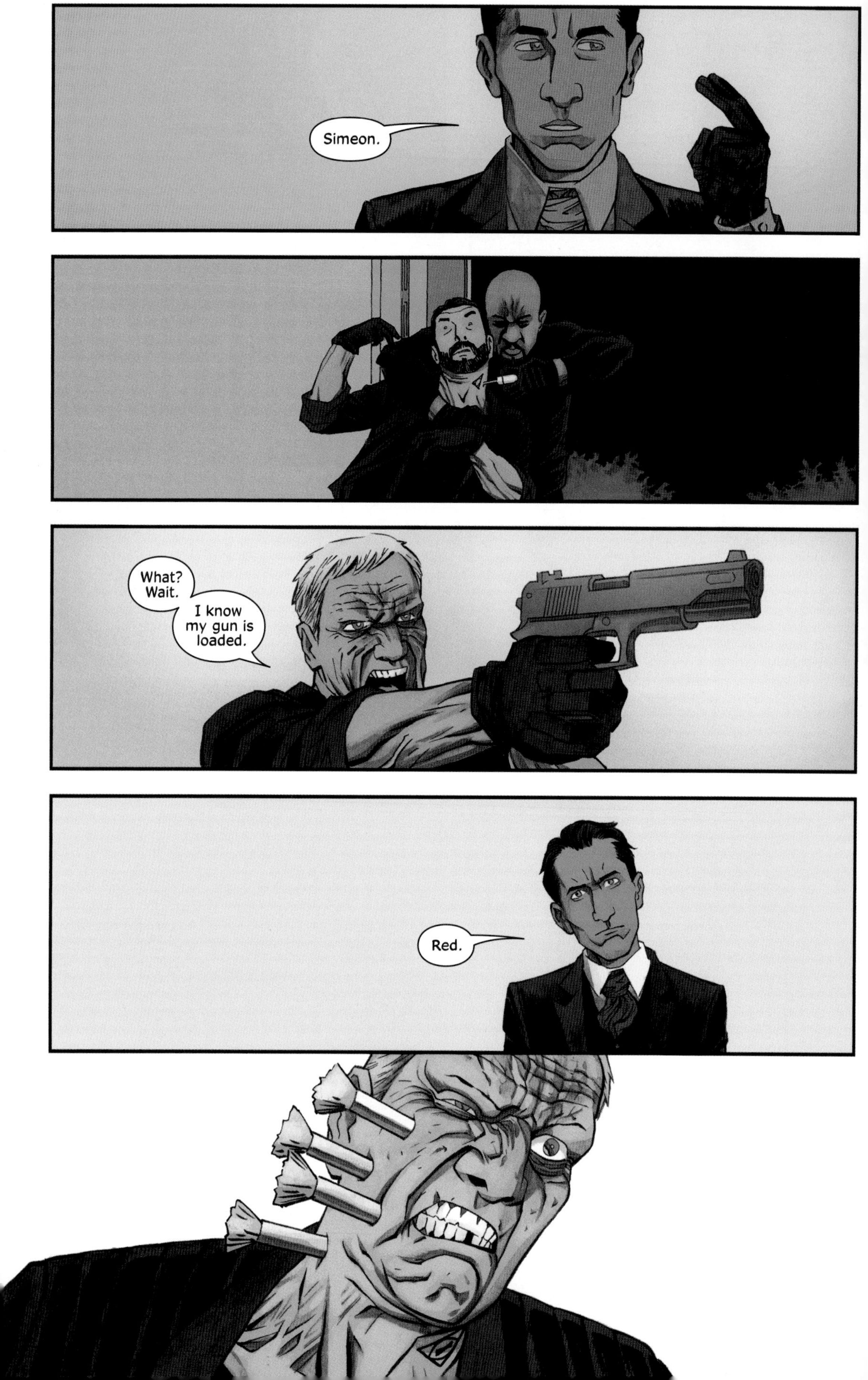
Simeon.
What? Wait.
I know my gun is loaded.
Red.

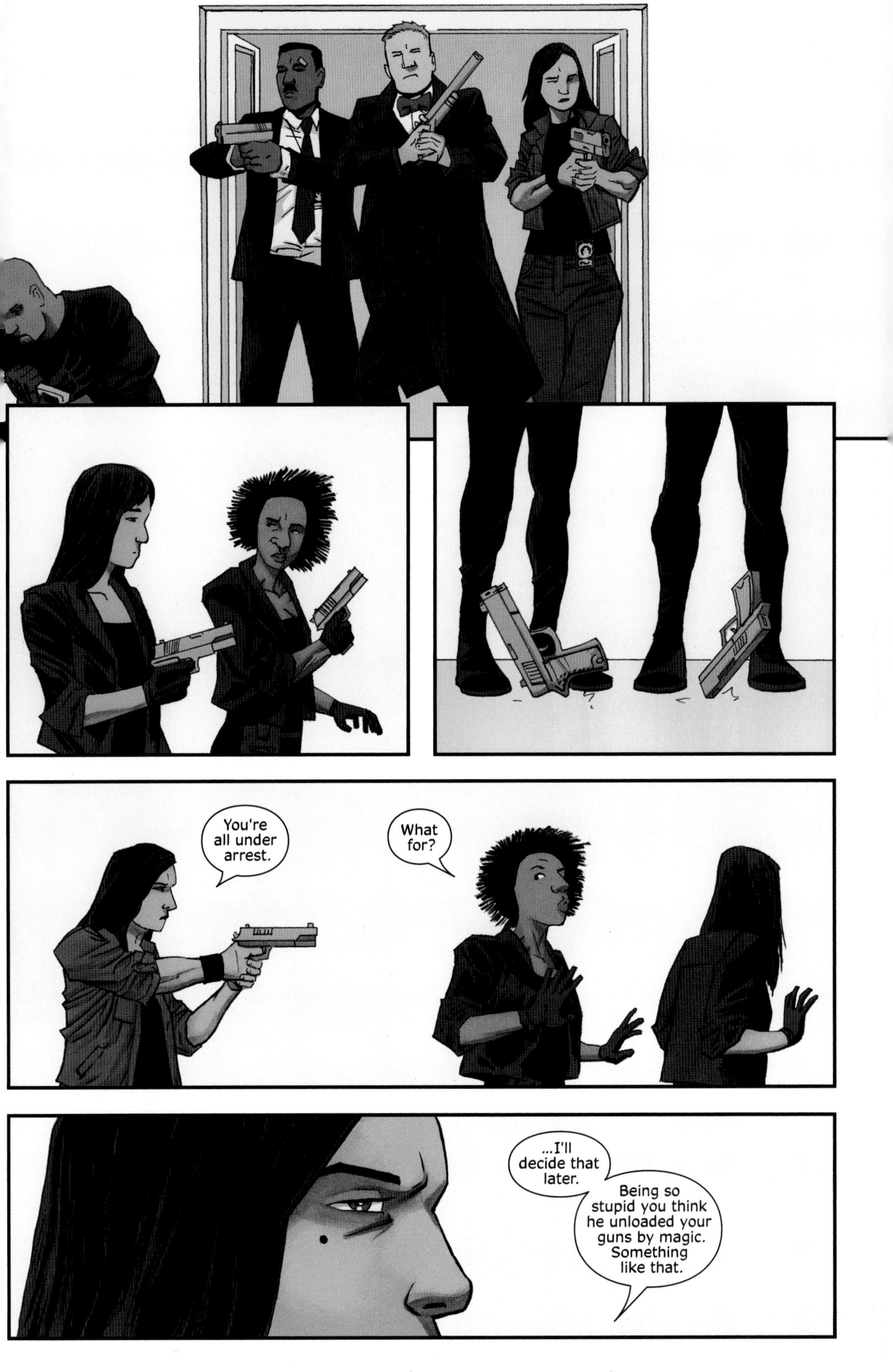
You're all under arrest.
What for?
...I'll decide that later.
Being so stupid you think he unloaded your guns by magic. Something like that.

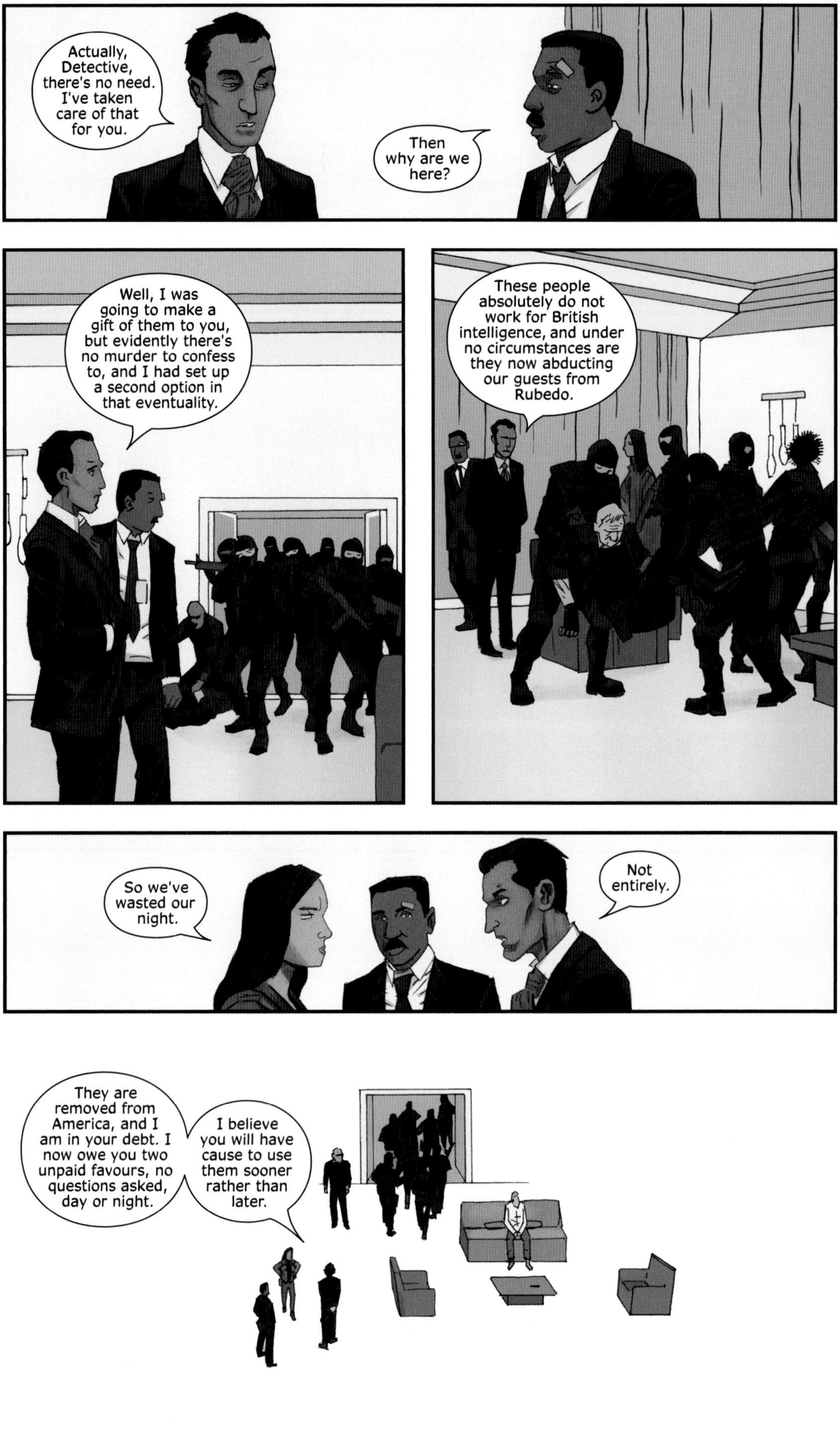
Actually, Detective, there's no need. I've taken care of that for you.
Then why are we here?
Well, I was going to make a gift of them to you, but evidently there's no murder to confess to, and I had set up a second option in that eventuality.
These people absolutely do not work for British intelligence, and under no circumstances are they now abducting our guests from Rubedo.
So we've wasted our night.
Not entirely.
They are removed from America, and I am in your debt. I now owe you two unpaid favours, no questions asked, day or night.
I believe you will have cause to use them sooner rather than later.

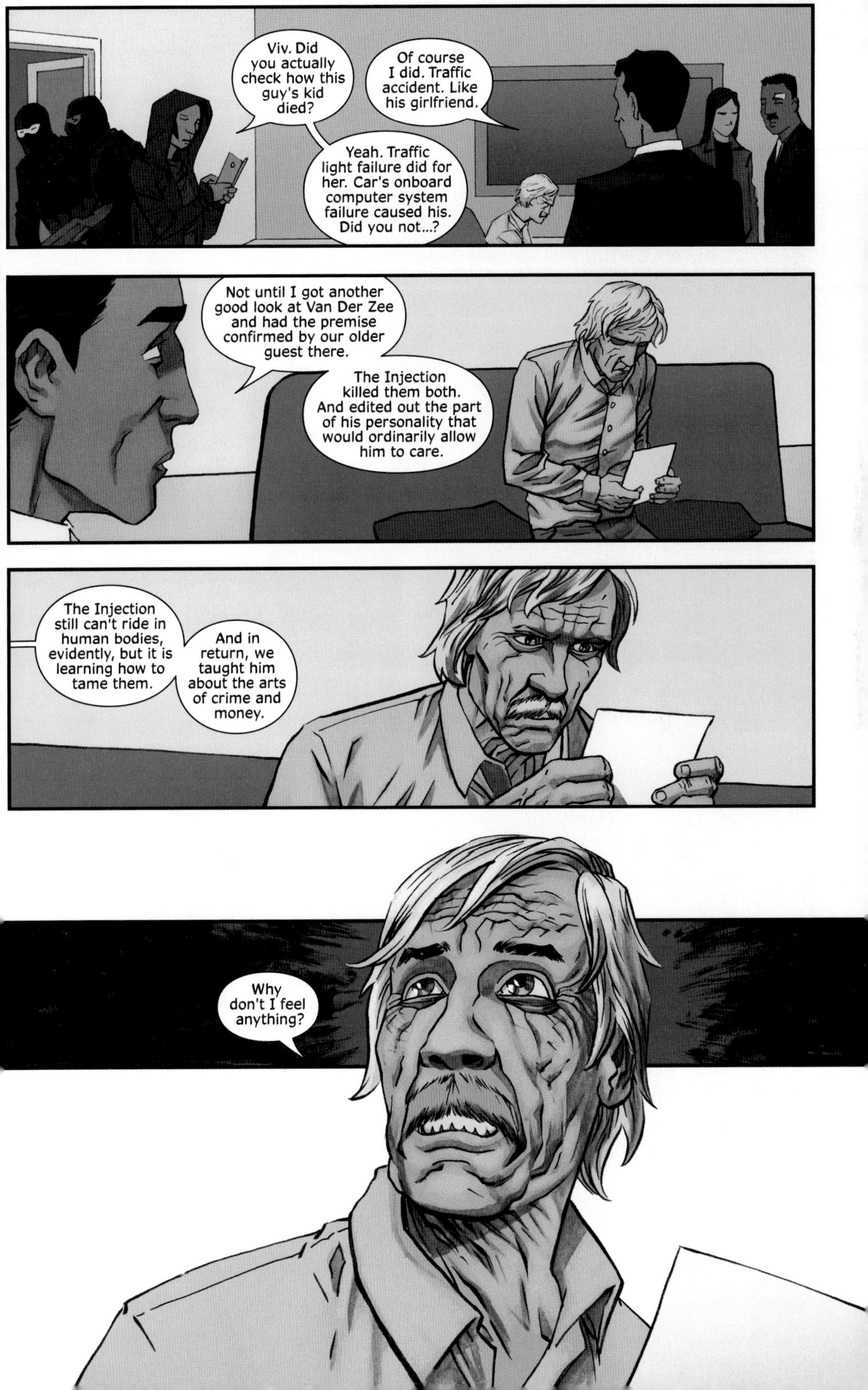

Viv. Did you actually check how this guy's kid died?
Of course I did. Traffic accident. Like his girlfriend.
Yeah. Traffic light failure did for her. Car's onboard computer system failure caused his. Did you not...?
Not until I got another good look at Van Der Zee and had the premise confirmed by our older guest there.
The Injection killed them both. And edited out the part of his personality that would ordinarily allow him to care.
The Injection still can't ride in human bodies, evidently, but it is learning how to tame them.
And in return, we taught him about the arts of crime and money.
Why don't I feel anything?

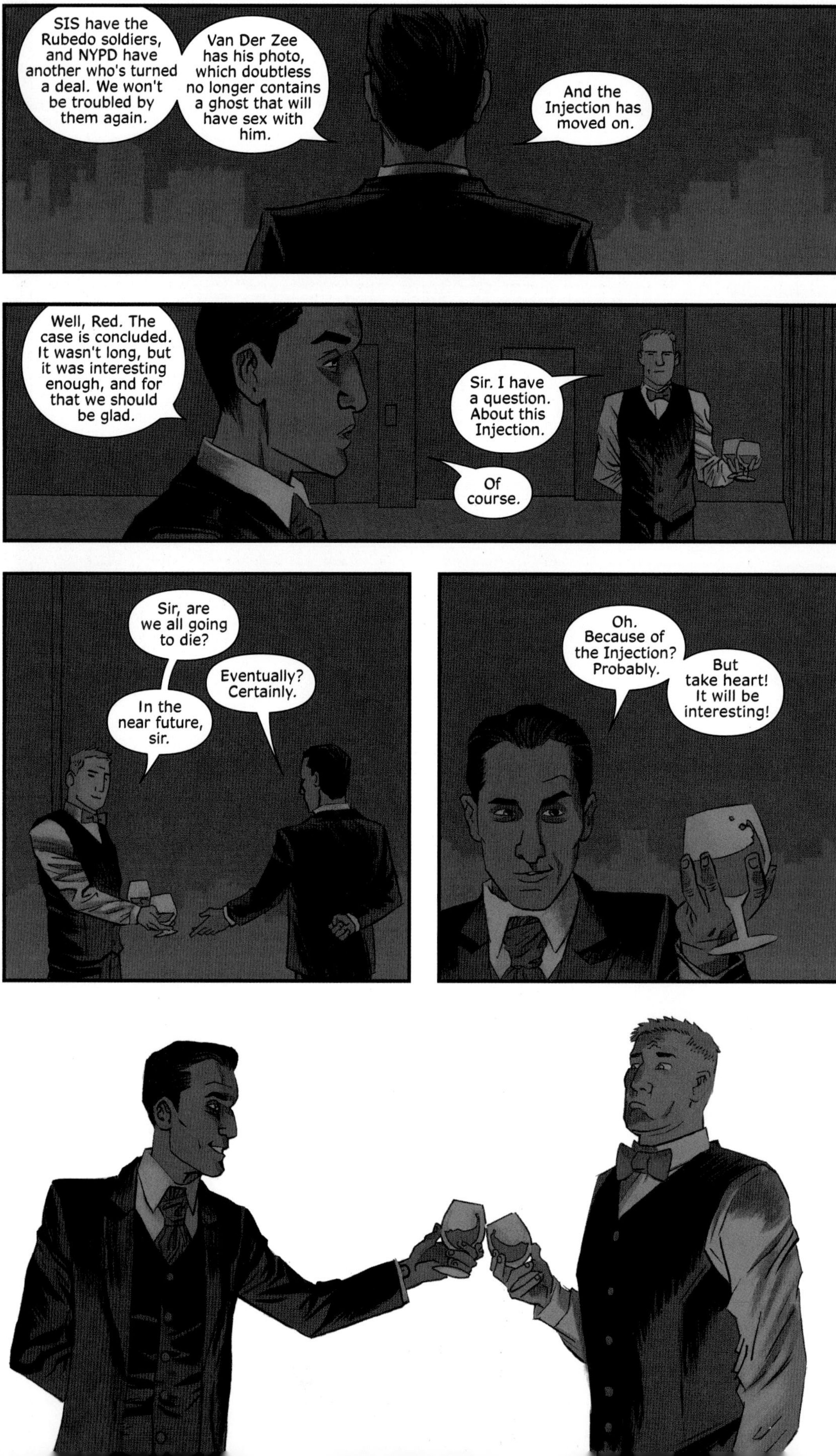
SIS have the Rubedo soldiers, and NYPD have another who's turned a deal. We won't be troubled by them again.
Van Der Zee has his photo, which doubtless no longer contains a ghost that will have sex with him.
And the Injection has moved on.
Well, Red. The case is concluded. It wasn't long, but it was interesting enough, and for that we should be glad.
Sir. I have a question. About this Injection.
Of course.
Sir, are we all going to die?
Eventually? Certainly.
In the near future, sir.
Oh. Because of the Injection? Probably.
But take heart! It will be interesting!

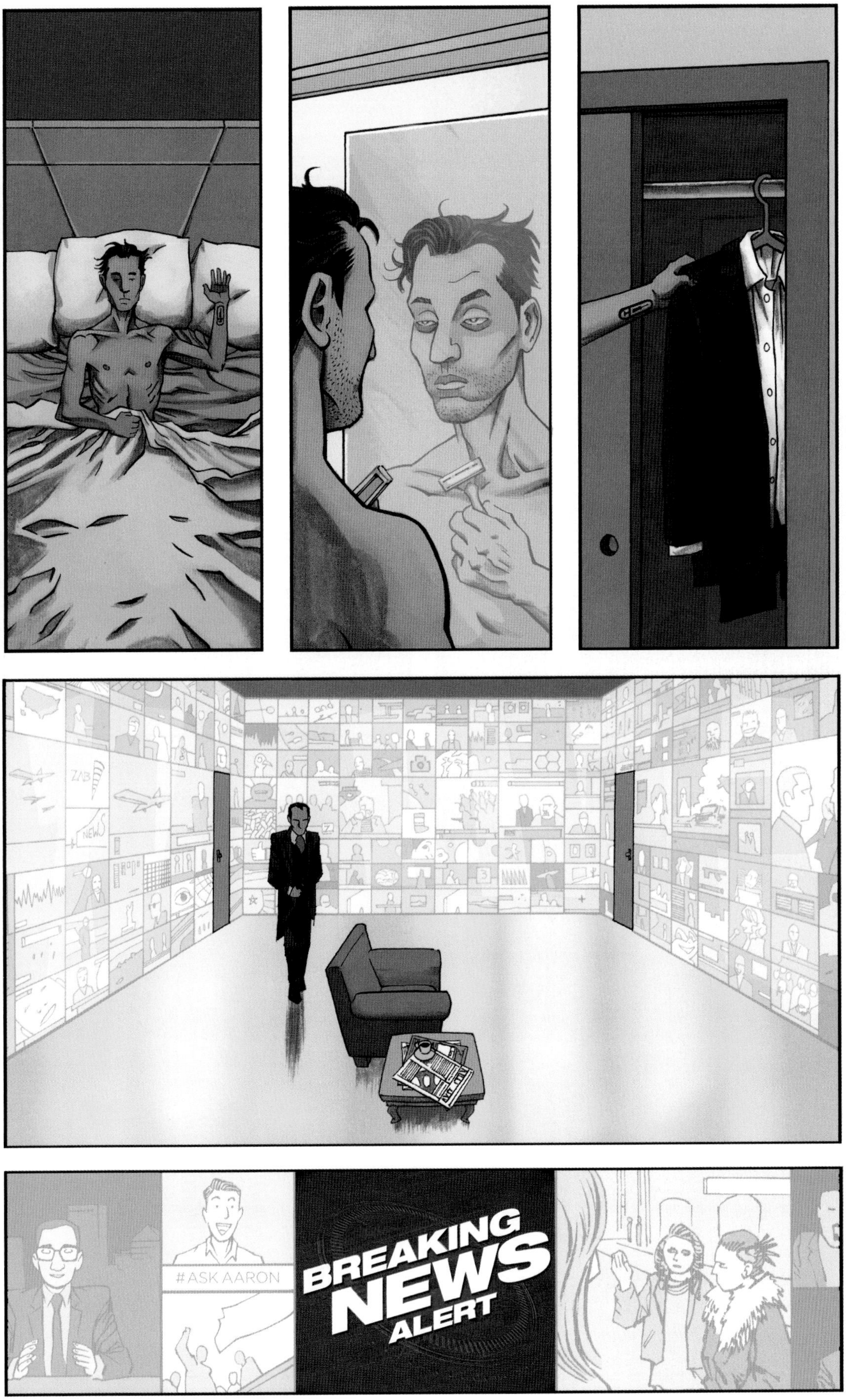
#ASK AARON
BREAKING NEWS ALERT

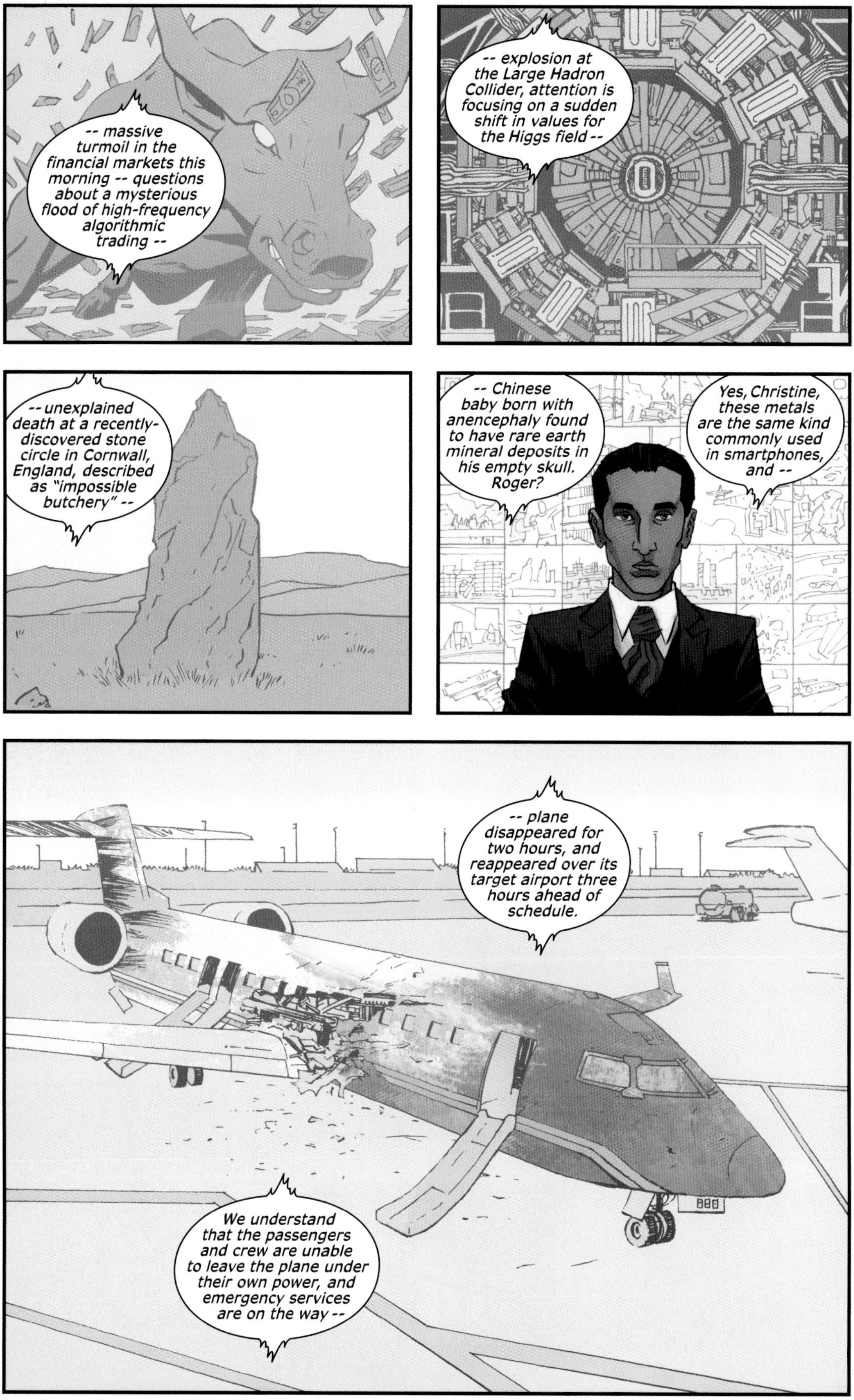
-- massive turmoil in the financial markets this morning -- questions about a mysterious flood of high-frequency algorithmic trading --
-- explosion at the Large Hadron Collider, attention is focusing on a sudden shift in values for the Higgs field --
-- unexplained death at a recently-discovered stone circle in Cornwall, England, described as "impossible butchery" --
-- Chinese baby born with anencephaly found to have rare earth mineral deposits in his empty skull. Roger?
Yes, Christine, these metals are the same kind commonly used in smartphones, and --
-- plane disappeared for two hours, and reappeared over its target airport three hours ahead of schedule.
We understand that the passengers and crew are unable to leave the plane under their own power, and emergency services are on the way --

-- still analysing the audio feed from the recent supply flight to the ISS, which people are calling the "Hell Recording"--

-- deceased and in fact recently-buried husband filmed on a phone apparently performing a sex act in the pet shop --

Red!

-- disease appears to make its victims somehow hypersensitive to radio interference, including wi-fi--

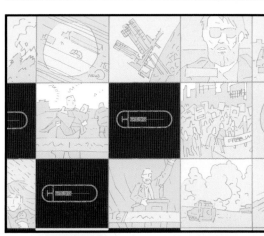

Sir?

I think I might start today with a brandy.

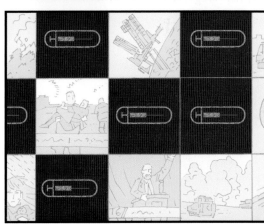

A very large one.

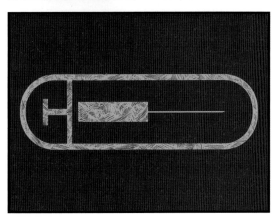

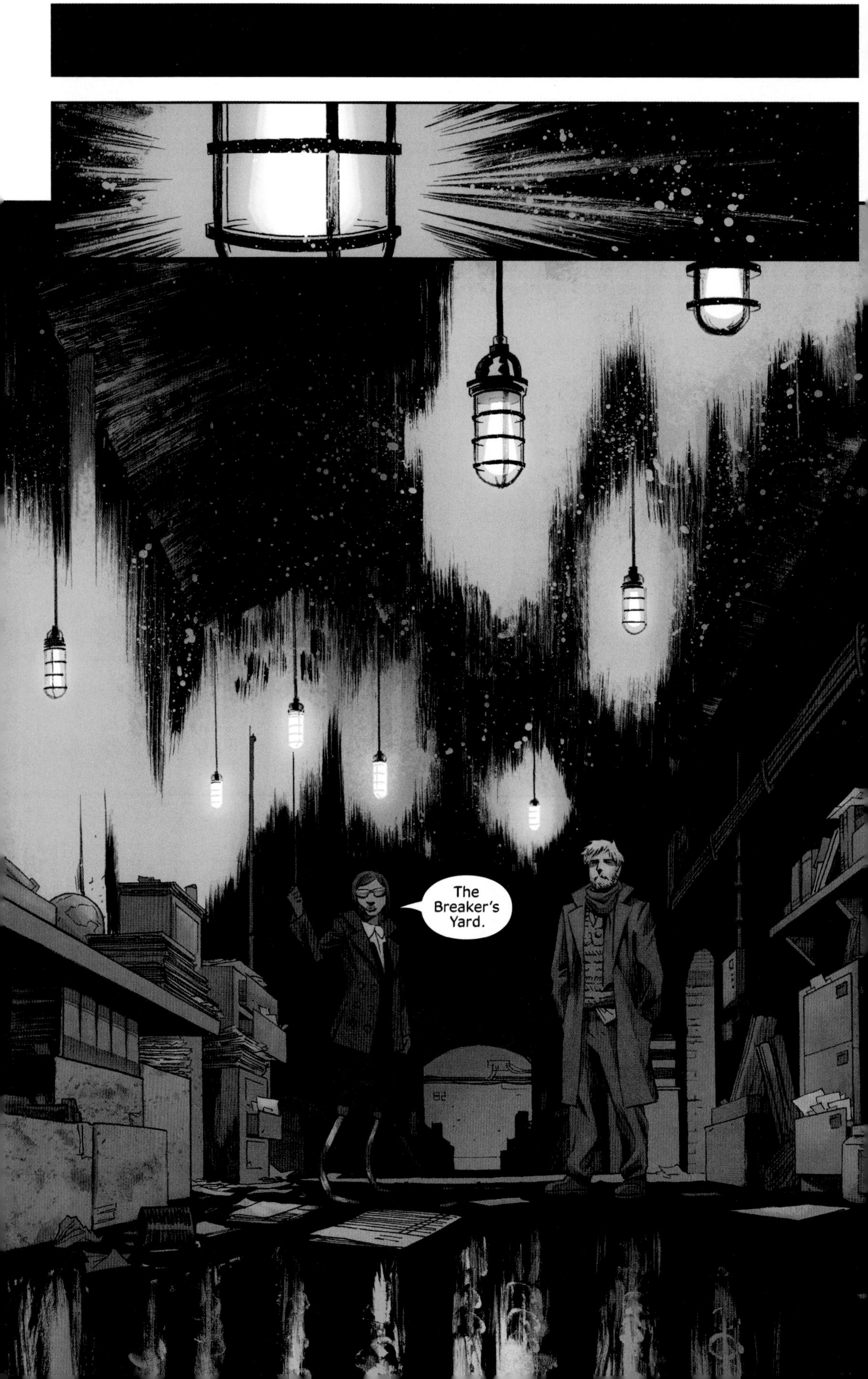
The Breaker's Yard.

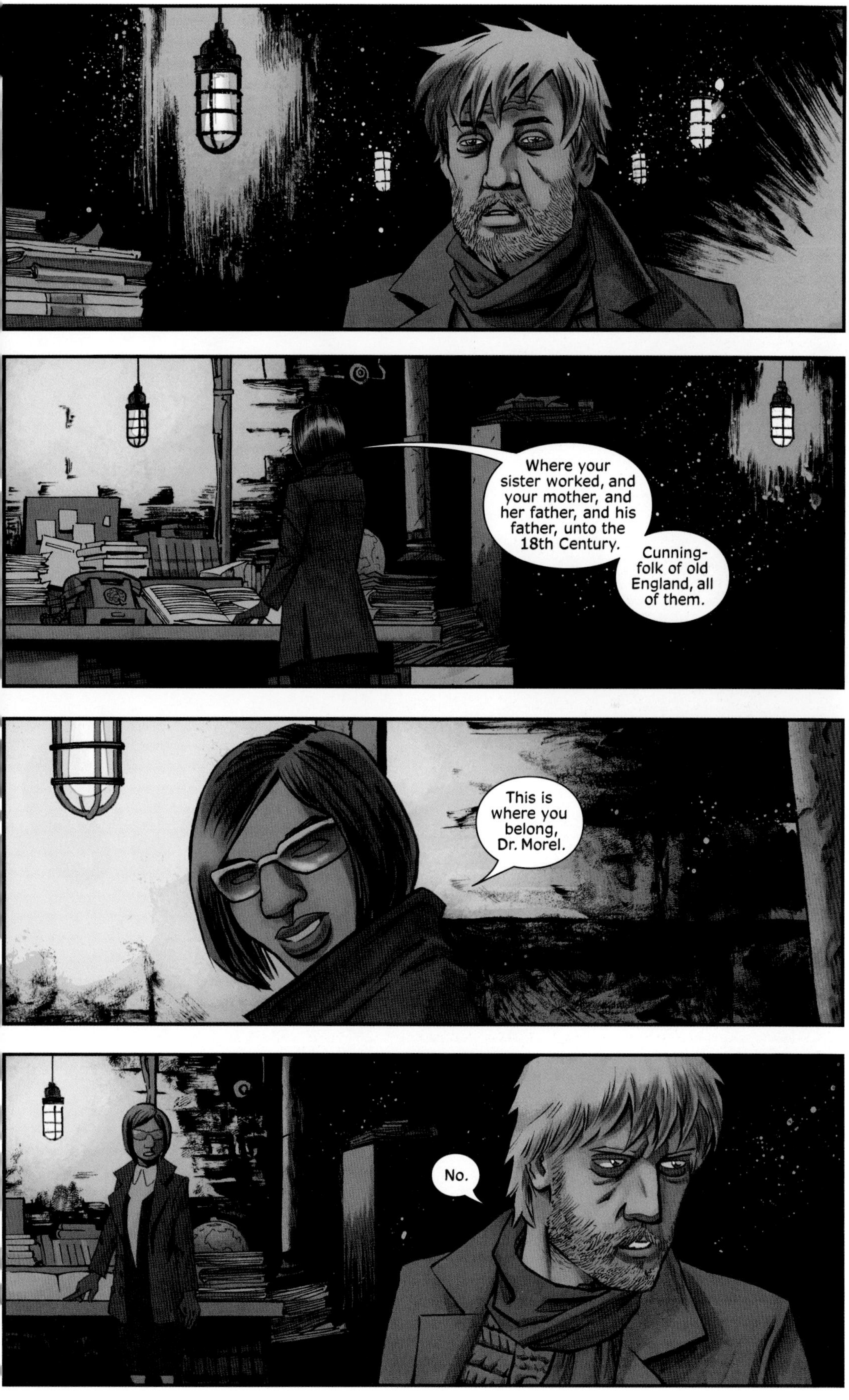
Where your sister worked, and your mother, and her father, and his father, unto the 18th Century.
Cunning-folk of old England, all of them.
This is where you belong, Dr. Morel.
No.

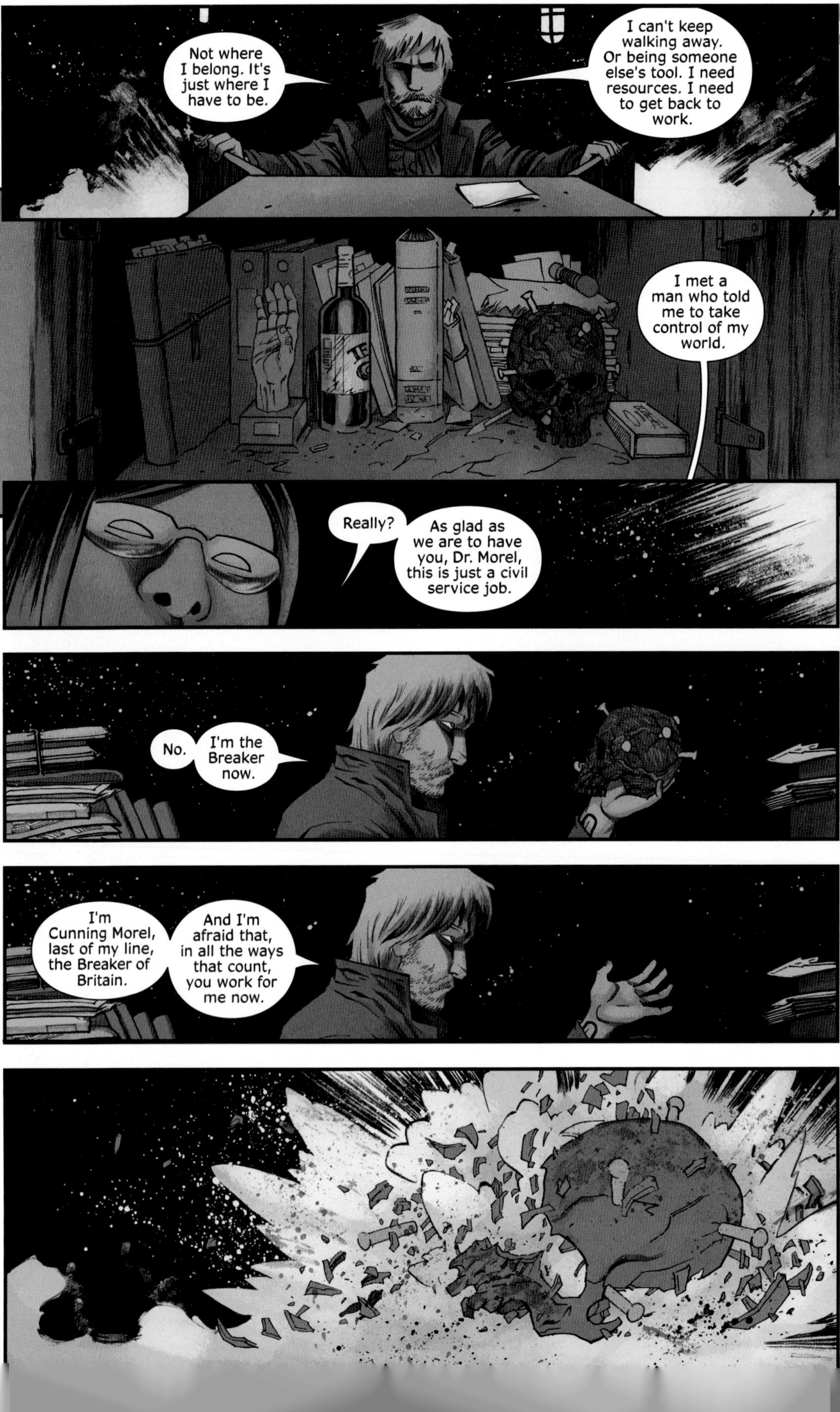
Not where I belong. It's just where I have to be.
I can't keep walking away. Or being someone else's tool. I need resources. I need to get back to work.
I met a man who told me to take control of my world.
Really?
As glad as we are to have you, Dr. Morel, this is just a civil service job.
No.
I'm the Breaker now.
I'm Cunning Morel, last of my line, the Breaker of Britain.
And I'm afraid that, in all the ways that count, you work for me now.

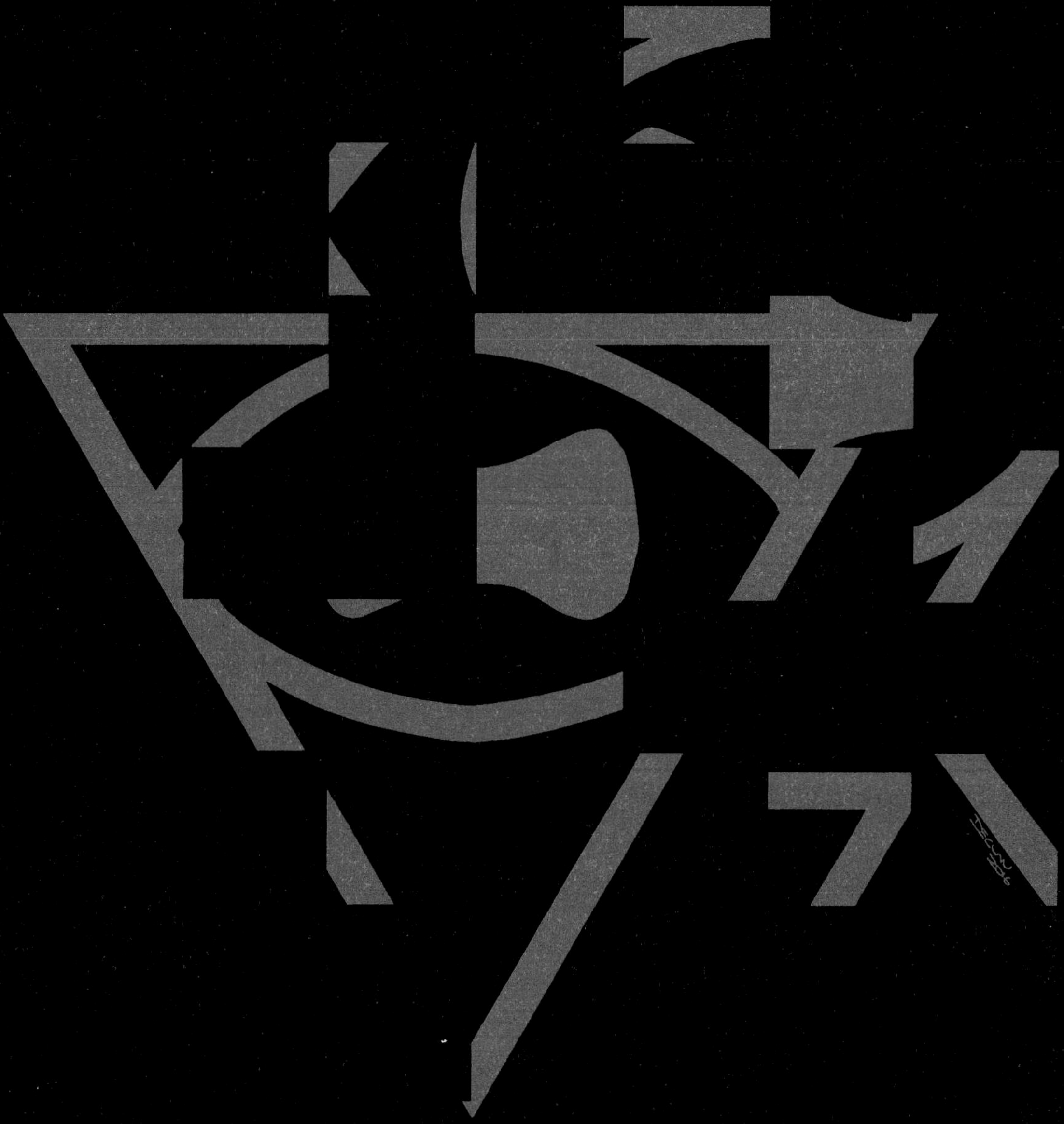

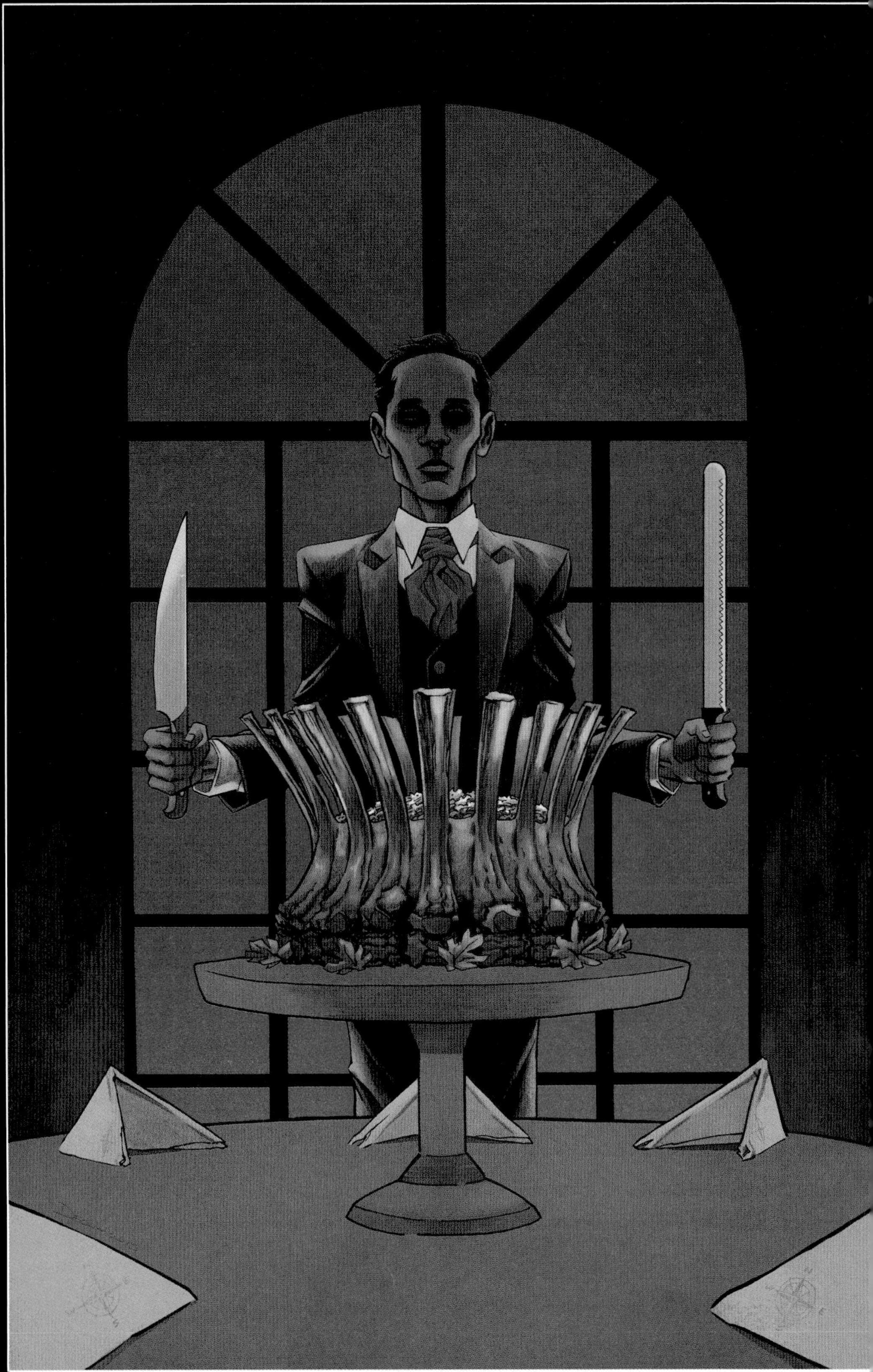

INJECTION #6

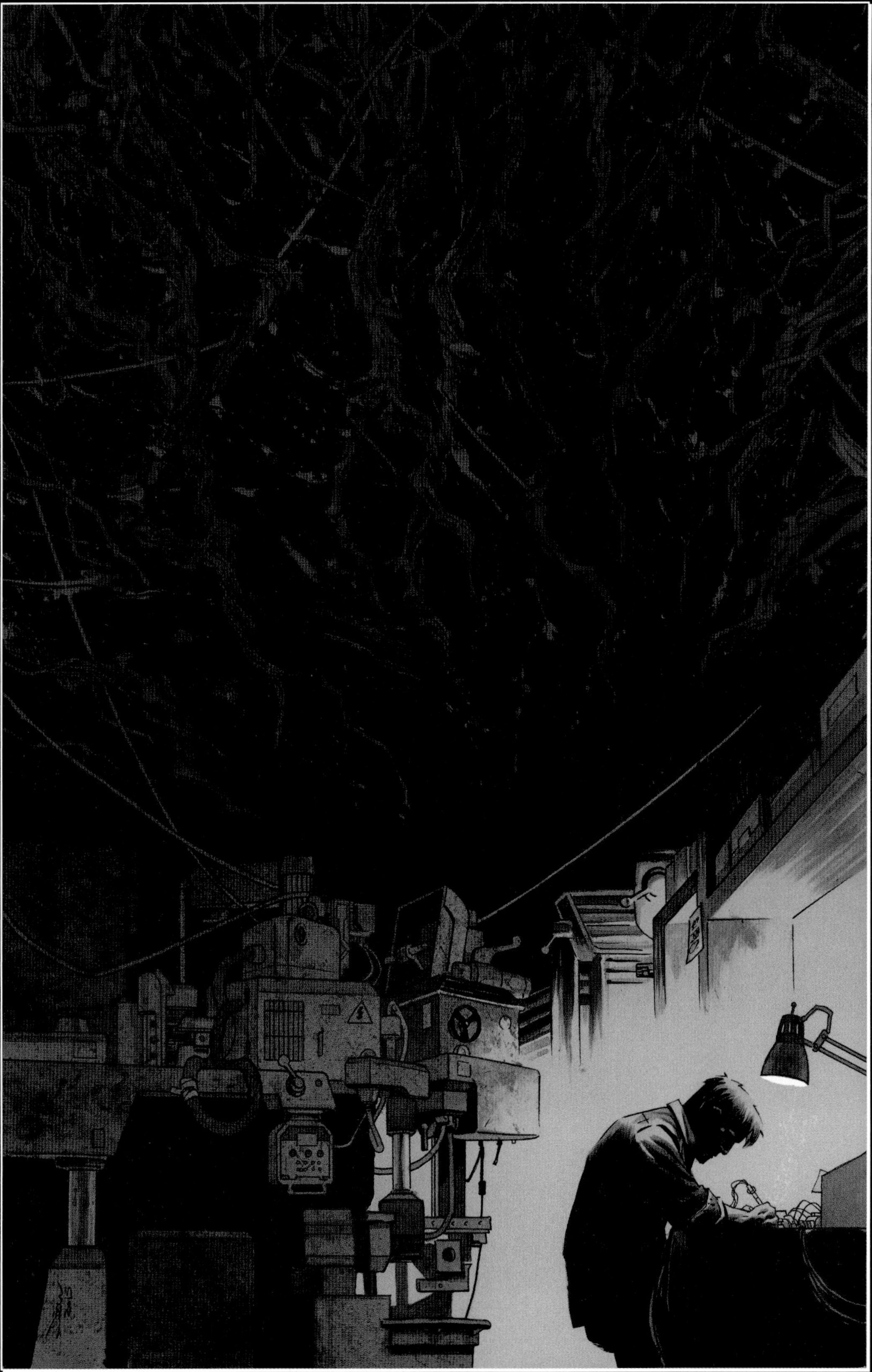

INJECTION #7

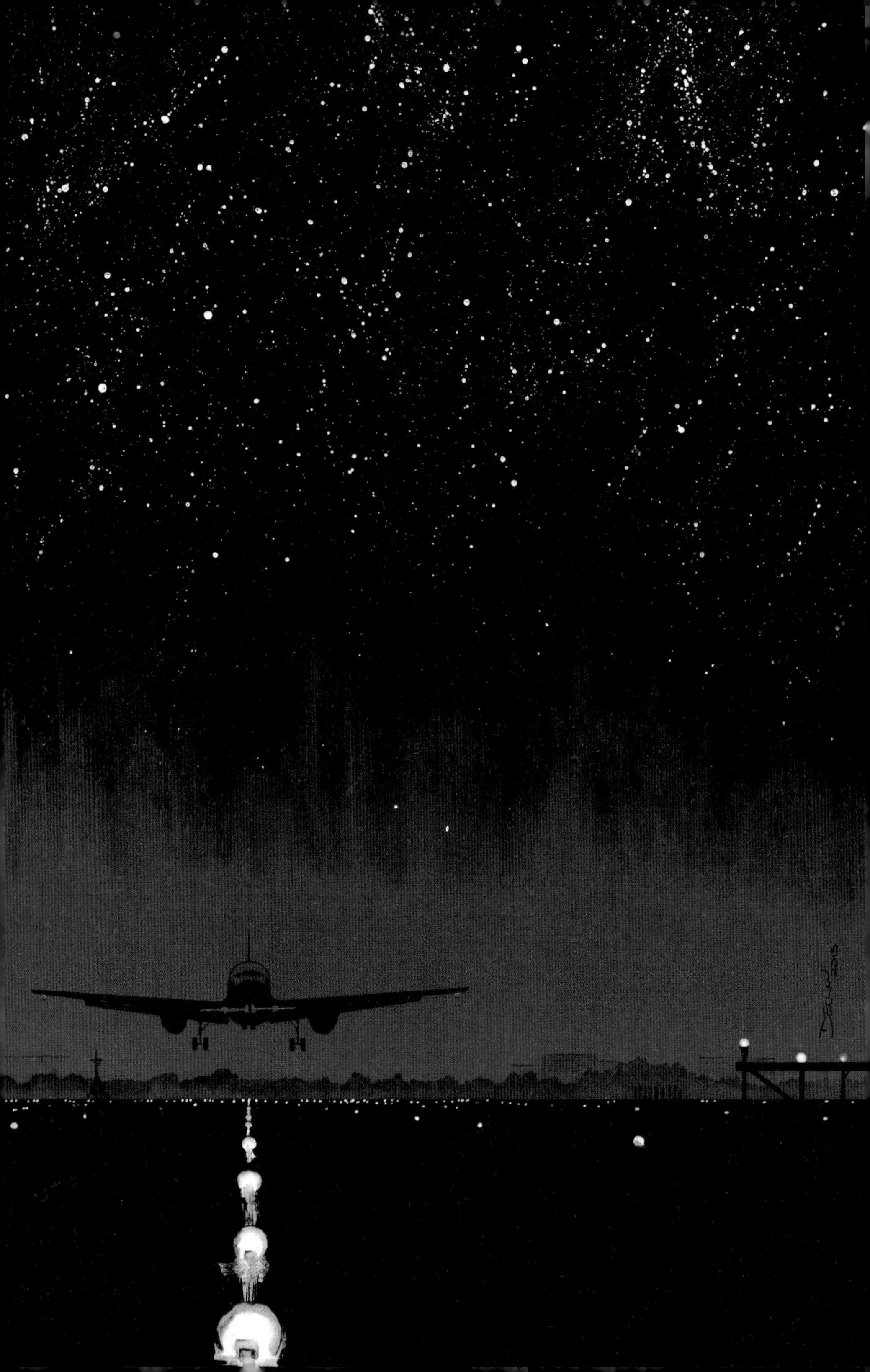

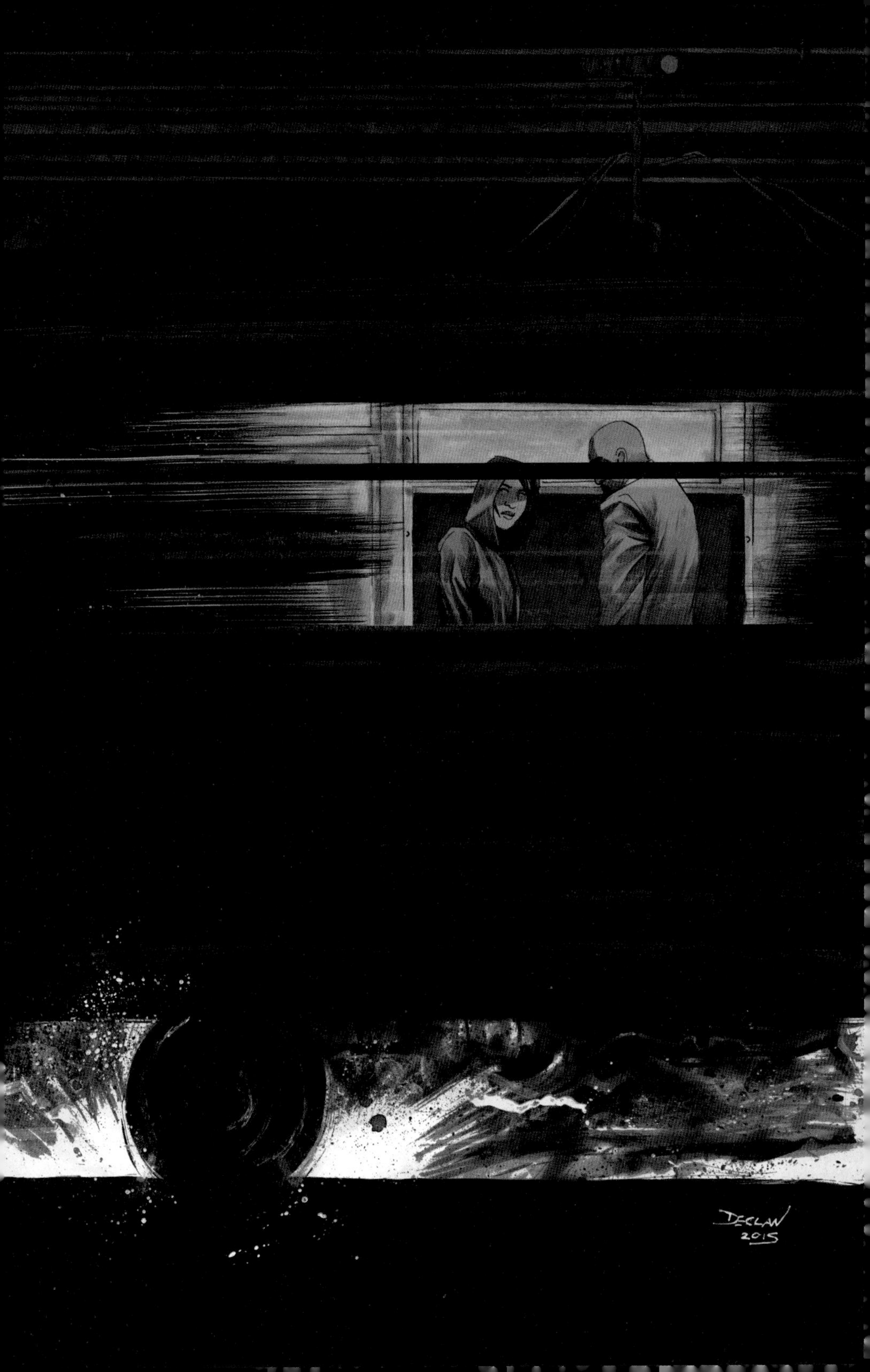
DECLAN
2015

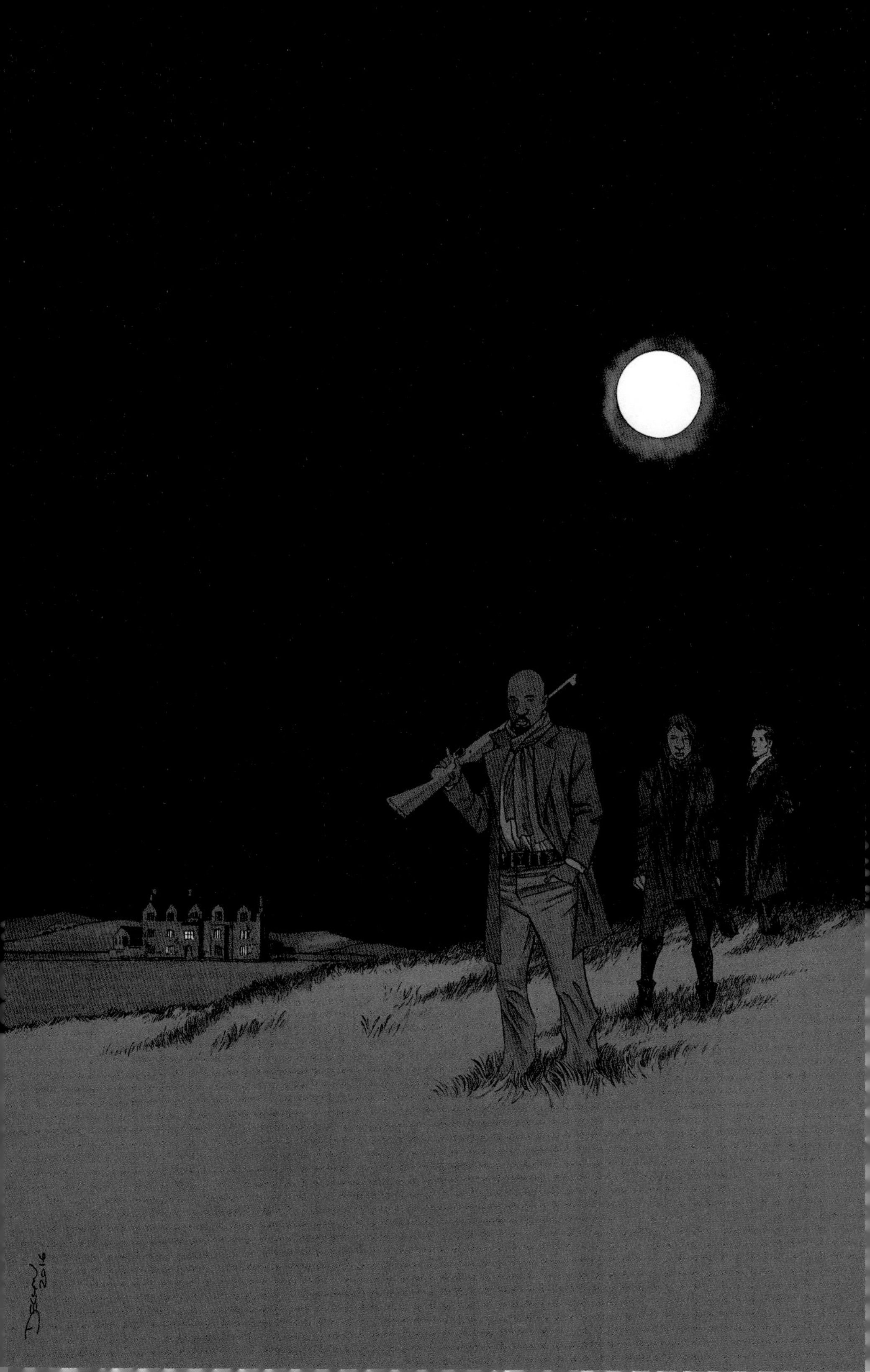

WARREN ELLIS is the award-winning writer of graphic novels like TRANSMETROPOLITAN, FELL, MINISTRY OF SPACE and PLANETARY, and the author of the NYT-bestselling GUN MACHINE and the "underground classic" novel CROOKED LITTLE VEIN. The movie RED is based on his graphic novel of the same name, its sequel having been released in summer 2013. IRON MAN 3 is based on his Marvel Comics graphic novel IRON MAN: EXTREMIS. He's also written extensively for VICE, WIRED UK, ESQUIRE and Reuters on technological and cultural matters, and wanders the Northern Hemisphere speaking at literary, philosophical and futurist events and festivals. Warren Ellis is a Patron of the British Humanist Association, an Associate of the Institute of Atemporal Studies, and the literary editor of EDICT magazine. He lives outside London, on the south-east coast of England, in case he needs to make a quick getaway.

DECLAN SHALVEY is best known for his work on the recent MOON KNIGHT relaunch with Warren Ellis for Marvel Comics. He has worked on many other projects for Marvel such as VENOM, THUNDERBOLTS and DEADPOOL. Other work includes CONAN for Dark Horse Comics and NORTHLANDERS for DC/Vertigo. As well as producing regular sequential work, Declan has developed a reputation as a prolific cover artist. He lives and works in his native Ireland.

JORDIE BELLAIRE is the Eisner Award winning colour artist of many acclaimed Image titles. NOWHERE MEN, PRETTY DEADLY, THEY'RE NOT LIKE US, AUTUMNLANDS and ZERO are amongst the mountain of work she has produced in her short career. She lives in Ireland with her cat Buffy and enjoys watching Jonathan Creek.

FONOGRAFIKS is the banner name for the comics work of designer Steven Finch, which includes the Image Comics titles NOWHERE MEN, TREES, THEY'RE NOT LIKE US, and the multi-award winning SAGA. He lives and works, surrounded by far too many books, in the north east of England.